W9-DEE-961

The New
Christian Counselor

DR. RON HAWKINS
DR. TIM CLINTON

HARVEST HOUSE PUBLISHERS
EUGENE, OREGON

We wrote this book with a deep sense of gratitude for all who have taught and mentored us along our journey. We dedicate this book to them and to all the people around the globe who have answered God's call to care for the millions of people in our world with wounded souls.

THE NEW CHRISTIAN COUNSELOR
Copyright © 2015 Ron Hawkins and Tim Clinton
Published by Harvest House Publishers
Eugene, Oregon 97402
www.harvesthousepublishers.com

Library of Congress Cataloging-in-Publication Data
    Hawkins, Ronald E.
    The new Christian counselor / Ron Hawkins and Tim Clinton.
        pages cm
    ISBN 978-0-7369-4354-3 (pbk.)
    ISBN 978-0-7369-4355-0 (eBook)
    1. Pastoral counseling. 2. Counseling—Religious aspects—Christianity. I. Title.
    BV4012.2.H39 2015
    253.5—dc23
                                                            2014049880

Printed in the United States of America

15 16 17 18 19 20 21 22 23 / ML-JH / 10 9 8 7 6 5 4 3 2 1

Contents

1

Introduction to a New Day

By your patience possess your souls.

Lᴋ. 21:19 ɴᴋᴊᴠ

It's a new day in the world of Christian counseling, psychotherapy, and mental health care. Like never before, Christian counseling is growing into a diverse, empirically grounded, and biblically based ministry-profession of worldwide prominence. It's encouraging to see the exponential growth of the modern Christian counseling movement as never before. Today, Christian counselors are equipped to respond to the diverse and complex needs of hurting people all over the world. However, we need to keep learning. We are challenged by advances in biblical, medical, and psychological research. Militant secularism and global opposition to Christian truth are on the rise.

Like the prophet Habakkuk, we seek to "write the vision and make it plain on tablets, that he may run who reads it" (Hab. 2:2 ɴᴋᴊᴠ). *The New Christian Counselor* offers a vision for the future of Christian counseling that provides definition, focus, and direction to Christian counseling practice in the 21st century. Author and scholar Leonard Sweet (1999) challenged all believers: "The future is not something we enter. The future is something we create."

As Christian counselors, we need to maintain pace with advances in research, practice, and treatment. If we properly respond to the challenges of militant secularism, which seeks to remove us from our rightful place in the public square, we will faithfully serve our spiritual calling and avoid becoming obsolete. This book is designed to assist in actively shaping our future so we respond to the Spirit in love and loyalty, honor God, and imitate Christ's kindness, humility, and strength in all we do.

The calling of the new Christian counselor, our high privilege and our compelling responsibility, is to be *distinctively Christian and thoroughly professional*. To effectively represent Christ and conduct counseling on the highest level, we are responsible to embrace and stay with the tenor of the times by keeping up with advances in research and in the treatment fields of counseling, psychotherapy, and pastoral care. Our foundation is the truth of God's Word, but we also gain critical insights from a variety of gifted counselors' and authors' theories and practices. We view all the resources available to us as God-given, and we rely on the Word of God and the Spirit of God to produce genuine, lasting change in us and in our clients.

We are partners with God in the grand and exciting adventure of seeing lives transformed. People usually come to us at their point of desperation. They are vulnerable and broken, but they have walked into our offices and our lives seeking a glimmer of hope. The potential for life-changing transformation is at its peak when people are in pain. Our desire and our challenge is to provide warmth, encouragement, and insights that help them to make their way toward God, finding him to be trustworthy, loving, kind, and able.

The time has come for us to speak with appropriate boldness, intellectual confidence, and spiritual astuteness in the work and ministry of counseling. Being a Christian counselor is more than having a title on a business card, and it's far more than a job. We are (or we can become) skilled, open, willing channels for God's grace to flow into other people's lives. The purpose of this book is to embolden and equip those who have a spiritual awareness but lack the knowledge and confidence to declare their position on the role of faith in emotional and psychological healing.

To understand our role more fully, we need to begin with a clear grasp of the universal longing—the cry of every person's soul.

The Cry of the Soul

Listening accurately to the client is a central counseling skill, a skill that enables the counselor to hear in stereo, attending to the client's words as well as the surrounding relational environment. The skilled, attentive Christian counselor hears the cry of the soul—the past hurts, present struggles, and future hopes.

When we listen, what do we hear? Depression, stress and anxiety, loss, abuse, relationship problems, divorce, loneliness, violence, and more. The world is full of brokenness that can be traced back to the opening pages of Genesis. The world started off well—really well. In Gen. 1:31 we read, "God saw all that he had made, and it was very good." Before long, however, a cataclysm shook the created order. The existential earthquake happened when sin entered the picture.

God had given Adam and Eve everything they could dream of wanting. He gave them only one restriction: Don't eat from a particular tree. Satan came along and whispered deception and doubt into Eve's heart— "Did God really say that?" He promised they could "be like God, knowing good and evil." Adam went along with Eve's choice to sin against

God. The problem wasn't that they ate a piece of forbidden fruit. The real issue—the sin of rebellion—was that they wanted independence from God. They chose something other than God to be in the center of their lives, and the results were disastrous. Since that day, people have lived with sin-darkened hearts, desperately in need of a Savior.

The fall of man affected us on every level. It distorted our thinking, warped our desires, wrecked our relationships, and infused our world with sin and death. Worst of all, it caused a separation between God and human beings. What a recipe for disaster and profound sorrow! Two verses in the book of Job describe this plight of man: "Man is born to trouble as surely as sparks fly upward" (5:7) and "Mortals, born of woman, are of few days and full of trouble" (14:1). Every day in our world, news accounts confirm these ancient observations.

Sin has disconnected us from God and made us strangers in the land he gave us. Instead of feeling deeply fulfilled and wonderfully connected, we now realize we don't belong. God created us for something else, something more, but sin has corrupted our world. When Dorothy landed in Oz, she told her faithful little dog, "Toto, I've a feeling we're not in Kansas anymore." Look around. We are all homesick for Eden. Ask the man caught in sex addiction, the single mother who's trying to get by, the couple who live in an armed truce, and the teenager who wonders if life is worth living anymore. The pace, pain, and pressures of modern life are robbing us of our joy.

However, all is not lost. Our Redeemer lives, and he offers us forgiveness, purpose, and ultimate hope. The apostle Paul reflected on the world's brokenness and the hope of eventual restoration:

> The whole creation has been groaning as in the pains of childbirth right up to the present time. Not only so, but we ourselves, who have the firstfruits of the Spirit, groan inwardly as

we wait eagerly for our adoption to sonship, the redemption of our bodies (Rom. 8:22-23).

As believers today, we still groan because we instinctively long for full, complete restoration. But someday we'll dance.

At this point in history, things aren't getting better. Frankly, the road ahead looks even more ominous than the past. Paul declared that in the last days things would only get worse:

> People will be lovers of themselves, lovers of money, boastful, proud, abusive, disobedient to their parents, ungrateful, unholy, without love, unforgiving, slanderous, without self-control, brutal, not lovers of the good, treacherous, rash, conceited, lovers of pleasure rather than lovers of God—having a form of godliness but denying its power (2 Tim. 3:2-5).

But all is not lost. The story of the Bible is a message of hope, a story of redemption and reconciliation. God is working at every turn to call our names and invite us to turn our hearts back from the destruction of sin. We can offer nothing to win his affection or twist his arm. His offer is pure grace.

One of the great love stories in the Old Testament is found in the book of Hosea. In the words of the prophet, we find God's unfathomable love for Israel:

> How can I give you up, Ephraim?
>   How can I hand you over, Israel?
> How can I treat you like Admah?
>   How can I make you like Zeboyim?
> My heart is changed within me;
>   all my compassion is aroused.

> I will not carry out my fierce anger,
>> nor will I devastate Ephraim again (Hos. 11:8-9).

The Israelites had turned their backs on God over and over again, but God still offered them his love and forgiveness. His great love moved him to action.

> Therefore I am now going to allure her;
>> I will lead her into the wilderness
>> and speak tenderly to her.
> There I will give her back her vineyards,
>> and will make the Valley of Achor a door of hope
>> (Hos. 2:14-15).

God isn't surprised by our sin. He knows the evil in our hearts far better than we know it ourselves. Jesus saw into people's hearts and understood their unique needs. He listened to the cry of their souls and was filled with compassion. The writer of the book of Hebrews describes him in this way: "For we do not have a high priest who is unable to empathize with our weaknesses, but we have one who has been tempted in every way, just as we are—yet he did not sin" (4:15). He doesn't stand back in fierce condemnation. He is the judge who pronounces us guilty, but he's also the Savior who pays the price we could never pay for our sins.

He not only sees but also understands and offers hope and healing. When Jesus was on the way to raise Jairus's young daughter from death to life again, a big crowd surrounded him. In this crowd stood a lady who had been bleeding internally for 12 years. As Jesus walked by, she reached through the crowd to touch the edge of his robe. Jesus healed her on the spot, and he stayed to talk to her to assure her of his love. Then Jesus continued on his way to raise Jairus's dear daughter back to life. God's gracious touch is always directed toward the need at hand.

As counselors, we are called to be ambassadors of Christ, to be his hands, feet, and voice. It is our privilege to hear the groans of our clients' hearts and step into their lives at their point of desperate need—to identify and relate to the troubles in their souls, to see the overwhelming burdens they carry and the bondage they are wrestling with, and then to help lead them on the healing path toward freedom. We aren't Christian counselors in name only, and we don't "do Sunday school with clients" by remaining on the surface.

We cannot go deeper with our clients, however, until we've gone deeper with God in our own lives. The most important factor in counseling is the emotional and spiritual vitality of the counselor. If we have hope, we can impart hope. But if we feel hopeless, we will have far less impact on our clients. God has called us to be conduits through which his love can flow to others.

Possessing the Soul

Just before Jesus was betrayed, arrested, tried, tortured, and murdered, he gave some last words of warning to his followers. He told them to expect persecution and hardships. Some, he predicted, would die for their faith—and in fact, all of the apostles but John died as martyrs. In the middle of this warning, Jesus gives his disciples a clear mandate: "By your patience possess your souls" (Lk. 21:19 NKJV).

Clients come to us as broken, needy people who have lost possession of their souls. They feel shattered, alone, and helpless. Jesus's encouragement to his disciples wasn't a promise of health and wealth. He promised a different kind of peace—not the escape from problems, but the experience of God's purpose, power, and pardon in the midst of problems. That's the perspective our clients need from us and from God.

But first, we need to possess our own souls. What does that mean?

It means we find our hearts' true home in Christ alone, and in him, we experience a deeper contentment and fulfillment than we ever dreamed possible. Soul transformation, for us and for our clients, involves taking responsibility for the possession of every element of the life of our souls, including the complicated process of cognition and the shaping of thought processes.

When the grace, truth, and power of God permeate our thinking and choices, they overflow into our practices and into every relationship. We use all the resources God has given us—including the eternal truths of God's Word, the power of the Spirit, and our growing understanding of human behavior—to guide us and effect change in our clients' lives. Through it all, we remain tenacious learners. We sharpen our helping skills and dig deeper into biblical principles, but we realize we always have much more to learn. The apostle Paul was the master theologian, discipler, and church leader, but he admitted that he, like all of us, was always in process.

> Not that I have already obtained all this, or have already arrived at my goal, but I press on to take hold of that for which Christ Jesus took hold of me. Brothers and sisters, I do not consider myself yet to have taken hold of it. But one thing I do: Forgetting what is behind and straining toward what is ahead, I press on toward the goal to win the prize for which God has called me heavenward in Christ Jesus.
>
> All of us, then, who are mature should take such a view of things. And if on some point you think differently, that too God will make clear to you. Only let us live up to what we have already attained (Phil. 3:12-16).

In Galatians, Paul explains the impact of grace, and he gives a necessary warning to avoid slipping back into empty moralism: "It is for freedom that Christ has set us free. Stand firm, then, and do not let your-selves be burdened again by a yoke of slavery" (5:1). Knowing, loving, and following Jesus are far more than going to a building once a week or adhering to some rigid rules. We have far more to offer our clients. Christ-centered, Spirit-drenched counseling is an arduous journey that starts with compassionate listening and heartfelt empathy.

Ultimately, the work of Christian counseling is holy work because it is soul work. Christian counseling, in its purest form, is a covenant between a caregiver and a care seeker to labor collaboratively for the pos-session of the soul—through the power of the Holy Spirit, under the authority of the Word of God, and within a context of accountability and encouragement—for the purpose of the imitation of Christ.

Searching for Hope

Brokenness begs for healing. People are searching for answers, reach-ing for anything to anesthetize the pain and fill the void in their lives. Sol-omon wrote, "All the labor of man is for his mouth, and yet the soul is not satisfied" (Eccl. 6:7 NKJV). Noted psychologist Ernest Becker observed, "Modern man is drinking and drugging himself out of awareness, or he spends his time shopping, which is the same thing" (Becker, 1973, p. 284). Author and professor Dallas Willard (1988, viii) may have said it best:

> Social and political revolutions have shown no tendency to transform the heart of darkness that lies deep in the breast of every human being....Amid a flood of techniques for self-fulfillment there is an epidemic of depression, suicide, personal emptiness, and escapism...all combined with an inability to sustain deep and enduring personal relationships. So obviously the problem is a spiritual one. And so must be the cure.

Most people live in some degree of denial because it's so painful and threatening to admit the depth of their hurt. To numb the pain, they use all kinds of anesthetics—not only drugs and alcohol but also sports, shopping, sex, television, and other pursuits. Many of these aren't wrong in themselves, but they are poor substitutes for the only thing that can really satisfy the longing of the human heart.

We were created for more—we were created to know, love, and follow God, and nothing else will satisfy. Only he can meet the deepest longings of a person's soul. Augustine prayed, "You have made us for yourself, O Lord, and our hearts are restless until they rest in you."

The Modern Search for God

Some people think the term *worship* is limited to religious practices, but it simply means that a person finds something supremely worthy of their time, affections, and resources. For many people, money, careers, children, pleasure, and power are the supreme values of their lives. They devote themselves to these pursuits as much as the desert fathers devoted themselves to God. The locus of their worship is simply in a different place.

God has put it in the hearts of people to seek transcendence. People everywhere are obsessed with God, however they define him. Solomon understood this when he wrote, "He has also set eternity in the human heart; yet no one can fathom what God has done from beginning to end" (Eccl. 3:11). An undeniable spiritual longing spans all of humanity. For example, every year three million Muslims visit Mecca to fulfill their call to a once-in-a-lifetime hajj. Every year hundreds of millions of Hindus trek to the Ganges River and surrounding temples to have their sins purified. And every year, Vatican City is the most visited place on the planet per capita. More than two billion people worldwide follow the teachings of the Bible. Conversely, only 2% of the world's population consider themselves atheists (Robinson, 2011).

This divine search is increasingly motivated by a deep thirst for the sacred. A recent Gallup poll indicated that 90% of Americans believe in God (Newport, 2013). Additional research shows that deeply committed believers seek counselors who explicitly incorporate prayer, the Bible, and other faith-based resources into their therapy (Wade, Worthington, & Vogel, 2007). In every generation before, care seekers have looked first to a pastor, priest, or rabbi even though secular resources have expanded enormously in the last 60 years (Clinton & Ohlschlager, 2002; Richards & Bergin, 2005). Confirming the Gallup poll observations, a recent Newsweek poll found that 91% of American adults claim a belief in God, while another Gallup poll reports that 73% of Americans "are convinced that God exists" (*Newsweek*, 2007; Newport, 2006).

What accounts for the global, pervasive pursuit of God? Is the earth's population exhausted by the pace, pain, and pressure of modern living? We believe that the past 100 years have created a sea of change in the hearts and minds of seekers everywhere because the grand promises of technology, information, and wealth have proved to be empty lies. People have more physical prosperity than ever, but their hearts remain empty. They instinctively sense something is wrong with the promises. Out of this vacuum, many are turning to God. We believe the future of effective caregiving belongs to those who dare to press in closer to the heart of God and to apply treatment strategies that are firmly anchored in Scripture and divine revelation. Godly change is transformational change—change that lasts and has a deeper impact—and people of faith are now demanding nothing less.

Many people are tired of religion, but they are fascinated with spirituality, the universal "God thirst." It's not surprising, then, that when people of faith consider mental health services, they want God in the equation. In fact, two thirds of Americans want their faith addressed in mental health care (Hage, 2006).

Overcoming the Faith Gap

Unfortunately, in the field of mental health care, there's been a serious faith gap between those seeking services and the service providers. Not long ago, if you talked about God or faith in mental health circles, you would have been laughed out of the room. Mental health providers often viewed faith as insignificant or even a hindrance to therapy. Many counseling theories taught in counselor training programs were biased against faith.

For example, Sigmund Freud, the father of psychoanalytic theory, viewed the idea of God as irrational and irrelevant, writing, "Religion is illusion and it derives its strength from the fact that it falls in with our instinctual desires" (Freud, 1932). Even Albert Ellis, one of the early leaders of cognitive theory, concluded, "The sane and effective psychotherapist should not...go along with patients' religious orientation...for this is equivalent to trying to help them live successfully with their emotional illness" (Ellis, 1980).

Seekers must be persistent when they search for professional counselors who value faith as part of the therapeutic process. Sadly, licensed therapists believe in God at much lower rates than do the general population (Aten & Leach, 2009; Pargament, 2007). The training and practice of therapy seems to be significantly secularized, but many people look for Christian counselors who understand and value spiritual life. Furthermore, the ethics codes of every professional counseling discipline have strengthened their commitment to religious diversity as part of the overall dedication to multiculturalism. Faith matters, and the faith of anyone seeking counseling must be respected and supported by all therapists today.

Good News About Faith and Mental Health

Recent research on the relationship of faith and mental health has shattered the prejudice that religion is pathological and should be avoided (Larson & Larson, 2003). Increasingly, outcome studies document the positive role of faith in mental health (Scalise & Clinton, 2015; Koenig, 2004; Wade, Worthington, & Vogel, 2007). Psychiatrist and researcher Harold Koenig (2011) shows that true faith enhances physical and mental health. Christian counselors are now aligning themselves to the truth revealed in this research—that faith-filled clients become stronger and healthier physically and mentally.

The research has found that most people want their faith to be addressed and integrated in the therapeutic process (Hage, 2006). In fact, recent studies are showing that therapeutic alignment in counseling is critical. Matching counselors of faith with clients of faith is significant to positive therapeutic outcomes. Clients who are deeply committed to their faith appear to prefer clinicians who can incorporate prayer, Scripture, and other faith resources (Wade et al., 2007). Therapist-client congruence is a powerful factor in counseling effectiveness. If spirituality is not considered, we're asking 98% of the world (those who believe in God) to set aside their deeply held personal values and embrace an irreligious therapist's view. That's neither rational nor helpful.

Practitioners have started to incorporate spiritual assessment and faith-based interventions in their counseling practices. Furthermore, empirical studies have supported the assertion that religious faith positively impacts physical and mental health (Koenig, 2004). Christian counseling, in fact, is right in the center of the developing force of religious faith and spirituality in psychotherapy (Keltner & Haidt, 2003; Koenig, 2004; Sandhu, 2007). The power of this positive relationship between faith and mental health is so great that many have begun calling it the fifth force—after the first four forces in psychotherapy: psychodynamic, behavioral, humanistic, and multicultural influences (Garzon, 2011).

Faith Matters

Many mental health organizations are now making provisions for spirituality in the counseling context. We believe that graduate counseling training programs should conduct sensitivity training to help therapists relate more effectively to religious clients.

Of the approximately 150 medical schools in the United States, 100 offer some variation of spirituality-in-medicine coursework, and 75 of those schools require their students to take at least one course on the topic (Booth, 2008).

The American Counseling Association and American Psychological Association each have a division to provide resources to professionals who recognize the significance of religion in the lives of their clients and in the discipline of psychology.* These organizations have concluded that faith matters in the therapeutic context. It's impossible to divorce counseling and psychology from its moral and philosophical roots.

To empower this fifth force in the 21st century, we need well-trained practitioners who are willing to wisely and persistently align themselves with Christ and learn to integrate God's truth and grace in their practices. We also need talented researchers who will help establish the efficacy of

---

* The American Counseling Association division is the Association for Spiritual, Ethical, and Religious Values in Counseling (http://www.aservic.org). The American Psychological Association division is the Society for the Psychology of Religion and Spirituality. It "seeks a broad dialogue on religion with all the areas of the social sciences" (http://www.division36.org/).

Christian counseling as applied to a variety of mental health disorders. We need gifted educators who will teach the ways, the truth, and the life of Christ to eager students. Christian ethicists are also critical. They can show us the way through deep and difficult issues that will trip up the naive and the unprepared.

Competent counselors and psychotherapists are needed to show others that God matters and that he is willing and able to assit with healing if we simply cry to him for help. We can echo Paul's prayer for the Colossians:

> For this reason, since the day we heard about you, we have not stopped praying for you. We continually ask God to fill you with the knowledge of his will through all the wisdom and understanding that the Spirit gives, so that you may live a life worthy of the Lord and please him in every way: bearing fruit in every good work, growing in the knowledge of God, being strengthened with all power according to his glorious might so that you may have great endurance and patience, and giving joyful thanks to the Father, who has qualified you to share in the inheritance of his holy people in the kingdom of light. For he has rescued us from the dominion of darkness and brought us into the kingdom of the Son he loves, in whom we have redemption, the forgiveness of sins (Col. 1:9-14).

Embracing Our Spiritual and Scientific Foundations

The work of Christ-honoring Christian counseling begins with a solid foundation. If our foundation is not sound, the work will totter and collapse, for "every city or household divided against itself will not stand" (Mt. 12:25). Scripture speaks repeatedly to the importance of building carefully and inviting God into our work.

> Therefore everyone who hears these words of mine and puts them into practice is like a wise man who built his house on the rock. The rain came down, the streams rose, and the winds blew and beat against that house; yet it did not fall, because it had its foundation on the rock (Mt. 7:24-25).

> But each one should build with care. For no one can lay any foundation other than the one already laid, which is Jesus Christ (1 Cor. 3:10-11).

As we seek to build "the house" of Christian counseling and soul-care ministry in the 21st century, we need to continually remind ourselves that without the foundation of Jesus Christ, the Word of God and the Spirit of God, our efforts will be based on human wisdom and strength instead of God's eternal truth and divine power. Christ is the chief cornerstone. He emphasized this simple truth to his disciples by saying, "Apart from me you can do nothing" (Jn. 15:5).

Throughout the development of Christian counseling, leaders sometimes have become enamored with the insights of psychology and neglected our biblical and spiritual foundations. Pioneering Christian counseling leader Arch Hart wisely lamented that Christian counselors often "run ahead of our biblical and theological roots" (Hart, 2001). Let this not be said of us!

Increasingly, those seeking mental health services are looking for counselors who align with them and partner with God on issues of faith, seeking to possess the soul and fully address spiritual issues as part of the counseling process. Mark McMinn (2011) has challenged members of our profession to be astute and accurate in three intersecting areas—the psychological, the theological, and the spiritual domains. A holistic focus demands we attend to biological, psychological, social, and spiritual factors when conducting assessment and treatment. Also, a significant movement in Christian counseling is developing the discipline of spiritual formation while pressing into the fundamental goal of change—cultivating vibrant intimacy with Christ (Col. 1:27-28).

Embracing the Revelation of Scripture

Christian counselors need to be students of the broad scope of biblical theology, and they need to be armed with key biblical passages that speak powerfully and graciously to the specific needs of clients. (See chapter 2 for an expanded outline on the biblical and spiritual foundations of Christian counseling.) Consider Paul's instructions in 1 Thess. 5:14-24 (NKJV):

> Now we exhort you, brethren, warn those who are unruly, comfort the fainthearted, uphold the weak, be patient with all. See that no one renders evil for evil to anyone, but always pursue what is good both for yourselves and for all.
>
> Rejoice always, pray without ceasing, in everything give thanks; for this is the will of God in Christ Jesus for you.
>
> Do not quench the Spirit. Do not despise prophecies. Test all things; hold fast to what is good. Abstain from every form of evil.
>
> Now may the God of peace Himself sanctify you completely; and may your whole spirit, soul, and body be preserved blameless at the coming of our Lord Jesus Christ. He who calls you is faithful, who also will do it.

The *ultimate* task of a Christian counselor is to be Christ's partner in the process of redemption and restoration. The first verse in this passage could serve as the *penultimate* goal, defining the core competencies of the Christian counselor—confronting, giving comfort, supporting and advocating for the weak, and extending patience to everyone. To warn the unruly—to confront the wrongdoer and point out the better way of Christ—reflects the heart of the nouthetic, or biblical counselor. To comfort the fainthearted is to give essential aid to fearful, faithless, and faltering people who are unable to walk on their own in the face of a daunting situation. Upholding the weak is very similar, calling for defense of and advocacy for needy people against controlling and abusive powers. And the call to be patient with everyone challenges any false assumptions (ours or our clients') that change is easy, quick, and simple. These are the four elements of a paracentric model for counseling—*to parakaleo*, or "coming alongside" someone who needs aid and calls out for help.

To his disciples, Jesus explained the intimate and powerful connection between him and our efforts to honor him. The motivation and the power to please God come from a vital connection with Jesus.

> I am the vine, you are the branches. He who abides in Me, and I in him, bears much fruit; for without Me you can do nothing. If anyone does not abide in Me, he is cast out as a branch and is withered; and they gather them and throw them into the fire, and they are burned. If you abide in Me, and My words abide in you, you will ask what you desire, and it shall be done for you. By this My Father is glorified, that you bear much fruit; so you will be My disciples.

> As the Father loved Me, I also have loved you; abide in My love. If you keep My commandments, you will abide in My love, just as I have kept My Father's commandments and abide in His love (Jn. 15:5-10 NKJV).

Advances in Theory, Research, and Practice

A growing cadre of researchers (see Worthington, Jennings, & DiBlasio, 2010; Garzon, Garver, Kleinschuster, Tan, & Hill, 2001; Koenig, 2011) are advancing Christian counseling on empirical frontiers. They have taken major steps to establish credible clinical outcomes of faith-based counseling in the ongoing development of Christian mental health care. Noted Christian counseling leader Siang-Yang Tan is calling for outcome-based research to identify the BEST therapies in Christian counseling (Biblically informed, Empirically Supported Therapies) (Tan, 2011). Recent advances in theory, research, and practice (Collins, 2007; Clinton & Ohlschlager, 2002; Garzon et al., 2001; E. Johnson, 2010; Koenig, 2004; McMinn & Campbell, 2007; Worthington, 2005; Worthington et al., 2010) are producing innovative thoughts, insights, and treatments, anchored and rooted in Judeo-Christian theology and salted with solid psychological science, to treat a wide array of clinical issues (Clinton & Hawkins, 2011; Worthington, Witvliet, Pietrini, & Miller, 2007).

In addition, advances in neurobiological research may provide a legitimate theoretical and practical structure for Christian counseling. Neuroscience offers a rich interplay between the mind, the brain, and the network of relationships, which helps us understand mechanisms of a wide array of therapeutic concepts, strategies, and techniques (Clinton & Sibcy, 2012). Additionally, the study of neuroscience fits well within the Christian worldview, especially in terms of the direct influence on cognition, affect, and behavior (Crabb, 2007).

Multicultural Care and Advocacy

The world is getting smaller by the day. People and concepts are more accessible than ever. Christian counselors are partnering with many different cultures and communities around the world in order to "proclaim good news to the poor...bind up the brokenhearted...[and] proclaim freedom for the captives" (Isa. 61:1). Technological advances are making *glocalization* possible—the process of thinking globally and acting locally. Web-based strategies and partnerships with local believers and churches all around the world enable Christian counselors to be informed, give input, and facilitate action to address issues with global consequences, including genocide, human rights, orphan care, refugees, persecuted and tortured Christians, the sex slave trade, and global environmental concerns.

Throughout the world, trauma is the new mission field. In war-torn and impoverished areas, people suffer tragic emotional wounds and have tremendous spiritual needs. Leaders in the field have observed that trauma is a unique problem and an opportunity for Christian counselors to offer hope and healing to those who have been abandoned, abused, traumatized, enslaved, or otherwise mistreated. Through the future development of a Client Bill of Rights, the American Association of Christian Counselors seeks to propel Christian counseling to the forefront of client advocacy to ensure the availability of compassionate care to everyone, including (and perhaps especially) the poor and disenfranchised, those persecuted for their religious or political beliefs, and victims of poverty, disease, and war.

WISDOM'S REVIEW

Solomon was the wisest of men, but he didn't have supreme confidence in people's ability to understand the complexities of the human condition. He knew that God is the ultimate source of wisdom, love, strength, and joy.

I applied my heart to know,
To search and seek out wisdom and the reason of things,
To know the wickedness of folly,
Even of foolishness and madness....
Truly, this only I have found:
That God made man upright,
But they have sought out many schemes.
Who is like the wise man?
And who knows the interpretation of a thing?
(Eccl. 7:25,29; 8:1 NKJV).

As Christian counselors, our responsibility is to pursue God and his wisdom with all our hearts. In this book, we want to bend your learning curve toward God's wisdom so you will become a mature and discerning believer, able to hear the truth from God and able to give it to those who come to you for help. However, like Solomon, we want to remind you that wisdom has its limits—sinful and finite minds can grasp only so much wisdom. We will close each chapter with Wisdom's Review to give some final thoughts about the material of the chapter. In Proverbs, Solomon again pursues wisdom and explains where it can be found. We can apply his encouragement to our role as Christian counselors.

[Christian counselor,] if you accept my words
    and store up my commands within you,
turning your ear to wisdom
    and applying your heart to understanding—
indeed, if you call out for insight
    and cry aloud for understanding,
and if you look for it like silver
    and search for it as for hidden treasure,
then you will understand the fear of the LORD

and find the knowledge of God.
For the LORD gives wisdom;
from his mouth come knowledge and understanding.
He holds success in store for the upright,
he is a shield to those whose walk is blameless,
for he guards the course of the just
and protects the way of his faithful ones.
Then you will understand what is right and just
and fair—every good path.
For wisdom will enter your heart,
and knowledge will be pleasant to your soul (Pr. 2:1-10).

This is our hope and prayer for you as you increasingly love God, study his Word, and apply the God-given insights gleaned from Scripture and study in your practice.

References

Aten, J., & Leach, M. (Eds). (2009). *Spirituality and the therapeutic process: A comprehensive resource from intake to termination.* Washington, DC: American Psychological Association.

Becker, E. (1973). *The denial of death.* New York, NY: Free Press Paperbacks.

Booth, B. (2008). More schools teaching spirituality in medicine. Retrieved from http://www.amednews.com/article/20080310/profession/303109968/7/

Clinton, T., & Hawkins, R. (Eds.). (2011). *The popular encyclopedia of Christian counseling* (pp. 125–131). Eugene, OR: Harvest House.

Clinton, T., & Ohlschlager, G. (Eds.). (2002). *Competent Christian counseling: Foundations and practice of compassionate soul care* (pp. 62–66). Colorado Springs, CO: WaterBrook Press.

Clinton, T., & Sibcy, G. (2012). Christian counseling, interpersonal neurobiology, and the future. *Journal of Psychology and Theology* 40(2), 141.

Collins, G. (2007). *Christian counseling: A comprehensive guide.* Nashville, TN: Thomas Nelson.

Crabb, L. (2007). Enter the mystery: Heart first, then with your head. *Christian Counseling Today, 15*(4), 58.

Ellis, A. (1980). *The case against religion: A psychotherapist's view and the case against religiosity.* Austin, TX: American Atheist Press. Retrieved from http://www.nasonart.com/personal/lifelessons/CaseAgainstReligion.html

Freud, S. (1932). A philosophy of life. Lecture 35 in *New introductory lectures on psycho-analysis.* Retrieved from http://www.marxists.org/reference/subject/philosophy/works/at/freud.htm

Garzon, F. L. (2011). Spirituality in counseling. In T. Clinton & R. Hawkins (Eds.), *The popular encyclopedia of Christian counseling* (pp. 22–24). Eugene, OR: Harvest House.

Garzon, F. L., Garver, S., Kleinschuster, D., Tan, E., & Hill, J. (2001). Freedom in Christ: Quasi-experimental research on the Neil Anderson approach. *Journal of Psychology and Theology, 29*(1), 41–51.

Hage, S. M. (2006). A closer look at spirituality in psychology training programs. *Professional Psychology: Research and Practice, 37*(3), 303–310.

Hart, A. (2001). Has self-esteem lost its way? *Christian Counseling Today, 9*(1), 8.

Johnson, B. A. (2010). *Addiction medicine: Science and practice.* New York, NY: Springer Science & Business Media.

Johnson, E. (2010). *Psychology & Christianity: Five views* (pp. 9–47). Downers Grove, IL: InterVarsity Press.

Keltner, D., & Haidt, J. (2003). Approaching awe, a moral, spiritual, and aesthetic emotion. *Cognition and Emotion, 17,* 297–314. doi:10.1080/02699930302297

Koenig, Harold G. (2004). Religion, spirituality, and medicine: Research findings and implications for clinical practice. *Southern Medical Journal, 97,* 1194–1200.

Koenig, Harold G. (2011). *Medicine, religion, and health: Where science and spirituality meet.* West Conshohocken, PA: Templeton Press.

Koenig, Harold G. (2011). *Spirituality and health research: Methods, measurements, statistics and resources.* West Conshohocken, PA: Templeton Press.

Larson, D. B., & Larson, S. S. (2003). Spirituality's potential relevance to physical and emotional health: A brief review of quantitative research. *Journal of Psychology and Theology, 31*(1), 37–51.

McMinn, M. R. (2011). *Psychology, theology, and spirituality in Christian counseling* (pp. 31–59). Carol Stream, IL: Tyndale House.

McMinn, M. R., & Campbell, C. D. (2007). *Integrative psychotherapy: Toward a comprehensive Christian approach* (p. 109). Downers Grove, IL: InterVarsity Press.

Newport, F. (2006). Who believes in God and who doesn't? Belief in God correlated with socioeconomic status. Retrieved from http://www.gallup.com/poll/23470/who-believes-god-who-doesnt.aspx

Newport, F. (2013). More than 9 in 10 Americans continue to believe in God. Retrieved from http://www.gallup.com/poll/147887/americans-continue-believe-god.aspx

Newsweek. (2007). Newsweek poll: 90% believe in God. Retrieved from http://www.newsweek.com/newsweek-poll-90-believe-god-97611

Pargament, K. I. (2007). *Spiritually integrated psychotherapy: Understanding and addressing the sacred* (p. 9). New York, NY: Guilford Press.

Richards, P. S., & Bergin, A. E. (2005). *A spiritual strategy for counseling and psychotherapy.* Washington, DC: American Psychological Association.

Robinson, B. A. (2011). Religions of the world: Number of adherents of major religions, their geographical distribution, date founded, and sacred texts. Retrieved from www.religioustolerance.org/worldrel.htm

Sandhu, D. S. (2007). Seven stages of spiritual development: A framework to solve psycho-spiritual problems. In O. J. Morgan (Ed.), *Counseling and spirituality: Views from the profession* (pp. 64–92). New York, NY: Houghton Mifflin.

Scalise, E., & Clinton, T. (2015). The case for faith: Celebrating hope in mental health care. *CounselEd* (a publication of the American Association of Christian Counselors).

Sweet, L. (1999). *SoulTsunami: Sink or swim in the new millennium culture* (p. 55). Grand Rapids, MI: Zondervan.

Tan, S.-Y. (2011). *Counseling and psychotherapy: A Christian perspective* (p. 318). Grand Rapids, MI: Baker Books.

Wade, N., Worthington, E. L., Jr., & Vogel, D. (2007). Effectiveness of religiously tailored interventions in Christian therapy. *Psychotherapy Research, 17,* 91–105.

Willard, D. (1988). *The spirit of the disciplines: Understanding how God changes lives.* San Franscisco, CA: Harper and Row.

Worthington, E. L., Jr. (2005). *Handbook of forgiveness* (p. 435). New York, NY: Brunner-Routledge.

Worthington, E. L., Jr., Jennings II, D. J., & DiBlasio, F. A. (2010). Interventions to promote forgiveness in couple and family context: Conceptualization, review, and analysis. *Journal of Psychology and Theology, 38*(4), 231–245.

Worthington, E. L., Jr., Witvliet, C. V. O., Pietrini, P., & Miller, A. J. (2007). Forgiveness, health, and well-being: A review of evidence for emotional versus decisional forgiveness, dispositional forgivingness, and reduced unforgiveness. *Journal of Behavioral Medicine, 30,* 291–302. doi:10.1007/s10865-007-9105-8

2

What Is Christian Counseling?

Definitions, Undergirding, Convictions, and Ethical Practice

When people walk through the doors of our counseling offices, what do they expect? Or maybe a better question is, what *should* they expect? Christian counseling has been defined and described by many respected authorities. It involves far more than a Christian who happens to be a counselor, and it's not injecting a verse from the Bible into a counseling session. In essence, Christian counseling is a form of discipleship designed to help free people to experience God's pardon, purpose, and power so they become fully devoted followers of Jesus Christ. It's nothing less than that. It involves the process of leading others to experience wholeness, spiritual maturity, relational competency, and a stability in intellect and experience (Collins, 1993).

People usually come to us because they have lost their way. They can be despondent, disturbed, desperate, and perhaps furious at God, others who hurt them, and even themselves. Our goal as Christian counselors is to help them "possess their souls" so they can trust God, love him with all their hearts, and respond to the challenges and difficulties in their lives with confidence and hope.

Those who offer overly simplistic answers do a disservice to their clients and to God. Life is complicated. The problems people suffer often have many layers of causation and impact. Few are unraveled easily. We have the unspeakable privilege of stepping into our clients' lives as God's representatives—his ambassadors in times of desperate need. To be equipped, we need to understand and appreciate the high honor and the daunting task of helping those who seek our assistance.

Everyone Needs God, But...

As a young pastor, I (Ron) became intensely aware of the paradox of living in a tragically fallen world that still reflects the perfection and beauty of God. I became convinced that what people really needed was God, because ultimately, spiritual issues are at the root of all of life's problems. Quite often, however, a person's troubles are connected to deeply habituated thought and behavior patterns that seldom vanish as soon as the person is saved and begins faithfully reading the Bible. In 1 Thess. 5:23, Paul says that genuine change requires attention to the whole spirit, the entire soul, and the whole body—no dimension of the person can be overlooked. People don't walk with God in a vacuum. We learn to follow him in every moment, every relationship, and every goal.

The grace of God changes everything. The default mode of the human heart is self-justification, trying to prove we are worthy and acceptable to God and to other people. Everyone needs God, but we would rather chart our own course—which brings disastrous results. The only hope of mankind is the forgiveness, love, and grace of God. When we reject or ignore him, we are left to ourselves. But when we have the courage to admit our need for a Savior, we find him to be beautiful, kind, and strong. He is a King who has earned our love and trust. As we grasp more of his greatness and grace, we are glad to follow him.

Many people, however, mistake keeping rules for a real relationship. Some see God as a business partner who'd better come through on our deal. Others treat God as a vending machine that dispenses blessings when they do their part. Our part, these people mistakenly assume, is to do the right thing to earn God's approval. Larry Crabb observed, "It's about time to go beneath the moralism that assumes the church's job is done when it instructs people in biblical principles and then exhorts them to do right" (Crabb, 1997, p. xvii). His deeper solution is the creation of true communities "where the heart of God is home, where the humble and wise learn to shepherd those on the path behind them, where trusting strugglers lock arms with others as together they journey" through this minefield called life.

People who come to us for help are often a mixed bag. They are sinners, and they are wounded. For years, they've lived with nagging fears or inflated arrogance (actually, arrogant people don't come to see us very often). In *Competent Christian Counseling*, I wrote about seven kinds of people populating the 21st-century church—people who require so much more than a Sunday school approach to growth and maturity (Hawkins, Hindson, & Clinton, 2002, pp. 409–414):

> people who are dead at the core of their personalities
> people who are "living in the flesh"
> people who have habituated thought patterns that need renewal
> people who are addicted and need to be set free
> people who are troubled by trauma and post-traumatic stress

people who are best described as the "walking wounded"

people who are beset by evil powers

If we can identify the profile of the people sitting across from us in our offices, we can tailor our biblical approach to each one. They're all wounded, and they're all sinners, but they need specialized insights, encouragement, and care.

The Modern Crisis in Church Ministry

The modern church has many programs and events for evangelism but very few successful programs for discipleship—for maturing the people of the church so they truly experience the freedom of forgiveness and the power of the Spirit to transform their lives. Attracting people is a worthy goal, but Jesus didn't stop there. He taught them, challenged them, and modeled a life of complete devotion to the Father. Discipleship is meeting people where they are, applying the life-changing message of Christ, and helping them take steps to follow God in every aspect of their lives. That involves much more than attracting a lot of people.

All of us are broken, and all of us have deep wounds and heartaches. Jesus isn't looking for people who have it all together. He's looking for those who will take his hand. Christian counseling is one of the most powerful forms of discipleship. It takes people at their point of need, nurtures them, and points them to the life-changing love of God.

Discipleship is the most challenging task a person will ever face. It requires complete honesty, dependence, and tenacity. If we don't understand the nature of discipleship, how can we help people follow Jesus? How could we help anyone move forward?

Hurts, distractions, resentments, and false hopes cloud the minds and hearts of the people God has called us to care for. It's our job and our great privilege to take the message of the gospel to them so that it frees them from the penalty and power of sin and motivates them to love their new King.

My Encounter With Psychology

My early encounter with psychology was positive and stimulating. When I began reading the psychological literature, I soon realized it described a way of relating to people that allows them to feel safe so they can be honest about areas of their lives in which they experience bondage. As I read more of the literature, I saw a strong correlation between biblical truth and some of the observations of psychology. Suddenly, I saw the principles and stories in the Bible with new eyes: People in the pages of Scripture struggled with negative habits and thoughts, with sins and wounds, and with fears and hopes.

The human heart cries out for love, justice, and mercy—exactly what God offers anyone who will believe in him. The Bible has a lot to say about the problem of bitterness. In many places and in many ways, the Scriptures show how God's forgiveness of our sins gives us the capacity and the motivation to forgive others. But of course, forgiveness, trust, and reconciliation are never simple and easy. As I accepted the reality of this complex world, I learned to appreciate people with different perspectives without judging them or falsely assuming I could show them an easy way to deal with life's most nagging problems.

Sin Mars Everything

People have offered many different definitions of sin. Many think of it as breaking God's law, but it's more than that. It's breaking God's heart. Sin isn't a list of terrible things we shouldn't do. It's putting our hope in anyone or anything other than God, and it's getting our sense of identity from anything other than him. People who walk in the doors of our counseling offices may have suffered deep wounds, but their real problem is even deeper. Sin is not about a moralistic code of behavior, but brokenness in our relationship with God. In many ways, the process of sanctification—Christian growth—occurs as the forgiveness of God becomes real and operative in our lives moment by moment. It's difficult, but we have the Word of God, the Spirit of God, and the people of God to help us take steps forward.

The journey of forgiveness, healing, and change is an arduous one, full of complex and difficult challenges. A proper understanding of psychology doesn't add anything to the Bible's teaching on human nature, but it can give insights into the complexities of human behavior, learning, and human physiology so people can apply the truth of the Scriptures more powerfully and specifically in their lives.

The Complexity of Life

In recent years, I've developed a new appreciation for the complexity of the human experience. New research has shown unique elements in personality, the way the brain works, and other aspects of motivation and relationships. In addition, some gifted pastors and authors have written eloquently about the wonderful grace of Jesus Christ. Their clear, compelling message of God's amazing love stirs our hearts and renews our hope. Still, countless people sit in churches week after week without encountering the life-changing power of God's love. They live in bondage to hopelessness, guilt, addictions, depression, bitterness, and other heart-numbing problems. Many of them know Christ, but they never have really experienced the measure of freedom that God wants for them.

Why is this? There may be many reasons, but one of them is that many pastors haven't clearly articulated the debilitating power of sin (so these people don't really understand their need for grace) or the beauty and power of the gospel. We need to do more than entertain people on Sunday mornings. We need to tell them the truth—the Bible's truth about their true condition and the hope they can find in Jesus Christ.

This book is designed to help you understand this complex interplay of truths and forces. That's why we are calling our model of counseling a biblical and transformational approach. There is nothing new under the sun—we're just providing language, some handles, and a clearer road map to help us understand this rich spiritual journey. We hope this book will enlighten you, inspire you, and challenge you to be clear and humble, gentle and strong as you help people with life's most pressing problems.

Grace and Truth Together

The new Christian counselor is committed to definitions of Christian counseling that do justice to biblical truth regarding sin and the brokenness and damage people experience because of sin. But the new Christian counselor is also committed to knowing God deeply—to the reality that transformational change is a challenging process that requires specific attention to all elements in the human personality.

In addition, we use counseling models that address the complexity of human nature, including hidden elements that are often the true sources of distress. In recognizing the complexity of human nature, we use every compatible resource in the medical community, the psychological community, and the pastoral community. The problems in people's lives are so vast and the resources so near that we can't afford to live in isolation. A narrow and simplistic approach doesn't honor God or help those who come to us for help. We can't become experts in all these fields, but we can become skilled in finding resources and making appropriate referrals. We can become experts at bringing a comprehensive array of healing balm to the distresses of people.

A Modern Ministry-Profession

Christian counseling as we know it today is approximately 70 years old. Most people who have studied the Christian counseling movement date it from shortly after World War II. But it is a mistake to think that the movement came out of nowhere after the war. It has a rich and long history (Johnson, 2009). Modern Christian counseling is rooted in pastoral care and congregant education in the church—soul care activities that reach back the entire two millennia of church history. Influenced in the 20th century by psychology and modern mental health care, we can identify the thread of Christian counseling running on the dual tracks of ministry and profession.

A few decades ago, pioneers in Christian counseling forged new biblical direction and professional development to help people grow and mature in Christ. We cannot forget the important early contributions made by Swiss physician Paul Tournier, American pastors Jay Adams and David Seamands, American psychologists Wayne Oates, Gary Collins, Bill Kirwan, Arch Hart, Bill Backus, and Larry Crabb, and such academic researchers and theorists as Ev Worthington, Mark McMinn, Scott Stanley, Ian Jones, Frank Minirth, Paul Meier, and Eric Johnson.

Three of the most influential pioneers in our ministry development are Gary Collins, Jay Adams, and Paul Tournier.

Gary Collins is a clinical psychologist and prolific author who delivered an "integrative model" of Christian counseling in his seminary courses. His primary model of "discipleship counseling" is outlined further in this chapter. It led to the development of the "How to Be a People Helper" system that became a significant model of lay training in churches around the world. He maintains international influence in the development of Christian counseling, coaching, and ministry through his writing, speaking, and consulting.

Jay Adams is a Reformed pastor who was challenged to teach a seminary course in counseling. He dug into the Scriptures and developed a model of "nouthetic counseling" that was wholly focused on and rooted in the Scriptures. Adams was opposed to an academic model of training that emphasized the sickness of the individual. He developed hands-on pastoral training that invited God into every session with a goal of pleasing God in all we say and do. His training model placed a premium on Christian hope overcoming the patterns and behavior of sin in a person's life. By faith, an expectation of change is encouraged in every session, and the counselee is taught to put off the "old man" and put on the "new man" redeemed in Christ.

Paul Tournier was a Swiss physician who developed a "whole person" worldview involving more than physical and biomedical change. In addition, he required investment in the soul and spirit of the person to bring about godly change. He wrote his first book, *The Healing of Persons*, to advance his person-centered model. *Christianity Today* (2006) included his book *The Meaning of Persons* on its list of the 50 most influential books for evangelicals in the 20th century. Tournier believed that God came alive in the dialogue between healer and the one helped, and that life was imparted and healing delivered in these "holy conversations."

The Message of the Triune God

Christian counseling is triadic in that it recognizes the complexity of body, soul, and spirit, and it also is triadic in another very important sense. In Christian counseling, God the Father, Jesus Christ, and the Holy Spirit are present by invitation in the counseling process. These three members of the triune Godhead each come, by invitation, to provide a special ministry and gifting for the counselor and client.

The Father comes to say, "I have loved you from before your creation, and I love you now and forevermore. I am providing all the resources you need to overcome in the present, and I promise you a future in my presence. This powerful promise will give you hope in the valleys and struggles of your life."

The Holy Spirit comes to say, "I am God, one of the Father's provisions for you. I am the God who brought Jesus Christ back from death and breathed life into his dead body. No matter how immense your challenges may be, I will give you the power to overcome them. Just trust me."

Jesus Christ comes to say, "I am the way, the truth, and the life. I am your Savior, King, and friend. I am the embodiment of forgiveness, love, and grace. I came that you might have abundant life. I will carry you to the place of peace and safety if you will hear my voice, embrace it, trust me, and allow me to carry you in my arms across the burning coals you are experiencing. I will never leave you, and we will live together in eternal peace and purpose."

Safe in Him and Seeking Scriptural Direction

Secular psychological interventions are naturalistic or sometimes mildly religious, and they often treat spirituality as vague, self-generated, and self-centered. Christian counseling, on the other hand, sees all of life through the scriptural lens of God the Father's passion for an intimate connection with the people he created in his image. He loves us and wants a relationship of love and trust. He has given us the sacrifice of Christ to cleanse our sins and provide us with a bridge we may cross to reconnect with him. He has provided the Holy Spirit to empower us to know, love, and follow him.

Some people ask, "Why don't we experience complete freedom and power now?" Good question. The kingdom of God was inaugurated at the cross, but it won't be fully consummated until we are with God in the new heaven and new earth. In between, our responsibility is to trust God so that his kingdom comes and his will is done on earth as it is in heaven. The rule of Christ in each believer today is accomplished by the Spirit's work and our tenacious (but often halting) trust in God, which enables us to experience more of a full, abundant life as God's beloved children. In his love and power, we gradually experience personal transformation through growth in emotional, psychological, and spiritual health. Christian counseling and caregiving is designed for nothing less than this.

Christian Counseling Defined

Definitions of Christian counseling have changed over time. Simply put, Christian counseling is a dynamic, collaborative process involving at least three persons—the counselor, the client, and the triune God of the Bible—aimed at transformational change for the purpose of producing higher levels of emotional, psychological, and spiritual health in persons seeking help. One of the unique features of Christian counseling is that the counselor is a junior partner with God, the senior partner. The collaborative undertaking between caregiver, care seeker, and the triune God, however, includes other important elements, including the foundational truths of the Word of God and a community of support and accountability.

Christian counseling is triadic at its relational foundation. God (by invitation), the client, and the counselor are engaged in a collaborative and highly interactive process moving along a continuum of change from dis-ease in one or more dimensions of the soul to higher levels of a sense of ease—safety, peace, forgiveness, joy, healing, and well-being. As the vehicle for the movement of God, the counselor is dedicated to teach the client how to invite God to be the redeemer and healer, and how to sense the presence and power of God.

Christian counseling proclaims *a living God who longs to comfort and console humans in the midst of their struggles in a broken world.* The Scriptures continuously portray the God of the Bible at the center of all initiatives directed at comforting the hurting. Paul announces this truth in his message to the Corinthians.

> Blessed be the God and Father of our Lord Jesus Christ, the Father of mercies and God of all comfort, who comforts us in all our tribulation, that we may be able to comfort those who are in any trouble, with the comfort with which we ourselves are comforted by God. For as the sufferings of Christ abound in us, so our consolation also abounds through Christ (2 Cor. 1:3-5 NKJV).

In a famous sermon, Pastor B. B. Warfield studied the gospels to identify every emotion described in the life of Christ (Warfield, n.d.). He found the full range of emotions in Jesus, but one stood out among the others—compassion. Jesus was often "moved with compassion" to reach out to the outcasts, touch lepers, welcome prostitutes and tax gatherers, and care for those who were forgotten or despised by society. When Jesus saw their needs, his heart broke, and he did whatever it took—including sacrificing himself on the cross—to meet their needs. He wept when a friend died. He defied the arrogant, narrow religious leaders who valued their strict rules more than healing a crippled man on a day of worship. Jesus wasn't a stained-glass guy. His heart broke because he cared so deeply.

As we experience the grace, strength, and kindness of God more deeply in our lives, we take on more of Christ's heart. As we meet with clients (and for that matter, every time we interact with family, friends, and strangers) we "put on" the compassion of Christ. Paul described this choice in his letter to the Colossians.

Therefore, as God's chosen people, holy and dearly loved, clothe yourselves with compassion, kindness, humility, gentleness and patience. Bear with each other and forgive one another if any of you has a grievance against someone. Forgive as the Lord forgave you. And over all these virtues put on love, which binds them all together in perfect unity (Col. 3:12-14).

We can't give away something we don't possess, so our first task is to dive deeply into the grace of God so that his life and love permeate our own hearts. Then we have the resources and motivation to choose to love the way Jesus loves, to care the way he cares, and to speak truth the way he spoke grace and truth to every person in every situation.

Power, Purpose, and Passion

The new Christian counselor believes in the God who has revealed himself and his truth in the Scriptures. This God moves with power to transform our lives when we believe and apply the Scriptures. Because he passionately desires to connect with people, God invites us to partner with him. As junior partners in the endeavor of applied compassion and redemption, we communicate his truth and grace in strategic and relevant ways to the hurts of people so they grasp the amazing truth that they are the recipients of his unfailing love and mercy. As God's partners, we become conduits of his power, his purpose, and his passion for hurting, doubting, struggling people.

Biblical Foundations of Christian Counseling

An analysis of a person's worldview outlines the presuppositions and core beliefs that undergird it. These core beliefs, however, are often hidden under layers of misunderstanding, hurt, and denial. In fact, explicit recitation of one's values and beliefs is exceptionally rare—even for

Christian counselors. Since Christian counseling has sometimes gotten off course and run far ahead of its biblical and theological roots, we need to begin with a clear outline of our biblical foundations.

Our worldview for Christian counseling begins with the proposition that the triune God of the Bible is alive and is the Creator of all things (Jn. 14:16-17; Heb. 1:2), is the source of all wisdom and truth (Isa. 25:1; Rom. 3:4), and seeks a love relationship with every person on earth (Jn. 3:16; 1 Jn. 4:8). Our second proposition is that God's main purpose for people is redemption in Christ. By his sacrifice on the cross, we are enabled by grace to experience redemption from slavery, sin, and death (Ex. 6:6; Gal. 3:13; Col. 1:14), and from the evil that pervades the world (Heb. 7:24-26). Our hope, however, is not limited to this life. Christian counseling serves, in part, to advance God's redeeming work so that believers may one day be resurrected from the dead and live eternally with the Father, the Son, and the Holy Spirit (Jn. 10:17-18; 1 Cor. 1:24; Eph. 1:7).

The Scriptures themselves are the key resource for knowing God and pursuing his plan for our lives. The psalmist queries, "How can a young man keep his way pure? By keeping it according to Your word" (Ps. 119:9 NASB). He further asserts, "Your commandments make me wiser than my enemies....I have more insight than all my teachers, for Your testimonies are my meditation. I understand more than the aged, because I have observed Your precepts" (verses 98-100 NASB). The well-known verses of 2 Tim. 3:16-17 reveal that "All Scripture is inspired by God and is profitable for teaching, for reproof, for correction, for training in righteousness, that the man of God may be adequate, equipped for every good work" (NASB).

Christian counseling, then, is not merely focused on the alleviation of painful, disturbing symptoms or the promotion of psychological health. Though these are important, the ultimate goal of Christian counseling is holistic personal growth that leads clients to become the people God created them to be—loved, forgiven, adopted children of God who are learning to love him above all else and love people as themselves. Speaking of his ministry to those he has helped, Paul describes being "in the pains of childbirth until Christ is formed in you" (Gal. 4:19). This kind of compassionate care is essential for revealing to our brothers and sisters the love that comforts their hurts but also challenges them to change at a very fundamental level. Similarly, Paul explains that he is "admonishing and teaching everyone with all wisdom, so that we may present everyone fully mature in Christ" (Col. 1:28-29). More than just behavioral change, Christian counseling is concerned with transformation of the self, redemption in relationships, and freedom from bondage to sin.

As we presented in the paracentric model in *Competent Christian Counseling* (Clinton & Ohlschlager, 2002, p. 50), helping that is grounded on the common New Testament Greek word *parakaleo* includes the ideas of admonishment and warning on one hand, and giving comfort on the other. Competent Christian counseling must include both comfort and warning at appropriate times. Models constructed on one end of the continuum to the exclusion of the other are incomplete and ultimately unhelpful. *Parakaleo,* which refers to "coming alongside" needy brothers and sisters and assisting them to health and holiness, is the better foundation of genuinely helpful Christian counseling.

A glimpse of *parakaleo* is seen in Paul's instructions to the Christians in 1 Thess. 5:14 (see also 2 Cor. 1:3-7). The wide-ranging behaviors identified in this verse includes comforting the brokenhearted, supporting the weak, encouraging the discouraged, exhorting those who aren't motivated, entreating and guiding the misdirected, and warning the rebel and the sinner. The full scope of Spirit-led counseling reveals the wide range of needed activities to help people grow up and become strong in Christ.

Counselors in training often show natural abilities at one end of the scale or the other—tending toward either tender caregiving or tough exhortation—and must learn to become competent at showing the other dimension of helpful counseling. Two clients may show up in our offices, one needing comfort and the other warning. Or an individual client may need comfort one time and exhortation the next.

The Process of Christian Counseling

The goals and the processes of counseling—trusting God to change thoughts, behaviors, and emotions—are thoroughly grounded in the Bible. The Bible-based and spiritually oriented cognitive-behavioral therapies of Chris Thurman (2003), Leslie Vernick (2000), Bill Backus (1987), and Siang-Yang Tan (2011) are variants of the admonition of Rom. 12:2: "Do not conform to the pattern of this world, but be transformed by the renewing of your mind. Then you will be able to test and approve what God's will is—his good, pleasing and perfect will." Mind change—putting off the lies of the world and putting on the truths of God revealed in the Scriptures—is a central pattern of sanctification for all believers, including those who benefit from Christian counseling. In this model, clients are trained to interrupt their normal thought patterns, reveal their lie-based thinking, renounce the lie, and forsake it. Then one is taught—and much counseling is a very personalized form of Christian education—to replace the lie with the appropriate truth of the Bible to confess, believe, and live by.

Many passages give directives to replace faulty thinking with God's truth. Phil. 4:6-9 is a critical passage used in the process of overcoming and managing anxiety.

> Be anxious for nothing, but in everything by prayer and supplication, with thanksgiving, let your requests be made

known to God; and the peace of God, which surpasses all understanding, will guard your hearts and minds through Christ Jesus.

Finally brethren, whatever things are true, whatever things are noble, whatever things are just, whatever things are pure, whatever things are lovely, whatever things are of good report, if there is any virtue and if there is anything praiseworthy— meditate on these things. The things which you learned and received and heard and saw in me, these do, and the God of peace will be with you (NKJV).

Many years of entrenched patterns of thinking don't change in an instant, but they can change if the person trusts the Spirit of God, does the hard work of replacing self-defeating thoughts with the powerful, positive truth of God's Word, and lives in a community of accountability and encouragement.

Three Biblical Antidotes to Anxiety

One of the most common complaints on intake forms is the prevalence of anxiety and worry. Many people who come for our help feel as if life is out of control. They've tried everything they can think of to manage people, circumstances, and their emotions, but they've finally given up. Their sense of desperation has brought them to our doors. Anxiety is a dense, pervasive cloud in our clients' thoughts about the troubling issues of family discord, death, disease, heartache, loss, and other worries. The Bible has much to say about anxiety. The psalms describe many situations when David and the other writers poured out their hearts to the Lord—sometimes in praise but often in despair.

In the New Testament, Paul reveals three crucial antidotes to fear-drenched anxiety. The first is prayer—entreating God to deliver help, encouragement, and resources. God's peace—which makes no sense in the midst of troubling circumstances—comes on the wings of prayer as we bring everything we need to God.

The second antidote is to refocus our thought life on the things that are good and true and worthy of our focus. Notice how Paul lists different types of good thinking. He understands that it takes a long chain of positive thoughts—thoughts we are called to meditate on, not just think about—to break the power of obsession and anxious thinking. We can help clients to make lists that define each element noted in Scripture and to systematically meditate through their lists. This is good antianxiety practice.

The third antidote is imitative learning—copying what our mentors, leaders, and others in the godly community of accountability and encouragement do and say as we address our own struggles and opportunities. Imitative learning is a powerful way to learn and serves, again, as a strong antidote to obsessive, anxious thoughts.

Christian Counseling Models

Over the past two decades, several Christian counselors have attempted definitions of Christian counseling. They have suggested models to forge counseling processes that appropriately honor the foundational principles of Christian counseling.

Larry Crabb

Early in his career, Larry Crabb (1977) developed a seven-stage process model that still has great influence today. The model encouraged Christians to (1) identify problem feelings, (2) identify problem behavior, and (3) identify problem thinking. Then the counselor (4) teaches biblical truth to (5) reshape and clarify biblical thinking and (6) secure client commitment to act biblically for problem solving. Finally, the counselor and client work together to (7) identify Spirit-controlled feelings.

In his more recent writings, Crabb (1997, pp. 200–201) has placed a great deal of emphasis on the importance of the church and the role of community in the healing journey. He challenges Christian counselors to reorient their practices more intentionally in and around the church.

> Serious students of psychotherapy are suggesting that *rich* talking, not necessarily *trained* talking, is helpful...
>
> I conclude that we have made a terrible mistake. For most of the twentieth century we have wrongly defined *soul wounds* as *psychological disorders* and delegated the treatment to trained specialists. The results for the church have been significant. Three stand out.
>
> 1. We no longer see the church as a place for the substantial healing of personal wounds....We regard relationships, the real business of the church, as having little to do with profound soul care and, in so doing, we have underestimated the power that God has placed in his family....
>
> 2. The work of discipling has been wrongly defined as less than and different from psychotherapy and counseling....
>
> 3. Professional training is thought to be more important in developing the "skill" of helpful talking than the sanctifying work of the Spirit....Only God can supply the medicine needed to heal someone's soul.

Gary Collins

An early leader in the field, Gary Collins (1993, p. 21) offered this definition of Christian counseling:

> Attempts to define or describe Christian counseling tend to emphasize the person who does the helping, the techniques or skills that are used, and the goals that counseling seeks to reach. From that perspective the Christian counselor is
>
> 1. a deeply committed, Spirit guided (and Spirit filled) servant of Jesus Christ
>
> 2. who applies his or her God given abilities, skills training, knowledge, and insights
>
> 3. to the task of helping others move to personal wholeness, interpersonal competence, mental stability, and spiritual maturity.

The Paracentric Model

In *Competent Christian Counseling* (Clinton & Ohlschlager, 2002, pp. 50–51) we proposed...

> a Paracentric focus that...melds two crucial aspects of Christian counseling....Our yieldedness to the Paraklete of God—the Holy Spirit—who is the invisible God present in counseling...[and our commitment] to Paraklesis...to "come alongside someone to help." These terms describe Spirit-directed and Christ-centered people committed to assisting others across a wide range of needs, from consolation to encouragement to confrontation....A Paracentric focus represents a centered convergence in Christ as our exalted model, and on the client as the clinical and ethical object of

our ministry. This focus...conveys the full arc of the helping process in which:

- The competent Christian counselor, yielded to an active, holy and merciful God (1 Cor. 1:18), meets the client at his or her point of need (diverging and becoming all things to all people, 1 Cor. 9:19,22), and connects with the client to create a working alliance.

- This activity includes comforting the brokenhearted, supporting the weak, encouraging the discouraged, exhorting those who are motivated, entreating and guiding the misdirected, and warning the rebel and sinner (the full scope of Spirit-led counselor behavior is described in 1 Thess. 5:14 and 2 Cor. 1:3-7).

- The counselor serves to refocus, facilitate, instruct and reinforce client action toward growing up into maturity (Eph. 4:12-16) and living in more intimate relationship (Jn. 17:9-13) with the divine object of our faith, Jesus Christ. This involves de-centering ourselves (Lam. 3:20-24) and converging or centering on Christ, the Author and Finisher of our faith (Heb. 12:2).

Everett Worthington

Everett Worthington (1999, p. 189) said this in giving a highly focused definition to our field:

Christian counseling is an explicit or implicit agreement for the provision of help for a client, in which the counselor has at heart the client's psychological welfare, but also the client's Christian spiritual welfare and tries to promote those goals through counseling methods, and the client can trust the counselor not to harm and to try to help the client psychologically and spiritually.

A Shorter and Simpler Definition

Possibly the best one-sentence description of Christian counseling was given recently by Siang-Yang Tan (2011, p. 363), emphasizing the role and work of the Holy Spirit: "Christian counseling or psychotherapy can be simply described as counseling conducted by a Christian who is Christ centered, biblically based, and Spirit filled."

Our Definition

In the opening pages of this book, we offered a definition for Christian counseling that we believe (1) does justice to the insights offered in the definitions we have examined and (2) provides a platform for the development of a strategic and comprehensive model for intervention. In our definition, Christian counseling is...

- collaborative, including a caregiver, a care seeker, and the triune God
- committed to a process of moving forward under the authority of the Word of God
- enabled by the presence and power of the Holy Spirit
- carried out in a context of accountability and encouragement
- aimed at the possession of all the elements in the soul for the purpose of pursuing the imitation of Christ

We believe this definition provides the goal and critical elements for the development of a model of intervention worthy of the best efforts of the new Christian counselor.

Implicit in the definitions and principles we have looked at is a commitment to several convictions that shape the work and character of the new Christian counselor. The new Christian counselor understands that each of these convictions helps develop a model that does justice to the complex dilemmas humans bring to the counselor. The new Christian counselor also realizes that appropriately applying these convictions to real-life counseling sessions requires great wisdom.

Wisdom. The new Christian counselor is guided by the conviction that meeting the complex needs of humans created in the image of God and living in a fallen world requires a wisdom that is beyond the capacity of mere mortals. Like Solomon, we find ourselves frequently confessing, "LORD... I am only a little child and do not know how to carry out my duties....Give your servant a discerning heart" (1 Ki. 3:7-9). And like Solomon, we find that such a confession brings us into an experience with the God who is always at work in his world and delights to give wisdom to those who ask him for it (1 Ki. 3:10-12; 1 Cor. 2:16; Jas. 1:5). The new Christian counselor with humility joins Solomon in his confession of need, his petition for wisdom, and his experience of God's gracious provision. The new Christian counselor receives this gift with thankfulness and depends on God's provision for the resolution of the great challenges he and his clients face.

Love. The new Christian counselor is guided in all his interactions by the conviction that God loves the peoples of the world and that God is deeply committed to the healing of persons (Hos. 11:1-4; Jn. 3:16). The counselor believes that like Hosea, he is called to be a conduit through which the love, grace, and truth of God can flow to the needs of broken people (Hos. 3:1). Christian counselors understand that this calling has come from God himself and that we are also called to mend the broken reed and bring to flame the embers that once burned brightly in the lives of those we are called to help (Isa. 42:3). Christian counselors love deeply and therefore pursue justice for those who cannot obtain justice for themselves (Mic. 6:8). This frequently includes filling up that which is lacking in the sufferings of Christ (Col. 1:24). Like our master, Jesus Christ, we discover that virtue (energy) flows from us as we engage with the hurting. We must know how to refuel, or we will surely come to ruin. Counselors who serve as a conduit for God's engagement in soul care must take care of their own souls, or they will surely be broken under the burden of such a demanding calling.

The Holy Spirit. The new Christian counselor approaches the counseling process with a spirit of expectation and optimism that often exceeds that of his secular peers. This high level of expectation and hopefulness is based on the conviction that by virtue of a prayerful invitation, the Christian counselor enters into partnership with the Holy Spirit, who raised the Lord Jesus Christ from the dead (Rom. 1:4).

This is the same Holy Spirit who breathed life into a valley of dry bones in Ezekiel's vision (Ezek. 37). This is the same Holy Spirit who hovered above the waters in Genesis and brought order out of chaos (Gen. 1:2). This same Holy Spirit is present in his transforming power to assist all Christian counselors as they help clients pursue change, and his presence provides a platform for optimism and expectancy.

The Creator God, who is also our Father, is always at work in our world. Just as he was committed to open a door of hope for Israel in the midst of its troubles, so he is committed to us today (Hos. 2:15; 1 Cor. 10:13). Christian counselors use appropriate self-disclosure to testify to their own personal experience with the transformational ministry of the Holy Spirit and the God who opens doors of hope for overcoming (2 Cor. 1:3-11; 12:7-10).

Scripture. The new Christian counselor is always guided by the conviction that the loving Father has spoken truth and wisdom into our profoundly fallen world. In the Scriptures, in the person of Jesus Christ, and in the world of nature and scholarship, God has revealed truth regarding the nature and character of God, humans, our world, and all things pertaining to life and happiness. Human ideas abound, but the Christian counselor is under the authority of the wisdom and truth found in the Bible. All other ideas advanced by persons, regardless of those people's credentials or impressive intelligence, must be filtered through the authoritative revelation of the mind and will of God found in the Bible.

God not only exists but also interacts with his creation. He speaks with absolute authority and demands obedience, which leads to the path of shalom and blessing for his creation. God is truth, and what he has spoken in Scripture is in every way consistent with his character and his passion for seeing His children prosper in every way possible. Christian counselors believe that the God of Scripture has a passion for connection and relationship with humans. We believe in his investment in the redemption and healing of persons, his gifts, his empowering Spirit, the reality of hope when founded on his person and character, and the power of human relationships to bring healing and wholeness to the most broken among us. We affirm our conviction to the truth of all these things because we find witness to these truths within the Scriptures, which we believe to be the inspired and inerrant Word of God.

A process. The new Christian counselor is guided by the conviction that he is a link in the chain of events operating under the control of a sovereign God. The counselor bows to the reality that counseling frequently is a short-term process, lasting two to four months. The counselor is limited by time and opportunity. We cannot therefore try to do too much too quickly. The question is, are we plowing up the ground, planting the seed, watering, weeding, or harvesting the fruit of our own and the work of others (Mt. 13:1-23)? Attempting to cut short the time often required for meaningful collaboration can result in a counselor attempting to force a client to go where he is not yet prepared to go.

Wisdom and humility are required as we attempt to determine what stage of the journey this particular client is in at this particular time and how our work fits into God's agenda for this person's life. Wisdom is again God's gift, giving us context and directing us to the best strategy for the care seeker at this time.

Listening. The new Christian counselor places a high value on listening well to the life story of the person who is seeking guidance. Careful listening and attentiveness honors the client. Scripture reminds us that it is a folly to answer a matter before it is fully heard (Pr. 18:13). Every individual is unique in some wonderful way, bears the image of the Creator God, and possesses value and dignity that makes her worthy of respect and honor. When we listen well, we affirm this unique value. Many people live their entire lives without experiencing the honor of someone wanting to know their story and hence know them at a deeper level.

Listening well also helps the Christian counselor to answer the *metatheoretical* question: What will work best for this particular person in this particular situation at this particular time? Sufficient attention to this question requires careful listening on the part of the counselor. Such listening is a necessary prerequisite for the collaborative development of preferences and action plans for change that the client is likely to take ownership for. Clients who do not take ownership for change are not likely to fully engage in the pursuit of counselor-desired outcomes.

Referral. The experienced counselor admits that he cannot accept total responsibility for change in the client's life. The Christian counselor knows that the client—not the counselor—is ultimately in charge of the outcomes achieved through the collaborative effort of counseling. The new Christian counselor appreciates the need to fully inform clients about theoretical orientation, principles guiding practice, and any other information that assists the client with making an informed decision.

The counselor values client self-determination freedom and will refer when in the best interest of the client. The attempts at collaboration are not always successful. Clients have the right to say no, and this must be respected. No one counselor is the best fit for all clients. Counselors will sometimes need to refer a client to others who are better fitted to assist this particular client at this particular time with this particular issue. The counselor will never seek to assign blame for such a referral. Rather, the counselor recognizes several good reasons for referral, such as an inability to forge a therapeutic alliance, a values differential, or a lack of counselor training for the issues at hand. The counselor will accept responsibility for doing everything possible to assure that the referral is managed professionally and successfully.

Multiple modalities. The new Christian counselor embraces the conviction that client challenges are rooted in multiple modalities that define and shape the human soul. No one modality causes the complex issues clients face. The complex interplay of elements that define and shape the soul must be carefully considered. The new Christian counselor prepares to identify, understand, and develop strategies to address these multiple modalities.

For example, it is not enough to say that all problems find their source in wrong beliefs or in sin. Of course, if sin had never entered the world, we would need no counselors, and people would experience no brokenness. But this particular client in this particular situation at this particular time may be facing something that has nothing to do with his sin. He may be a legitimate victim, suffering from someone else's sinful and narcissistic lifestyle.

Likewise, although beliefs are central to the fueling of emotions and actions for clients, merely hearing what a client says he believes or teaching him new ideas may not lead the client to emotional, psychological, and spiritual health. Often, particularly for people who have experienced some form of abuse, trauma, or a period of suffering, the underlying metacognitions are actually fueling their emotions, thwarting their ability to apply newly learned truth and generating crippling anxiety.

Learning. The new Christian counselor appreciates the complex interplay of factors contributing to the absence of emotional, psychological, and spiritual health in persons. Therefore he believes he must be a lifelong student of human nature, theology, the Bible, and the world of information that surrounds us. He never stops reading and listening to his peers and clients. He continues to pray that he will connect with and understand the needs of hurting persons, and that he will be able to apply his increasing knowledge to the healing of their wounds.

He first devours the Scriptures. In them he finds the definition of personhood, the truth regarding God and humans, the record of the Fall, and the promise of the renewed heaven and earth. In them he finds the path and the means to emotional, psychological, and spiritual health. This careful and thoughtful engagement with Scripture gives the new Christian counselor a filter for sifting the work of peer scholarship. He reads what others say about the Bible and finds that some of it resonates with what he has come to believe about the Bible and some does not. Some scholarship does justice to the infallibility and authority of the Word, and some does not.

He moves into the literature that abounds on the nature of the soul and soul care. He finds some information and insights that pass successfully through the filter of the Scriptures and much that does not. He values dialogue with peers of all persuasions in his quest for strategies and insights that will enhance his ability to care for the souls of those he is privileged to serve. He does not neglect any of these interactions or intentionally alienate any of those who seek the healing of persons. In these interactions he often finds information and strategies that enhance his ability to help persons and that are not found in the Scriptures but do not contradict them.

Restoration. The new Christian counselor believes that the central dilemma of humans is the marring of their core identity. Human beings at their core are fashioned in the image of God (Gen. 1:26-27). Sin has not effaced that likeness but has significantly damaged it. With the entrance of sin in the core of the individual human soul, humanity has experienced a death and darkness that separates us from our Creator (Rom. 1:18-32). Humanity is helpless to eradicate that damage, but God has made provision in Christ for the redemption of the person and the restoration over time of the image of God in the core of the human personality (Rom. 5:8).

The appropriation of this provision, which is rooted in God's free offer of grace and love, is a matter of individual choice. It can be chosen or rejected, but it is open to all humans. The new Christian counselor is sensitive to the right of choice. His heartfelt desire for all clients is that they might experience life in the core self, embrace the process of being restored to the image of God, and experience shalom in every area of life. Some clients are readied by the Spirit of God to hear this message, and some are not. The new Christian counselor does not prioritize his agenda in the counseling event. He has a vision, as do all counselors, of what would be best for the client, but does not squeeze the client into his agenda. That is the difference between preaching and counseling. Preaching is a highly directed experience with a sage on the stage. Counseling is a collaborative experience with a guide by the side.

Choice. The new Christian counselor listens carefully and begins where the client wants to begin. Together, they find opportunities to develop a plan of action that will help the client reach the goals he is committed to achieving at this stage in his journey. We may get to deal with many issues in the client's life or just one and then he is gone. God is always at work, we have served as his conduit, and he will complete his purposes in the life of this person and us.

The new Christian counselor believes that the imitation of Christ is the highest and best possible goal. However, although the guide knows exactly which path and goal he would like to pursue, the fellow traveler is always given information and then afforded the right of personal choice.

Presence. The new Christian counselor believes in the power of presence. He is convinced that the most powerful force in the counseling process is his relationship with the client. Often, more than any words spoken, this is what the client remembers years later. This is often what brings the client back to hear more, to receive additional assistance, or to work on a new issue. When a counselor stays in one geographical area over many years, he is likely to see clients come, go, and come back multiple times over many years due in large part to the relationship they have formed with the counselor. The new Christian counselor doesn't feel the need to fill the silent spaces with words. He has prayed for the healing power of presence and experiences this with his client.

Strength based. The new Christian counselor appreciates the truth that all persons are fearfully and wonderfully made by the Creator God to serve a specific purpose in his world and are gifted to fulfill that purpose. Therefore persons come to counseling with areas of strength and weakness. The new Christian counselor helps the client to develop action plans that are solution focused and founded on client strengths. There is less focus on pathology, naming, and exploration of the unconscious, and more focus on identifying strengths and strategies that have brought the client a measure of success in the past.

Evaluation. The new Christian counselor evaluates the methodologies he employs. He accepts the responsibility to do no harm as well as the parallel responsibility to demonstrate the efficacy of the models of intervention he employs. He supports and engages in research that empirically demonstrates the efficacy of the approaches he utilizes. When possible he shares the results of his research in peer journals and opens up his work to the scrutiny of fellow professionals. He sees himself as part of a larger group of professional and pastoral counselors and feels a responsibility to be accountable to his peers.

Counseling and the church. The new Christian counselor believes that counseling is greatly strengthened when the counselor is anchored in the mission of the church, utilizing the resources of the church, held accountable for change, and receiving daily encouragement through life-giving relationships in a vibrant church community. He believes that the church's efforts in evangelism and discipleship are stronger when counseling is a valuable ally and not just an occasional afterthought or even an enemy. Christian counseling often serves as a gateway into the family of God. Discipleship is frequently abortive because Christian leaders attempt to disciple persons who are suffering from stubborn addictions and other deep-seated challenges requiring counseling services. These can go underground in the blush of conversion and resurface later during periods of stress, destroying all the good work that has been accomplished on the foundation of conversion. The Christian church is sometimes naive enough to believe that all things psychological and emotional are resolved when someone is saved. The new Christian counselor, often swimming against the tide in the evangelical church, seeks to dispel this naiveté.

The Ethical Christian Counselor

For new Christian counselors, high standards of integrity are extensions of our commitment to be disciples of Jesus Christ. As we follow him and emulate his example, we live, speak, and act with the powerful blend of grace and truth. God calls all believers to a high standard of integrity. As counselors, we have the unique role of stepping into people's lives at the point of pain and vulnerability. Our clients count on us to treat them with the utmost respect and offer assistance according to the highest standards of professional care.

Too often, discussions of ethics are incredibly dry. For the Christian counselor, however, the topic of ethics takes on rich dimensions. The Bible gives us the astounding, inspiring, and challenging truth that every person we help represents Jesus Christ. The apostle Paul tells slaves and masters to treat each other the way they'd respond to Jesus (Col. 3:22–4:1). The implication is that in every relationship, we need to respect, love, and honor the person the way we respect, love, and honor Jesus Christ, our Savior and King.

Jesus told a parable about a king giving his servants a report card. The servants fed the hungry, refreshed the thirsty, welcomed strangers as guests, clothed the naked, and visited those who were sick and in prison. The king praised the servants and explained, "Truly I tell you, whatever you did for one of the least of these brothers and sisters of mine, you did for me" (Mt. 25:40).

The people who come to our counseling offices are in desperate need emotionally, spiritually, and relationally. When we love them, care for them, and patiently meet their needs, we're actually pouring out our love for Jesus himself. This realization radically changes our perspective (especially of annoying clients), our motivation, and our prayers for them.

Ethical excellence in counseling marries *working knowledge, competent skills,* and *ethical awareness.* To consistently achieve demonstrable gains from treatment, every new Christian counselor must embrace the ethical challenge of doing good (beneficence) while doing no harm (nonmalfeasance) to all those served. Let us be the first to tell you that no one achieves ethical perfection, not even the very best and most honored of our practitioners. Yet therapists with the highest integrity can and do count any failed cases on one hand (when they are completely honest with themselves), and we commend them to you as examples to follow.

It is no great secret why our best therapists consistently terminate cases with satisfied clients and show demonstrable gains year after year. These are therapists who aspire to excellence—not the impossible standard of human perfection, but that which flows out of a radical yieldedness to the Holy Spirit—and who yield each client to the love and grace of God himself. These are the master therapists who are worthy of emulation because they...

- only take on cases within the purview of their expertise and experience,

- make liberal use of opportunities for consultation and referral (and have intimate knowledge of the resources available within their communities),

- are clear with clients about ethical and personal boundaries, neither crossing those of the client nor letting the client cross those of the therapist,

- work diligently to maintain the therapeutic alliance, always sensitive to issues of client consent and control of their lives,

- do not push their own beliefs or agenda, but instead patiently draw the best out of their clients, challenging them to plan, decide, and act on their own,

- are diligent about maintaining client confidences and are clear with clients about likely outcomes when confidences must be legally breached,

- prayerfully prepare for each case by reviewing past session notes (and keeping these notes up-to-date) while yielding each session to the guidance and the power of the Holy Spirit, and

- display the requisite humility that admits to wrongdoing when it happens, and work diligently to correct or make restitution in these cases.

Core Elements of Ethical Excellence

The five *C*s of ethical practice that every therapist must embrace include competence, consent, consultation, confidentiality, and contracting for services (see American Association of Christian Counselors, 2014). Learn to review these issues for every case across the five fingers of your hand, and your practice and reputation will blossom.

Competence. This entails a multilevel analysis of counselor knowledge, skill, and relatability. Competence is not just the knowledge of your strengths—which is an essential part of building confidence—but also the humility of having a clear awareness of your weaknesses and areas where you lack proficiency. Competent counselors know their limits and live by them. Amazingly, some Christian counselors take cases involving suicide, abuse trauma, post-traumatic stress, bipolar disorder, or serious family crisis without expertise in these areas. This is shockingly unethical.

Competence also goes to the counseling environment. The essential "feel" that you and your office project should be one of *relaxed and inviting grace*, not one of pressure, confusion, or distress. (Think of times when you have been client or patient, and note which environments invite you to stay and which arouse so much anxiety that you want to get out of there!)

Grace (instead of stress) will flow from you because you...

- have yielded yourself to God and invited him to be present,
- are committed to speak the truth in love in everything you communicate,

- are relaxed, even a bit playful, as you remain focused in your initial interview,

- are dedicated to listening intently while displaying great respect for your client,

- are dedicated to creating a safe-haven experience for your clients, letting them know they are completely safe and welcome to be who they are with you, and

- avoid all judgments and criticisms of your client during the process of initial interview and create a trustworthy alliance.

Consent. Consent is the ethical-legal expression of the cardinal counseling value of client self-determination, a revered right in all medicine and psychotherapy because it respects the patient-client's right to determine, in the end, what shall be done to one's own mind, body, and soul. Consent is far more than a routine signature on paper—it is the ongoing psycho-spiritual dynamic that respects clients' control of their own life's choices. Clients should be fully apprised of goals, process, methods used, costs, risk of failure, and alternative ways of achieving their goals, and they should be given opportunity to signify their informed consent to these things.

Consultation. The maintenance of your competence is based on knowing where the boundaries of your expertise lie and when consultation and referral is indicated. This counters the puffed-up and self-aggrandizing tendency of our fallen human nature. In the early years of practice, the best counselors are those who can craft an argument for the need of consultation in nearly every case. Good consultation is the quickest and most valuable road you can take to become an expert in your practice.

Confidentiality. The high value of maintaining a client's secrets is often demonstrated by those who express anger and heartache at the breach of their privacy by previous counselors. Church settings are notorious for divulging shared secrets, and a person's resistance to allow you to consult with a pastor or former therapist can be a significant problem. Never promise your patients or clients absolute confidentiality, but disclose to them the major exceptions to the rule—child or elder abuse, suicide threats, and homicide threats. Be sure to speak about these exceptions in a frank and matter-of-fact tone.

Contract. Fundamentally, the counselor and client should have an agreement that is formalized in a good and accurate contract. And if possible, the client should lead in defining what he or she wants from the relationship. Far too many therapists—including far too many Christian counselors—do not do an adequate job of disclosing their values and detailing the nature and operation of their services. A contract outlining these disclosures is an essential ethic in counseling—essential to the task of securing from your client a freely given consent to the work they are about to entrust to your care. (See the contracts in the appendix of Clinton, Hart, & Ohlschlager, 2005, p. 463.)

WISDOM'S REVIEW

In this book we seek to offer a definition for Christian counseling that does justice to the insights and definitions we have examined. We also provide a platform for the development of a strategic and comprehensive model for intervention that may be used to enhance counselors' efficiency and effectiveness. We believe that ours is a practical, transformational approach and that counselors engaged in this fresh biblical and transformational approach are aligning themselves with the purposes and direction of God's Spirit. Christian counseling is truly about God's transformational work in people's lives. As a part of that challenge, we need to know God, ourselves, and our clients at a deeper level. That challenge should move us to prayer for ourselves and intercession for those who come to us seeking help.

Embracing this challenge changes us from the inside out. We develop a heightened sense of our need for grace working through the power of the Holy Spirit, the power of the Word of God, and the power of our faith community. The overarching goal isn't temporary relief—it's transformational change. The dynamic resources of the Spirit, the Word, and the family of God bring power and order in our lives and in the lives of those who seek our help. Transformational change doesn't happen simply because a counselor and a client meet in the consulting office. This kind of change occurs in a context that is much richer, operates so much deeper, and is much more comprehensive. It is as if the client and the counselor are inside a circle, and around them are the Holy Spirit, the Father, the Son, and the believing community—all working together for meaningful change. Ultimately, the battle is the Lord's, and we are called to be warriors and trusted friends. We are partners with God in the great work of helping persons to achieve healing and transformation.

References

American Association of Christian Counselors. (2014). *AACC Christian counseling code of ethics* (pp. 46–47). Forest, VA: American Association of Christian Counselors.

Backus, W. D. (1987). *Finding the freedom of self-control.* Bloomington, MN: Bethany House.

Christianity Today. (2006). The top 50 books that have shaped evangelicals. Retrieved from http://www.christianitytoday.com/ct/2006/octo ber/23.51.html?start=1

Clinton, T., Hart, A., & Ohlschlager, G. (Eds.). (2005). *Caring for people God's way: Personal and emotional issues, addictions, grief, and trauma.* Nashville, TN: Thomas Nelson.

Clinton, T., & Ohlschlager, G. (Eds.). (2002). *Competent Christian counseling: Foundations and practice of compassionate soul care* (p. 50). Colorado Springs, CO: WaterBrook Press.

Collins, G. R. (1993). *The biblical basis of Christian counseling for people helpers.* Colorado Springs, CO: NavPress.

Crabb, L. (1977). *Effective biblical counseling.* Grand Rapids, MI: Zondervan.

Crabb, L. (1997). *Connecting.* Nashville, TN: W Publishing Group.

Hawkins, R., Hindson, E., & Clinton, T. (2002). Pastoral care and counseling: Soul care centered in the church. In T. Clinton & G. Ohlschlager (Eds.), *Competent Christian counseling: Foundations and practice of compassionate soul care.* Colorado Springs, CO: WaterBrook Press.

Johnson, E. (2011). *Foundations for soul care: A Christian psychology proposal.* Downers Grove, IL: IVP Academic.

Tan, S.-Y. (2011). *Counseling and psychotherapy: A Christian perspective.* Grand Rapids, MI: Baker Books.

Thurman, C. (2003). *The lies we believe.* Nashville, TN: Thomas Nelson.

Vernick, L. (2000). *The truth principle: A life-changing model for spiritual growth and renewal.* Colorado Springs, CO: WaterBrook Press.

Warfield, B. B. *The emotional life of our Lord.* Retrieved from www.moner gism.com/thethreshold/articles/onsite/emotionallife.html

Worthington, E. L., Jr. (1999). Christian counseling and psychotherapy. In D. Benner & P. Hill (Eds.), *Baker encyclopedia of psychology and counseling* (2nd ed.). Grand Rapids, MI: Baker Books.

3

Anthropology and Identity

What is man that You are mindful of him?

Ps. 8:4 NKJV

W hat does it mean to be human?
In the modern world of specialization, people's wounds, sins, and pathologies are often viewed in fragmented pieces with little serious effort to fit all the pieces into a meaningful whole. One group of professionals believes problems originate primarily in the physical realm. Their solutions focus on medications, diet, and similar strategies. Yet another group of professionals is trained to locate most of the problems humans experience in the psychological realm. Their primary objective is to help people relate in a better way to themselves, to others, and to their world. Still other professionals view human dilemmas primarily through the prism of spirituality, emphasizing the issue of sin as it impacts the interpersonal and intrapersonal worlds.

The new Christian counselor recognizes that all these pieces play a role in human suffering and that each is often present and active in varying degrees as we seek to understand a care seeker's difficulties. A comprehensive view isn't new or unique. More than three centuries ago, the Puritan pastor Richard Baxter preached on the complex causes of depression. Though he didn't have access to modern advances in biochemistry, pharmacology, physiology, and psychology, Baxter observed a full range of physical, emotional, relational, environmental, and spiritual causes for "melancholy and overmuch sorrow"—and often, a combination of two or more of these (Baxter, n.d.). In the world of helping professions today, however, the spiritual element is often minimized. And even when Christians attempt to bring God into the counseling equation, they sometimes have a superficial understanding of how spirituality fits with the other aspects and shapes them all. A comprehensive approach to answering the question of what it means to be fully human is greatly aided by a careful and thorough investigation of the biblical and theological literature.

In chapter 1, we saw that Jesus told his followers that after he was executed on the cross and they began to take the message of the gospel to every corner of the world, they would suffer intense persecution. They would experience betrayal, rejection, and hardships. He instructed them, "By your patience possess your souls" (Lk. 21:19 NKJV).

Throughout the Bible, the authors refer to the immaterial part of human existence, commonly called our souls. This aspect of human existence involves a wide array of processes and responses. The condition of our souls determines how we relate to God, our connections with other people, our goals and purposes, and our reactions to the difficulties and joys of life. Christian counselors need to grasp the complex and profound nature of the soul. This is foundational for understanding the elements requiring attention in a comprehensive and holistic approach to counseling.

The Larger Story of Humanity—from Glory to Glory

The Bible presents a comprehensive backdrop for defining human nature. Created in the image of God, humans have the potential for great good and for great evil. These two great impulses pervade the human condition, and all of humanity is divided into these two opposing forces. Many different terms identify these groups, including children of darkness and children of light, lost and found, sheep and goats, family and aliens, fruitful and unfruitful trees, and living stones and shattered rocks. All bear irrevocably the divine image, but some people have turned from sin and embraced God's forgiveness, love, and strength. Others have become indifferent or hostile toward God. The apostle Paul explains that those who are lost remain solely "in Adam" and are identified with his sin. The people of God find their identity in Jesus Christ (Rom. 5:12-21) as their Savior and King. Those who have rejected God's offer of forgiveness are dominated by the deceiver, Satan, the enemy of our souls (Eph. 2:1-3). But the people of God, through no merit of their own and the mystery of the divine purpose unfolding on their behalf, have been bought with the price of Christ's blood and experience the regeneration of their inner core through the indwelling presence of the Holy Spirit (1 Cor. 6:19-20).

To his followers—then and now—Jesus addressed this issue when he said, "By your patience possess your souls." We learn to possess our souls as we find the gospel intellectually coherent, emotionally compelling, and volitionally directing. As the gospel takes hold of our hearts, we experience the thrill of being God's beloved children, we increasingly want to honor him, we endure suffering with grace and confidence, and we devote our lives to God's purposes. Out of hearts overflowing with love from God and for God, we want our lives to count for him. The apostle Paul emphasized the goal and the motivation of those who are overwhelmed with God's grace.

> Follow God's example, therefore, as dearly loved children and
> walk in the way of love, just as Christ loved us and gave him-
> self up for us as a fragrant offering and sacrifice to God.
>
> But among you there must not be even a hint of sexual immo-
> rality, or of any kind of impurity, or of greed, because these are
> improper for God's holy people (Eph. 5:1-3).

A transformed heart inevitably produces a transformed life.

The Process of Possessing

Jesus indicated that we possess our souls by our patience. Patience is
one of the marks of a person who is gaining God's perspective on life.
Paul included patience in the fruit of the Holy Spirit's work—evidence
of his indwelling presence (Gal. 5:22). The Holy Spirit's work in the life
of a disciple provides supernatural empowerment as the Spirit produces
love, joy, peace, patience, kindness, goodness, faithfulness, gentleness,
and self-control.

Patience doesn't occur in a vacuum, and it isn't displayed only in
easy times of obvious blessing. In Rom. 5:1-5, Paul reminds the Roman
Christians that they are to glory (take great delight) in tribulations. This
is certainly strange advice! Paul explains his counterintuitive instructions.
God's purpose for taking us through times of difficulty is to deepen our
dependence on him, which is a prerequisite for possessing our souls.

> We also glory in our sufferings, because we know that suffer-
> ing produces perseverance; perseverance, character; and char-
> acter, hope. And hope does not put us to shame, because
> God's love has been poured out into our hearts through the
> Holy Spirit, who has been given to us (Rom. 5:3-5).

Trusting God in times of suffering, betrayal, and other heartaches begins a sequence of spiritual growth. Trust produces perseverance, which produces godly character, which then produces genuine hope and a refreshing, deeper experience of God's love. Our culture treasures peace, prosperity, and plenty, but God's curriculum to strengthen, deepen, and tenderize our souls takes us through the hard school of tribulation. These courses are essential if we are to possess our souls and our clients are to possess theirs.

Spiritual growth is not a self-improvement program. From beginning to end, God is the source of power and life. Jesus was with his disciples for about three years. As he prepared to ascend to heaven, he promised "another advocate" would be with them. Jesus explained that the Holy Spirit would instruct the disciples in the ways of the Father. The Spirit speaks the truth he receives from the Father and the Son. This truth proclaims freedom from the *penalty* of sin, growing freedom from the *power* of sin as we trust God, and eventually, freedom from the *presence* of sin when we see Jesus face-to-face. The Spirit regenerates our hearts so we can respond to the gospel, awakens faith so we can trust in Christ for forgiveness, adopts us into God's family, and gives us the motivation and power to live for God. The long process of sanctification, or spiritual growth, is the work of the Spirit to inspire awe at God's majesty and obedience out of love for him.

The concept of possession was familiar to those who listened to Jesus that day. They probably thought back to the most important story in the Old Testament—the Exodus from Egypt and entry into the Promised Land. The tribes of Israel spent 40 years wandering in the desert, but finally, Joshua led them in the conquest of Canaan. As they fought, they gradually possessed the land God had promised long before to Abraham.

As the people of Israel stood on the banks of the Jordan before cross-ing to fight for their new land, they had a challenge and a promise. For generations, they had longed for the promise to be fulfilled, and now they stood on the edge of this reality. Still, the people who lived in Canaan weren't going to pack up and leave simply because a ragtag bunch of wan-derers came out of the wilderness and claimed the land as their own. The children of God had to *dispossess* the inhabitants before they could *pos-sess* the land. Moses told the people at the Jordan, "You are now about to cross the Jordan to go in and dispossess nations greater and stronger than you, with large cities that have walls up to the sky" (Deut. 9:1). The story of Joshua and the conquest is long and bloody, but ultimately, the people live in safety in the new land. They finally possessed the land God had promised them.

Against this backdrop of Israel's history of dispossession and posses-sion, Jesus articulated his encouragement and directions to his disci-ples. Like the Israelites centuries before, they were on the verge of a new adventure. Their Lord and Master was about to leave. He had often pre-dicted he would be crucified and raised from death back to life, but he would be with them for only a few weeks after his resurrection. Then he was going to ascend to the Father. In response to the gospel of grace, the majesty of God, and the example of Christ, the disciples were to take possession of their souls—to entrust to God the direction of their lives, their values, their treasure, and their purpose.

Taking possession would be as difficult for them as it was for Joshua and his people to conquer the Promised Land. The same pattern is true for Jesus's disciples today. We have to fight to dispossess the forces of darkness, indwelling sin, and destructive habits so we can possess God's peace, purpose, and joy. Paul described our daunting struggle.

> For our struggle is not against flesh and blood, but against the rulers, against the authorities, against the powers of this dark world and against the spiritual forces of evil in the heavenly realms. Therefore put on the full armor of God, so that when the day of evil comes, you may be able to stand your ground, and after you have done everything, to stand (Eph. 6:12-13).

Possessing our souls means having the spiritual insight to see the choices we need to make, the courage to make them, and the humility to admit when we've failed. Like the children of Israel fighting to possess the land, we fight every day to…

- repent of our desire for possessions, power, positions, and popularity, and choose to love God with all our hearts and love our neighbor as ourselves (Deut. 6:4-5; Jer. 9:23-24; Mt. 22:36-40),

- realize our blindness and develop spiritual perception (Mt. 6:22-23; 2 Cor. 4:16-18),

- reject moralism and the desire to prove ourselves by living by rules, and obey out of hearts of gratitude (Lk. 18:9-14; 2 Cor. 5:14-15), and

- pour out our lives in humble service to those in need (Mic. 6:8; Jas. 2:14-17).

God sometimes gives us peace and unfettered blessings, but he often accomplishes his purposes in our lives through pain and struggle. In these times, we have to make hard choices. Moses summarizes this choice for Israel on the brink of Canaan.

> And now, Israel, what does the LORD your God require of you, but to fear the LORD your God, to walk in all His ways and to love Him, to serve the LORD your God with all your heart and with all your soul, and to keep the commandments of the LORD and His statutes which I command you today for your good? (Deut. 10:12-13 NKJV).

Joshua commanded his officers to tell the people of Israel, "Prepare...to go in to possess the land which the LORD your God is giving you to possess" (Josh. 1:11 NKJV). Solomon realized, "What is crooked cannot be straightened; what is lacking cannot be counted" (Eccl. 1:15). Jesus described an upside-down kingdom in which the people who suffer poverty, hunger, grief, and rejection are blessed above those who value riches, plenty, ease, and popularity (Lk. 6:20-26). The soil of spiritual life is a rich compost of blessings and heartache, dirt and manure. We can expect both, accept both, and trust that God will use both to accomplish his purposes.

If people believe that they are exempt from struggles or that God's job is to protect them from all hassles, they will quickly become disillusioned in difficult times. Philip Yancey (2000, p. 69) states, "Gregory of Nicea once called St. Basil's faith 'ambidextrous' because he welcomed pleasures with the right hand and afflictions with the left, convinced that both would serve God's design for him."

The principles of possession apply clearly and powerfully to Christian counseling. First, we counselors have to be in the process of possessing our own souls. As our hearts are gripped by the amazing grace of God, the Spirit gradually transforms us, reveals wrong values, changes our desires and motivations, and empowers us to make choices that honor Christ. Then, the work God is doing *in* us flows *through* us into lives of those in need.

Taking possession of our souls, however, isn't a strange or mysterious process. The apostle Paul explains that just as we can change clothes, we can "put off" selfish, destructive choices (such as lying, stealing, wounding and manipulating with our words, and being bitter), and we can "put on" thoughts, words, and behaviors that honor God (Eph. 4:17–5:21). Our responsibility and our privilege is to help clients "change clothes" so they experience God's love and power, thereby gradually possessing their souls.

Defining and Shaping the Soul

To understand human nature, we must carefully explore the components of the soul. An analysis of the parts and the process of development reveals important connections among the components. This exploration facilitates understanding for the counselor and the client. The elements should be clearly explained to the client within a global, multimodal assessment strategy for health and growth. Our multimodal assessment strategy is broad enough to cover the numerous areas in the human experience contributing to the etiology of dis-ease and dysfunction in the soul and specific enough to arrive at focused and strategic interventions.

This holistic model focuses attention on the development of counselor adaptiveness. Counselors can adapt their approach to particular clients by determining which set of modalities provides the largest potential for client engagement and the formation of a working alliance. Counselor adaptation and alignment occur when counselors assess the most appropriate modalities addressing the needs of a particular client. Alignment with client preferences for engagement of persons and challenges contributes to the creation of a powerful working alliance.

Illustration 1
Elements Contributing to the Defining and Shaping of the Soul

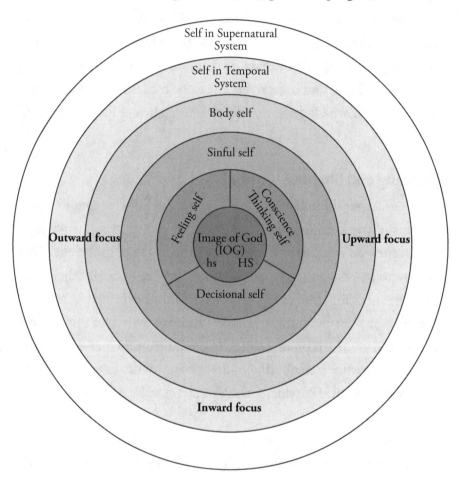

Illustration 1 provides a visual representation of the modalities that should receive attention in a structured, formal diagnosis. Across my journey as a child of God, I (Ron) have increasingly sought to understand myself better. I have labored, often haphazardly, to grow as a God follower in ways that were worthy of the great love he has shown me. At times, I have enjoyed some measure of success in my journey, but often I have known times of great failure. One day, when reading the words in Lk. 21:19, I heard the challenge of Jesus to possess my soul, and I heard him saying additionally, "I never ask you to do anything I have not equipped you to accomplish." After that encounter with Scripture, I developed the concentric circles. I reasoned that if I aim at nothing, I will surely hit it every time. I began the process of detailing the elements found in Scripture that contributed to the defining and shaping of my soul and the souls of my clients. The delineation of those elements is what you now see in illustration 1.

At our core, or human spirit (hs on the illustration) we are spiritual and eternal beings created in the image of God. In the core soul of those who have been regenerated through faith in Christ is the indwelling Holy Spirit (HS on the illustration). Moving outward toward the body dimension of the soul, we are engaged in challenges related to the possession of the thinking, feeling, decisioning, and sinning dimensions of the soul life. Then, beyond the body dimension, we encounter the need to take possession of the soul/self in temporal and supernatural relationships. In our counseling, each of the elements will, at levels unique to each particular client, require our skillful attention. I now propose to discuss in greater detail the significance of each of these elements/modalities in the promotion of heightened levels of spiritual, psychological, physical, and relational health.

The new Christian counselor appreciates the broad spectrum of modalities that may be contributing to the care seeker's pain and the need for a comprehensive multimodal approach to sourcing the pain. Arnold Lazarus (2008) pioneered a multimodal assessment and treatment model following the acronym BASIC ID, which includes seven interactive and reciprocally influential dimensions of personality and psychology. These modalities are Behavior, Affect, Sensation, Imagery,

Cognition, Interpersonal relationships, and Drugs/biology. The multimodal approach enables us to understand and explore the complex origin of our clients' problems. Then we can we develop an effective strategy for change.

For each dimension, counselors can assess the client's overinvolvement or deficit. Intake questions can focus on the past (family of origin, experiences, and so on), the presenting problem, and the preferred future the client envisions. This analysis provides a full and helpful matrix to evaluate and diagnose the client.

Purpose and Context

While engaging in a comprehensive exploration of the possible sources for the problems faced by the care seeker, the Christian counselor is always framing her efforts within a larger context in which she is intent on modeling the Christ and drawing the care seeker into a desire to imitate Christ. It is for the purpose of imitating Christ and drawing others into an affection for that imitation that we dedicate ourselves to the great work of Christian counseling.

The concept of imitating Christ is daunting to some and confusing to others, yet it remains a clear goal of the Christian life. Mark McMinn comments on the imperative for viewing the imitation of Christ as the ultimate goal in Christian counseling.

> Any Christian model for soul care is only comprehensive if it is Christocentric....Jesus, the Great Physician, cared for whole persons, body and soul, which lends credence to....engaging more than intellect in structural-domain interventions....Jesus, full of grace and truth, serves as the one perfect examplar of how we are to treat one another....Our greatest freedom is discovered by identifying ourselves as beloved

children of God, those who are being re-formed into the *imagio Dei* that is revealed perfectly in Jesus Christ (McMinn & Campbell, 2007, p. 390).

This focus on the imitation of the Christ may in one sense seem unreasonable or beyond the reach of mere humans. Truly, flawed human beings can never approach the majesty, omniscience, and supreme power of the Son of God. We are finite; he is infinite. Certain incommunicable qualities of God, then, are out of our reach. Other qualities, however, are communicable. That is, God imparts them to us as we trust him and follow him.

As we commit to possess our souls and pursue the imitation of Christ, we are empowered by the Holy Spirit. To cooperate with the Holy Spirit as he forms Christ in us, we choose to live in communities of encouragement and accountability under the authority of the will of God revealed in Scripture. As counselors we choose to imitate Christ by loving the unlovely, forgiving those who have hurt us, speaking truth to people who are wandering, standing strong against injustice, reaching out to outcasts, and patiently bearing with annoying or boring people. Once again, Paul uses the metaphor of changing clothes.

> You were taught, with regard to your former way of life, to put off your old self, which is being corrupted by its deceitful desires; to be made new in the attitude of your minds; and to put on the new self, created to be like God in true righteousness and holiness (Eph. 4:22-24).

In a thousand choices each day—some seemingly minor, some cataclysmic—we choose to put off sinful, selfish habits and put on attitudes and behaviors that reflect the righteousness and holiness of Christ. It's not magic; it's the discipline of dispossessing and possessing. To be like

Christ is to fulfill our destiny as humans who bear his image. As Christian counselors we believe in the power of presence. In our presence with our clients we seek to model Christ and call them to do the same. We believe him to be the healthiest human who has ever lived and find him totally worthy of our (and our clients') imitation.

We don't depend on sheer willpower to imitate Christ, follow him, and live for him. Transformed from the inside out, we love others because Christ loves us (1 Jn. 4:10-11), we forgive out of the deep well of our experience of God's forgiveness of our sins (Eph. 4:32), and we accept people with warmth and humility because God has accepted us as his own (Rom. 15:7). Everything we are, everything we own, and every talent we possess is a gift of grace from the hand of God. As partners with God, we grow and serve by the power of the Spirit of God, with encouragement and direction from the Word of God, and with support from the people of God.

Now that we have explained the unique and ultimate goal for the counselor and care seeker in the Christian context, let's return our attention to the elements in the soul contributing to the care seeker's health or lack of health.

Brown (1971) explains that in Scripture the soul...

> is the sensitive part of the life of the ego, the seat of the emotions, of love (Cant. 1:7), of longing (Ps. 63[62]:1), and of gladness (Ps.86:4).... The "soul" reveals its life in movement and the most various expressions of the emotions. It is the uniting factor for the inner powers of man: hence the phrase "with all your soul" (Deut. 13:3). Within the soul dwell the desire for food (Deut. 12:20,21), the lust of the flesh (Jer. 2:24), and the thirst for murder and revenge (Ps. 27[26]:12). The soul expresses feelings: it weeps (Ps. 119:28), is poured out in tears

(Job 30:16), is "made long" in patient endurance (Job 6:11). But knowledge and understanding (Ps. 139[138]:14), thought (1 Sam. 20:4) and memory (Lam. 3:20) have their seat in the soul as well. To such a degree is the soul the summing up of the whole personality, of the whole self of a person, that "soul" can be equivalent in meaning to "I myself" or "yourself" (1 Sam. 18:1)....

In 2 Cor. 1:23 Paul pledges his "soul"...as a solemn form of asseveration. The reference here is not only to the life, but to the whole man, with all that he believes, hopes, and strives for.

In the Bible the soul is conceived as the writers' attempt to sum up the various components of psychological, spiritual, and relational health in human beings, which also affect the physical aspects of life. The concentric circles in illustration 1 (p. 78) focus on these aspects.

The Spiritual Dimension and the Shaping of the Soul

Christian counseling includes a distinctive emphasis on the spiritual modality at the core of human personality. As with an apple, all of life emanates from the seeds. At the center of human personality is the human spirit (hs), originally created in the image of God. The core, the heart, however, is fallen, "desperately wicked" (Jer. 17:9 NKJV), and in need of a Savior. The Holy Spirit (HS) regenerates the human heart so the person can respond in faith to the gospel of grace and become a child of God. Real, supernatural power for lasting change comes from the Holy Spirit. Christian counselors recognize a spiritual core at the heart of what it means to be human, and they give attention to that core in a comprehensive approach to holistic health. All counselors who value the power of faith for producing holistic health want the freedom, where appropriate, to engage the power of spirituality to recover hope and healing in the lives of wounded people. As Mark McMinn (McMinn & Campbell, 2007, p. 392) has pointed out, "Every therapist—religious or not—has a worldview." Christian counselors are not unique because they have a defined anthropology. All counselors have commitments to a doctrine of humanness and a doctrine of change. Clients must be informed of these therapeutic commitments and be free to dissent from them.

Upholding the need for informed consent, respecting the clients' values, and striving to do no harm, Christian counselors are anchored to the importance of the spiritual dimension for the development of full humanity. Just as the life of an apple proceeds from the seeds in its core, so all that is truly human emanates from the center or core of the human personality. In this core reside the human spirit (hs), the image of God (IOG), and in the regenerated child of God, the Holy Spirit (HS).

The human spirit was generated in the beginning when man first breathed in the breath of God. The energy that flows from the life of God into the body of man creates a new kind of being in the universe. The human is not angel, animal, or deity. To be human is to be male or female and to bear the imprimatur of the divine image. The principle of life (hs) is received as God breathes out and the human breathes in life from God.

As male and female, humans are fitted to serve the Creator in unique ways. They are uniquely designed to exercise dominion over the created order, to multiply, and to create a kingdom people who live in shalom while ruling the planet for the glory of the Creator God. The divine intention and the human experience of shalom is frustrated, for a time, by humanity's decision to focus on self-glorification and self-exaltation. The decision for the self in opposition to the divine directive and purpose damages not only the relationship between the Creator and created but also the core being of humans. The core being of humanity is changed.

The image of God is not destroyed but is marred. The life-giving energy of the human spirit that makes humanity eternal remains in place (Eccl. 3:11,21). Yet another principle, the principle of sin, enters into the fabric of the core self, bringing death and the need for atonement and redemption. These are actions and gifts that are clearly beyond the humans' ability to create and offer. In short, humanity is fallen from its relationship with the Life Giver, banished from the experience of shalom with the loss of that relationship and Eden, and in desperate need of a Redeemer who can create a path to the restoration of all that is lost.

Christian counselors understand the relevance of the work of Jesus Christ and the ministry of the Holy Spirit for putting themselves and those they seek to help on the path to restoration, renewal, and the experience of shalom. This path holds potential not only for renewing relationship with God but also for the total transformation of the self.

The Holy Spirit enters the core self to regenerate and to animate the life of the human spirit. In his coming there is the power to overcome sin, to bring light where darkness has dominated, to commence the process of the restoration of the image of God in the core self, and to provide the energy and empowerment to obey the Word of God and reshape the self in all its relationships from the *inside out*. The Holy Spirit is received through the gospel message by humans in need of redemption. This redemption has the power to set free those who are captive to sin and to the self. It frees humanity to make choices that lead to the restoration of the image of God in the core self and weaken the power of sin in its desire to dominate the human will.

This redemption begins by receiving the gospel message of the death, burial, and resurrection of the Lord Jesus Christ. It includes the indwelling and regenerating work of the Holy Spirit. These are at the core of meaningful change, the recovery of Eden, the experience of shalom, and the ultimate healing of persons. The real power for lasting change comes when the Holy Spirit, who is at the foundation of biblical spirituality, is joined to truth-based thinking, a commitment to obeying the truth revealed in Scripture, and life in a community of encouragement and accountability.

Lasting, substantive change isn't added on. It comes from internal transformation. Therefore, change in behavior occurs from the inside out. This core self is the central feature of our human personality and being.

In a remarkable act of love, God created mankind in his own image (Gen. 1:27). In creation before the Fall, one feature separated humans from all of the other works of God: Adam and Eve bore the imprimatur of the image of God. No other created thing possessed this image. In sin, however, the image of God was tarnished.

> Even in the fallenness, humanity bears the mark of God's image....We live in a paradoxical state—carrying dual conditions within our single personage that emphasize both the dignity and fallenness of humanity....Thus, our specialness as humans resides not in what we may do but in who we are, because God who formed us placed his image and his gifts within us (Clinton & Ohlschlager, 2002).

Christian counselors see all people—believers as well as unbelievers—through the lens of God's creation. Every person still has the marks of the image of God—tarnished, marred, and sometimes hidden but present nonetheless. For this reason, we give all humans great respect and treat them with grace and truth. The new Christian counselor views all people through this unique prism because each one is of supreme value to God. Jesus Christ stepped out of heaven, humbled himself, and died for each individual we meet. If he values them that much and we are imitating him, we will value them too.

The human spirit lives in the soul. God breathed into man, and he became a living soul (Gen. 2:7). Living souls will live for eternity. All humans are unique, valuable (Ps. 139:13-18), and eternal. Solomon commented that God has put a sense of eternity in people's hearts (Eccl. 3:11). This, however, can be good news or bad news. Every individual will live for eternity—either in the presence of God or separated from him and all that's good.

Under the umbrella of his divine sovereignty, God has given every person the right of self-determination. One of the mysteries of faith is that both are true: God chooses us, and we choose him. We prefer to think of this dilemma as either/or, but in the mind of God, it's both/and.

When a person expresses faith in Christ, the Holy Spirit comes as the divine light to conquer death and dispel darkness. We have a new relationship with God, a new identity as citizens of heaven, a new purpose to honor him, and a new destiny to be with God in the new heaven and new earth. We become partners with God in bringing his kingdom to earth. The Holy Spirit works collaboratively with counselors and with our clients who trust in him. The inside-out process requires God's supernatural work and our obedience. Paul explained our response to the glory of the gospel.

> Therefore, my dear friends, as you have always obeyed—not only in my presence, but now much more in my absence—continue to work out your salvation with fear and trembling, for it is God who works in you to will and to act in order to fulfill his good purpose (Phil. 2:12-13).

The importance and eternality of the human spirit has filled the literature of humanity across all times and cultures. Counselors are obligated to identify how this dimension of the human soul has affected the client's past. How is it affecting the present—as an overemphasis or a deficit? What positives might this dimension contribute to enhanced client health in the future?

> Seeking for the Divine...has been a major aspiration and force in all cultures and periods of history, yet it has been virtually ignored by traditional psychology....Regular people with ordinary problems who are also on a spiritual path...are looking for therapists who will honor their seeking for something sacred and who can respect their whole being—in its psychological and spiritual fullness—rather than belittling or minimizing their spiritual seeking, as much of traditional psychotherapy has historically done (Cortright, 1997, pp. 13–14).

The Cognitive Dimension and the Shaping of the Soul

Corsini (2008) conducted a clinical factor analysis of more than 300 articles attempting to identify the elements in psychotherapy that are critical for producing change in people. The results of this analysis led him to emphasize the importance of cognitive factors, affective factors, and behavioral factors. This is his conclusion:

> Close examination...reveals that the cognitive factors imply "Know yourself," the affective factors tell us "Love your neighbor," and the behavioral factors essentially suggest "Do good works." Perhaps there is nothing new under the sun, for this is what philosophers have told us for millennia: Know thyself, love thy neighbor, and do good works (Corsini & Wedding, 2008 p. 9).

The Christian counselor cannot help but note the way such thinking coincides with a worldview and a model of self-possession that accords well with the teaching of the Bible.

Christian counselors recognize multiple levels in cognitive functioning. The brain is like a giant sponge. It soaks in experiences and information, and it seldom forgets. An experience may lose its place of prominence in mental attention and move, so to speak, to the background, being replaced by newer ideas, words, and thoughts. But it is rarely totally lost to recall. Such ideas often crystallize and coalesce with other ideas to form schemas constellations of control beliefs, producing a mindset that governs the person's choices and actions. McMinn and Campbell (2007, p. 246) remind us of the difficulty attached to changing these core beliefs or schemas, describing them as "mostly unconscious, very general and highly resistant to change."

When hurtful thoughts are allowed to proceed unchallenged, the amygdala will generate a hormonal cascade accompanied by intense and pervasive feelings of fear and anxiety that compromise a person's ability to make rational decisions. Adequate knowledge of brain physiology and the biochemical processes that accompany decisions, emotions, and behaviors (neuroscience) enhances therapists' ability to create effective interventions.

Therapeutic intervention must include helping clients realize that their destructive, overwhelming thoughts do not define who they are and are not permanent. Left unchallenged and unchanged, anxiety-producing thoughts often spiral out of control and contribute to additional anxiety, depression, and doubt. The therapist's task is to help the client develop rational, truth-based beliefs and the skills to empower the mind to discredit irrational, lie-based beliefs. Clients who formulate action plans based on rational, truth-based beliefs can (1) interrupt hormonal cascades that produce fear and anxiety, (2) disempower lies that produce fear, devalue the self, and damage ability to form healing relationships, and (3) contribute to a pattern of responding to life's challenges that can lead to higher levels of freedom, personal efficacy, and a growing sense of hopefulness. Learning to conduct *pattern interruptions* empowers a person to direct thoughts and behaviors in a healthier way. Habits of the heart, then, are actually habits of the mind. This explains why Paul admonishes Christians not to conform to world-based thoughts, but to participate in processes directed at the renewal of the mind so that they may be properly related to the good and acceptable will of God (Rom. 12:1-2).

Visualization, memorization, personalization, and meditation on truth-based statements and passages of Scripture can aid in the development of the mind of Christ, which can eventually trump previously held control beliefs. Cognition as a dimension of the self includes the amazing capacity of *imagination*. Imagination is a beautiful and creative aspect of human nature and part of our inheritance as image bearers. God loves variety. In creation, he imagined and produced a seemingly infinite variety of colors, stars, planets, trees, flowers, and animals for the blessing of human beings and for his enjoyment. Imagination and image bearing are connected. The amazing capacity of our imagination is in our DNA and fuels creativity in art, medicine, science, and relationships.

The power to imagine, though, can be used for good or ill. Imagination inspired the dubious desire to build the tower of Babel, a symbol of man's defiance and rebellion that resulted in God's curse. But healthy imagination has led to incredible advances in philosophy, medicine, and technology. The use of the imagination allowed Abraham to see the heavenly city (his promised destiny) and withstand the challenges he faced on his journey of faith in a world often hostile to the purposes of the covenant God (Heb. 11). Christian counselors can help clients use their imaginations to create relaxed minds and bodies and to get a picture of a better future—of hope instead of despair, love instead of bitterness, and joy instead of guilt.

The counselor must assess how the cognitive dimension has affected the client's past; how is it affecting the client's present feelings, behaviors, and relationships; the role of this dimension in creating a better future for the client.

The Conscious Dimension and the Shaping of the Soul

A person's sense of right and wrong is embedded in human cognition as a gift from the Creator. In Rom. 2:15, Paul states that the requirements of the law are written in the people's hearts, their consciences bearing witness to its truth and accusing them when they violate it. The conscience is strengthened and weakened by family and cultural experiences, but God endowed humanity with a powerful sense of justice. This is part of being created in the image of God. Experience and instruction can confirm the child's desire for justice and morality or repudiate it. This is why Christian counselors are concerned and involved with education, politics, and other aspects of the culture. We must ever be concerned for the protection and advancement of justice and those family and cultural initiatives that preserve and enhance it (Mic. 6:8).

Like the other dimensions of the soul, a person's conscience often slides to one of two extremes and is either too sharp or too dull. Some clients (and counselors) are driven by perfectionism. They never feel they can do enough. Perfectionism can be valuable for a surgeon, engineer, or attorney, but perfectionism fueled by the fear of failure can consume a person's life (Parrott, 2003, pp. 61–75). On the other end of the spectrum are those who have, to some degree, "arrested moral development." Past trauma, poor modeling, personality disorders, addiction, or overwhelming grief and depression can cause consciences to be seared—dull and unresponsive.

Typically, it doesn't take long for a counselor to assess the acuity of a client's conscience, and quite often, both extremes are present in a family system.

The counselor must assess how this dimension has affected the client's past, how it is affecting the present—as an overemphasis or deficit—and the role of this dimension in the creation of a better future for the client.

The Emotional Dimension and the Shaping of the Soul

Emotions are gateways to the soul. Many people who come to us for help have become emotionally numb because they've been traumatized. Others are controlled by their emotions. Imparting the ability to perceive and process emotions is one of the goals of therapy. Although some strands of Christianity play down the role of emotions in spirituality and mental health, this is not a helpful position. True health—living the life God created us to live—requires a deep appreciation for the significant role of emotions in the maintenance of psychological, biological, and spiritual health.

Some clients come to us with the conviction that they need to "get over negative emotions." Their goal is suppression, which leads to denial and eventual implosions or explosions of long-repressed feelings. The emotional life of the Christian isn't ancillary. The psalms show that emotional authenticity includes joy and praise but also honest expressions of despair, anger, impatience, and heartache.

A healthier, more productive view of emotions is to see them as indicators and motivators. Like the gauges on an automobile, emotions signify something—either health or warning. When the engine is running at the right temperature with sufficient lubrication, the gauges tell us everything is fine. When the temperature runs too high and the engine is in danger, the gauges go to the red zone. Failing to take immediate action by adding water or oil may have devastating consequences. In automobile maintenance and emotional life, people ignore the gauges at their peril!

Emotions, then, aren't negative or positive. They are signs and symptoms of a deeper reality, a blessing or a threat. Hurt, anger, anxiety, and fear are indications something is not right in our souls. The human engine may be conceived as the person with all of its biochemical and physical parts, including the brain, thoughts, spirit, decisions, goals, values, and relationships. Like all the functions in a car, the components of human life work together in an integrated manner. When one or more of these areas overheats, we experience an emotion that functions as a warning signal. When a car temperature gauge goes above the redline, it would be foolish to try to correct the problem by focusing on the gauge. In the same way, attempts to control emotions usually ignore the deeper, more substantive problems.

As counselors, one of our goals is to surface a client's emotions, to give validity to them and normalize them, and then to use them to uncover the underlying challenges. Emotions are often (but not always) among the first important topics we can comfortably discuss with clients. Then the counselor and the client begin the quest to explore the root causes of the discomfort. The painful feelings may have been birthed from trauma or loss, in a physiological dysfunction (such as an addiction or compulsive behavior), in a pattern of sin or bitterness, or in faulty thinking anchored in irrationality. For our clients to possess their souls, they need our assistance to interpret the redline of their emotions.

Painful emotions have probably led to unhealthy coping mechanisms, which produced even more raw, painful feelings. Healthy emotions have a self-feeding quality too. Joy, love, and gratitude usually produce positive responses from others that lead to more joy, love, and gratitude.

The counselor must assess how emotions have evolved in the client's past and how they are affecting the client's present. Helping clients appreciate the value of knowing what they are feeling, the source of those feelings, and the power healthy emotions have for assisting with the building of a better future—these are important goals for the Christian counselor.

The Volitional Dimension and the Shaping of the Soul

The Scriptures describe God as anything but passive. From the dawn of creation, he has been an engaged decision maker and communicator, and he continually takes action to bless or correct. He made choices about the creation of our world with all it contains. He chose the human family. He chose where he would place that family and communicate their purposes, resources, and limitations. He entrusted care of his creation to us as stewards. After the disruption in his relationship with Adam and Eve, God chose to continue pursuing us, to share his heart with us, and to offer forgiveness and hope.

Created in the image of God, humans share his capacity for decision, engagement, and communication. The ability to decide (the freedom to exercise the will) is embedded in our DNA. Why, we might ask? The answer is clear. Image bearers must have the capacity for decision if they are to resemble their Creator. With freedom comes responsibility, so we are accountable for decisions. Our choices have direct and indirect consequences—on us and those around us.

God respects the human right of choice, and he is affected by our decisions. The Bible says he delights, grieves, and becomes angry in response to our choices. But God is also incredibly patient. If he judged us harshly for every sinful word or action, we'd be in real trouble! In him, mercy and justice are wedded. His love guides his decisions. From Genesis to Revelation, we find God delaying judgment to give people plenty of opportunities to repent. To Israel and to us he says, "I will not surrender you. I will not give you up, for my love for you is inflamed, and my heart is turning over because of my love for you" (Hos. 11).

We are free to embrace, ignore, or reject God's love and purposes. We can choose to yield to or resist the Holy Spirit, to obey or disobey the words of Christ, and to accept or reject God's invitations and warnings.

Paul described a process of change through choice and discussed at length the dehabituation-rehabituation process. Some of our clients come to us because they are addicts or are in a relationship with an addict. One of the most common traits of addiction is complete self-absorption, which leads to lying and stealing to get the substance to get high. This behavior offends and confuses others, generating anger and harsh words. If these aren't soon resolved (and they fester for years in most addictive families), the family suffers from the poison of bitterness. Every person in the family invests in self-protection and manipulation.

In Ephesians, Paul gives clear directives for all these habits. As we've seen before, he draws a line to illustrate choices, and he offers the promise that decisions anchored in true repentance and commitment to the practice of new behaviors within a community of accountability and encouragement will lead to a transformation, moving the person in the direction of the imitation of Christ.

> Therefore each of you must put off falsehood and speak truthfully to your neighbor, for we are all members of one body. "In your anger do not sin": Do not let the sun go down while you are still angry, and do not give the devil a foothold. Anyone who has been stealing must steal no longer, but must work, doing something useful with their own hands, that they may have something to share with those in need.
>
> Do not let any unwholesome talk come out of your mouths, but only what is helpful for building others up according to their needs, that it may benefit those who listen. And do not grieve the Holy Spirit of God, with whom you were sealed for

the day of redemption. Get rid of all bitterness, rage and anger, brawling and slander, along with every form of malice. Be kind and compassionate to one another, forgiving each other, just as in Christ God forgave you (Eph. 4:25-32).

The choices Paul describes are very clear. They require courage and support, but they aren't confusing in the least. Stop lying and speak the truth. Be honest about your anger and resolve it quickly. Don't steal, but instead, work and give. Don't use words to condemn or control, but to affirm and build. Don't let bitterness ruin your relationships. Instead, go deeper into Christ's forgiveness so you'll have the capacity and motivation to forgive those who hurt you.

Honesty, humility, and repentance should become normal parts of believers' lives. When the Spirit shows us we're selfish or more intent on controlling people than loving them, we need to agree with him about that sin and about the need for forgiveness. We have a new motivation for honoring God—a glad response to the beauty of grace and the majesty of God.

The counselor must assess the general direction of the client's will. Is it focused on self-satisfaction, or does it allow room for participation in the well-being of others? Is the client's will fenced in by an addiction to a substance or to symbols of success? Does the client understand at any level the need for godly sorrow over the bondage of self-absorption or hurt inflicted on others? What is the potential for harnessing the power of the will of this client for securing a more hopeful future?

The Sin Dimension and the Shaping of the Soul

Mankind has jouneyed a long way from the purity, humility, and joy of his original home. Sin has supported him on the journey. Sin is more than breaking God's laws—it also breaks God's heart. It's not merely our failure to follow a rigid list of rules. Sin is the compelling desire and the concerted choice to get our identity from something or someone other than God. It is idolatry of the soul. Tan (2011, p. 330) summarized a Christian theology of sin:

> From a biblical perspective humanity's *basic problem is sin.* All human beings have sinned and therefore are fallen people (Rom. 3:23), yet they have been created in the image of God (Gen. 1:26-27), with a freedom or capacity to choose (Deut. 30:19; Josh. 24:15). Disobeying God's moral laws as revealed in Scripture and believing the satanic deception or lie that we can handle our own lives and fulfill our basic needs and longings without God underlie most psychological or emotional problems that do not have obvious organic bases.

Although sin as a human dilemma is at the root of all that is broken in our world, the sin of an individual is not always the source of personal brokenness.

> Sin is not confined to the destructive choices that humans make; it also refers to our general state of brokenness and the consequences of living with other broken people. So a Christian theology of sin tolerates various explanations for psychopathology (McMinn & Campbell, 2007, p. 241).

Cornelius Plantinga (1995) calls sin the "vandalism of shalom." In the Bible, shalom isn't merely the absence of conflict. It implies far more—it is the presence of joy, meaning, and well-being. The vandalism of shalom bears its awful fruit every day in human history. Jeremiah describes sin this way: The heart of man is "deceitful above all things, and desperately wicked" (Jer. 17:9 NKJV). People are foolish and deluded. They follow paths that lead them away from God and the blessings of knowing and following him.

In response to our rebellion, God could have obliterated us. He did it once with the flood, and he would be fully justified in doing it again. Instead, God was motivated by love to provide a path to reconciliation through the life, death, resurrection, and ascension of Christ. The amazing story of the gospel is that God placed our sins on the sinless Son, and he paid for them by sacrificial atonement. He lived the life we couldn't live, and he died the death we should have died. He is our substitute.

When the beauty and power of the gospel invades our souls, our hearts melt in gratitude as shalom floods the inner world of our soul. Paul explained the normal response to the glory of grace.

> For Christ's love compels us, because we are convinced that one died for all, and therefore all died. And he died for all, that those who live should no longer live for themselves but for him who died for them and was raised again (2 Cor. 5:14-15).

The counselor must assess how sin has impacted the client in the past and how the fruit of past choices and harm inflicted by the sin of others against the client are impacting the client's ability to experience shalom in the present. The counselor will need to explore with the client the relevance of such themes as forgiveness of self and others, grace extended toward self and others, attachment styles and the client's ability to experience God as loving Father, and the power of confession and repentance for the reclamation of shalom in the soul.

The Physical Dimension and the Shaping of the Soul

The Christian response to the body has varied throughout the history of Christianity. Ascetics have seen the body as a vessel to be severely disciplined and denied every form of pleasure. Manicheans viewed the body as evil. These and similar views have led to extremes from self-denial to self-gratification. As recently as the last century, some pastors taught that except for procreation, sex, even between marriage partners, was sinful. Many others today view sex as a normal, animal appetite to be enjoyed without guidelines or restraint. Neither of these views is biblical or healthy.

The human body is a special gift from God, designed to play a prominent role in his purpose for humanity. Adam and Eve were created with male and female bodies so they could multiply and build a culture that glorifies God in its work, sexuality, creativity, and worship. Through its physical engagement of creation and experiences of pleasure, the body was designed to be an instrument of service and delight. In response to God's grace, we gladly give everything—including our bodies—to serve and honor him.

The body, like the soul, has been used as an instrument of sin in rebellion against God. When the sentence of death fell as judgment for sin, age and disease began to destroy the vitality of the body. Instead of growing in strength, we stand at gravesides and grieve the physical death of those we love.

Sin has turned the world upside down. Solomon saw a world in which the number of things that are wrong is so immense they cannot be added up, and the crooked cannot be made straight (Eccl. 1:15). We long for love, purpose, and transcendence, but we suffer from alienation, hopelessness, and death. To numb the pain, people look for an anesthetic. Solomon identifies some of the painkillers people utilize (Eccl. 2). Some, such as alcohol and sex, are opiates for the body. They provide a shadow of shalom by temporarily changing the biochemistry of the body. The acquisition of possessions and positions—bigger houses, faster chariots or cars, swimming pools, promotions, and the achievement of awards and praise—briefly offers thrills and a type of shalom.

Nothing is inherently wrong with most of the things we enjoy, but when we use them to mask pain or take God's place in our hearts, they fail miserably to deliver on their promises, and they frequently carry us into enslavement from which we are unable to free ourselves. They simply aren't designed to perform this function. As we'll see in the chapter on addictions, the downward spiral of use, misuse, abuse, and addiction gradually puts us in bondage to the thing we hoped would provide freedom, peace, and joy. Our bodies become enslaved to the adrenaline rush or the sense of safety promised by the smell, the touch, the sight, or the experience of our anesthetic of choice. Eventually the thing, the pursuit, or the experience owns us. Our bodies and minds start to crave the anesthetic, and we become powerless to break free.

When God is at the center of our lives, everything can take its proper place. We accept sex, careers, prestige, popularity, power, and pleasure as God's gifts. As we increasingly trust in God, changes occur in our bodies. Our level of stress declines, and we sleep better, feel better, relate better, and look better.

In our culture, many people worship their bodies. They either want them lean and fit, or they feed them to the point of obesity. People spend billions in their obsession with their appearance. Instead of obsessing, we need to recognize our bodies are instruments of God. Then we can use our bodies for his honor in everything we do.

The counselor must assess whether the client's view of their body is healthy or unhealthy. It is impossible to experience shalom if I am unhappy with the body in which my soul resides. The counselor must assess the affect attached to the body image held by the client. Assessment of this dimension must also include attention to any addiction designed to produce a change in biochemistry that is ultimately unhealthy for the client and his relationships.

The Relational Dimension and the Shaping of the Soul

God has created us with a yearning and capacity for relationships with him and with other people. Our deep desire for connections isn't a flaw, and the pain we feel when those we trust abuse or abandon us is entirely normal. We cannot be whole without meaningful relationships. In the Garden, God created Eve to be Adam's partner in the mission and to meet his need for companionship. Adam could not multiply, fill the earth, and have dominion over it without Eve. God announced, "It is not good for man to be alone; I will make for him one who completes him" (Gen. 2:18 paraphrase), and then God delivered on his promise.

Many of our clients come to us because their relationships are broken or severely strained. They have trusted untrustworthy people or failed to trust those who have proven to be trustworthy. They've loved but felt betrayed in return. They've hoped, been vulnerable, and sacrificed, but they've been abused. Many have built strong, thick walls of self-protection. Others have almost given up on loving and being loved. Our task is to assess their past patterns and present condition and to offer them hope for a better future—to reconcile broken relationships or heal the wound and start something new. They've come to us because they still have some hope. It's our privilege to give them direction and to fan the embers of their hope. Solomon observed,

> Two are better than one,
> > because they have a good return for their labor....
> A cord of three strands is not quickly broken (Eccl. 4:9,12).

Counselors appreciate the powerful role relational systems play in the formation of the human personality. These systems—such as family, school, church, neighborhoods, and the broader community—are mirrors that reflect important perceptions to each person. Affirmation, truth, and love are mirrors that build strong, confident, honest individuals. Condemnation, deception, rage, and apathy poison minds and hearts. The nature of the systems experienced by children and adults creates a strong bias for or against God and his truth. To the extent they are healthy and positive, they enhance the development of a lifestyle of confidence, humility, and service. But consistent condemnation, discouragement, and shame bind a person to fear, anxiety, and depression and often do great damage to their ability to trust God and others.

As counselors, we step in to identify these relational systems, reveal their power, dislodge any lies, and replace them with healing truths. However, as we step into the lives of wounded, sinful people, we need to remain aware of the possibility of transference, which can complicate the counseling process.

The counselor must assess how and to what extent the client has been damaged or encouraged in past relationships. The counselor must understand how client's past relationships are impacting their ability to trust counselors, God, and others in the present. The caregiver will need to develop for each client a hopeful vision for doing relationships in the present and future. To aid in the assessment of the positive and negative patterns the client brings to her relationships, we make use of Erikson's metaphors describing psychosocial development as a series of stages occurring across the lifespan:

trust vs. mistrust	identity vs. role diffusion
autonomy vs. shame	intimacy vs. isolation
initiative vs. guilt	generativity vs. stagnation
industry vs. inferiority	ego integrity vs. despair

More detailed discussions of these stages can be found in any textbook on theories of personality. The metaphors are powerful and speak for themselves. My desire is to gauge the general disposition of the person in relationships. Is he trusting, capable of exercising autonomy, initiating action, accomplishing an intimate connection with other humans, and so on?

The Dimension of Supernatural Systems and the Shaping of the Soul

Christian counselors often mirror the culture's view of good and evil forces in the supernatural world. Some focus on it far too much, and some not at all.

> There are two equal and opposite errors into which our race can fall about the devils. One is to disbelieve in their existence. The other is to believe, and to feel an excessive and unhealthy interest in them. They themselves are equally pleased by both errors and hail a materialist or a magician with the same delight (Lewis, 1941).

Psychiatrist and author John White (1976) warned Christians to be on guard against the unseen forces of darkness.

> You have also established a new relationship with the powers of darkness. Whatever you were before you were a Christian...you are now the sworn foe of the legions of hell.

> Have no delusions about their reality or their hostility. But do not fear them. The God inside you terrifies them. They cannot touch you, let alone hurt you. But they can still seduce and they will try. They will also oppose you as you obey Christ....If you are serious about Christ being your Lord and God, you can expect opposition.

Even a casual reading of the Bible shows conflict between God and the forces of evil. This evil takes many forms, including temptation, deception, accusation, and demonization. In Western cultures, the idea of someone being possessed or obsessed with demons is often derided, but biblical accounts, church history, and current reports from many parts of the globe tell of this warfare.

An important Old Testament account of spiritual conflict is in the life of Daniel, one of the most beloved biblical characters. He lived in captivity, but he remained true to his faith in God. At one season, he prayed diligently for three weeks without receiving an answer. Finally, an angel appeared to him and explained the delay.

> "Daniel, you who are highly esteemed, consider carefully the words I am about to speak to you, and stand up, for I have now been sent to you." And when he said this to me, I stood up trembling.
>
> Then he continued, "Do not be afraid, Daniel. Since the first day that you set your mind to gain understanding and to humble yourself before your God, your words were heard, and I have come in response to them. But the prince of the Persian kingdom resisted me twenty-one days. Then Michael, one of the chief princes, came to help me, because I was detained there with the king of Persia. Now I have come to explain to you what will happen to your people in the future, for the vision concerns a time yet to come" (Dan. 10:11-14).

Centuries later, Jesus cast out demons as he inaugurated the kingdom of God with truth, grace, and power. Luke records one of these events.

> Then he went down to Capernaum, a town in Galilee, and on the Sabbath he taught the people. They were amazed at his teaching, because his words had authority.

In the synagogue there was a man possessed by a demon, an impure spirit. He cried out at the top of his voice, "Go away! What do you want with us, Jesus of Nazareth? Have you come to destroy us? I know who you are—the Holy One of God!"

"Be quiet!" Jesus said sternly. "Come out of him!" Then the demon threw the man down before them all and came out without injuring him.

All the people were amazed and said to each other, "What words these are! With authority and power he gives orders to impure spirits and they come out!" And the news about him spread throughout the surrounding area (Lk. 4:31-37).

In Paul's letters, he explained that Jesus isn't just marginally stronger than the forces of darkness.

[He is] far above all rule and authority, power and dominion, and every name that is invoked, not only in the present age but also in the one to come. And God placed all things under his feet and appointed him to be head over everything for the church, which is his body, the fullness of him who fills every-thing in every way (Eph. 1:21-23).

Evil shows its presence in many different ways. Some of our clients manifest the signs of demon possession. Most of our clients have been deeply wounded by evil deeds, and all of us bear the scars of sin caused by the foolish, sinful choices we made when we were tempted and deceived. Christians struggling with psychological, physical, and spiritual pain will encounter "the enemy of our souls" in their most difficult relationships. In his letter to the Ephesians, Paul describes the armor God has given us for the battle (Eph. 6:10-20). One of our tasks in counseling is to help our clients recognize this armor and suit up.

Deception, accusation, temptation, and demonic possession and oppression are real issues and parts of a comprehensive assessment strategy. Satan uses his lies to deceive minds and hearts so he can retain possession of souls. Even when he has lost and the person trusts in Christ, he still uses every tactic at his disposal to blind eyes, distort facts, and hinder the person's grasp of God's truth, grace, and power. Certainly we don't interpret all of our clients' problems as demonic, but we cannot overlook this modality as we engage in a comprehensive assessment. "The one who is in you is greater than the one who is in the world" (1 Jn. 4:4). These words are a clear pronouncement that God is in charge. All things are subservient to him.

And so a comprehensive assessment of all of the elements contributing to the shaping of the soul in any given moment includes an evaluation of the influence of the supernatural on the client and the situation in which the client finds himself.

WISDOM'S REVIEW

In a multimodal approach, we look carefully at each dimension of the client's soul life and commit to making a comprehensive assessment. We are careful to avoid being too narrow in our approach to assessment lest we omit elements contributing to the overall soul life of the client that may be causing specific challenges. Professionalism requires us to be thorough and inclusive in our understanding of our clients' needs. There is a broad consensus among secular and Christian therapists regarding the majority of the modalities that we have discussed in this chapter. Of course, all major theories differ to some extent on the causes of pathology. Christian counseling is no different. However, many areas of commonality exist between secular and Christian approaches to therapy, and these areas of agreement provide fertile ground for dialogue.

Some people may see an apparent contradiction between Jesus's encouragement to "possess your souls" and his directive, "Whoever wants to be my disciple must deny themselves and take up their cross and follow me. For whoever wants to save their life will lose it, but whoever loses their life for me will find it" (Mt. 16:24-25). These, however, are complementary, not contradictory. Ultimately, we possess our souls for the purpose of surrendering ourselves to Jesus. However, if we are to surrender our best selves to Jesus, it is incumbent upon us to first take possession of our bodies, our relationships, our thoughts, our emotions, our wills, our sin, and our spiritual core. Having accomplished the possession of these elements of the self, we are then free to offer up to him a living sacrifice—under the management of a self, empowered by the Holy Spirit, under the authority of the Word of God, and functioning within a community of encouragement and accountability (ideally a church)—pressing toward the goal of the imitation of Christ.

People who cling to selfish goals and behaviors suffer the disintegration of the soul through resentment, self-pity, and estrangement from God and others. Those who lose their lives in the wonder of God's love find more love, purpose, and adventure than they ever imagined. Many of our clients come to us crushed, angry, despairing, and with only a shred of hope left. They've lost their souls to the heartache they've endured—as a result of their own sins, the sins of others, unforeseen accidents, or natural disasters. In order to deny themselves, they first need to find a new or refreshed identity as beloved, forgiven children of God.

Not every person is ready for the message of self-denial. We must first receive before we can give, must possess in order to give up, must have a place before leaving it. Many Christians, diminished by misguided theology, need a healing emphasis on self-possession before they can think about self-sacrifice. Wounded children must be healed before becoming capable parents (Yancey, 2000, p. 224).

References

Baxter, R. The cure of melancholy and overmuch sorrow, by faith. Retrieved from www.puritansermons.com/baxter/baxter25.htm

Brown, C. (Ed.). (1971). *The new international dictionary of New Testament theology* (Vol. 3, pp. 680, 683). Grand Rapids, MI: Zondervan.

Clinton, T., & Ohlschlager, G. (Eds.). (2002). *Competent Christian counseling: Foundations and practice of compassionate soul care* (p. 107). Colorado Springs, CO: WaterBrook Press.

Corsini, R., & Wedding, D. (Eds.). (2008). *Current Psychotherapies* (8th ed.). Belmont, CA: Brooks/Cole.

Cortright, B. (1997). *Psychotherapy and spirit: Theory and practice in transpersonal psychotherapy*. Albany, NY: State University of New York Press.

Lazarus, A. A. (2008). Multimodal therapy. In R. J. Corsini & D. Wedding (Eds.), *Current psychopathies* (8th ed.) (pp. 153, 368–401). Belmont, CA: Thompson.

Lewis, C. S. (1941/1996). *The Screwtape letters* (p. ix). New York, NY: HarperOne.

McMinn, M. R., & Campbell, C. D. (2007). *Integrative psychotherapy: Toward a comprehensive Christian approach*. Downers Grove, IL: InterVarsity Press.

Parrott, L. (2003). *Shoulda, coulda, woulda: Live in the present, find your future*. Grand Rapids, MI: Zondervan.

Plantinga, C. (1995). *Not the way it's supposed to be* (p. 7). Grand Rapids, MI: Eerdmans.

Tan, S.-Y. (2011). *Counseling and psychotherapy: A Christian perspective.* Grand Rapids, MI: Baker Academic.

White, J. (1976). *The fight* (p. 16). Downers Grove, IL: InterVarsity Press.

Yancey, P. (2000). *Reaching for the invisible God.* Grand Rapids, MI: Zondervan.

4

Attachment and Relationships

People may pursue many different kinds of goals, but no one thrives without meaningful relationships. Why? At the deepest levels of our souls, we instinctively know that we are created for connections—with God and with people. God exists in relationship—an unshakable connection of love and truth that forever binds togetehr the Father, Son, and Holy Spirit. This relationship—this divine unity, this tri-unity among the three persons of the Godhead—existed long before God ever considered sharing it in the act of creation, and it will continue long after the creation is transformed into the new heaven and new earth. This affection for connection embedded in the heart of God is transmitted to humans in the image of God he has shared with humanity.

Clients may come to us because they suffer from depression, family strife, sexual dissatisfaction, financial ruin, or a hundred other presenting problems, but under the surface, their highest desires and deepest wounds are relational. Today's Christian counselors realize this truth and tailor their therapy to heal relational wounds and build relational bonds.

Our understanding of relationships doesn't begin with horizontal, human connections. First, we attempt to plumb the immeasurable depths of the relationship in the Trinity.

God Exists in Relationship

The conceptual basis for the primacy of relationships begins with the Trinity. God exists as a community (Icenogle, 1994) within the eternal relationships of the Father, the Son, and the Holy Spirit. When God created the universe, he created man and woman for relationships—especially for relationship with himself. At the beginning, human relationships were pure. In the Garden, God created Adam and Eve in perfect harmony with each other and with him. But anything that has that much propensity for beauty also has the propensity for pain and brokenness when life is not as it should be. It was a bit of heaven in a perfect life on earth, but it didn't last (Gen. 1–3). Man broke the shalom of Eden by disobeying God in foolish pride and eating the fruit of the one tree God had said not to eat from. The results were disastrous for them and have been for all who followed them. Sin entered and marred the equation, breaking into all relationships, separating man from God, and causing division and distress in human relationships.

Relationships are broken and strained by such issues as pride, fear, jealousy, resentment, and greed, but the need for connections hasn't gone away. In fact, we need relationships more than ever to heal, restore, comfort, and direct us. God said, "It's not good for the man to be alone." That analysis is still true today. An ancient Jewish proverb states, "He who goes too far alone, goes mad." Loving, affirming relationships make a difference in every aspect of our lives—emotionally, spiritually, and physically. A wide array of studies has shown that people (especially men) who enjoy a rich web of healthy and caring relationships live nearly a decade longer than those who live alone (Biebel & Koenig, 2004). In counseling and helping ministry, we continuously cycle back to a theory of relationship.

The power to choose. Why did God allow sin to enter the world and mar the perfection he created? God didn't create people to be robots who have no free moral choices. He created people with not only the capacity to choose to love him but also the option to ignore or reject him. God was determined to honor humanity's free will—which is a reflection of his image—by always respecting their choice to go their own way. True love is also a function of true choice—it can't be given or received by an automaton.

Valuing redemption or taking God for granted. There may be another reason God gave people the freedom to choose. He may have wanted man to experience the deficit caused by sin so that we would supremely value the wonder of God's redemption. Love is shown by the level of sacrifice, and God reveals his love most clearly through the ultimate sacrifice of his Son to pay for our sins. When this truth permeates our hearts, everything changes. We marvel at the love and justice of God. We delight in God's amazing grace. Our pride is dissolved in the wonder that Almighty God humbled himself to die a horrible death for us. We deserve only condemnation and shame, but through the cross, God offers forgiveness and adoption as his beloved sons and daughters. In so doing, God models the love of grace and forgiveness that are required to bring healing in some of the complex relationships in which we have been wounded. No wonder so many great songs through the centuries shout gratitude and wonder!

Relationship as a Central Principle

In the opening chapters of Genesis, we find an interesting irony. Adam existed in complete harmony with God, lived in a perfect environment, and was given an important role. Still, something wasn't right. In creation, God had pronounced each new marvel as "good" and "very good," but now he announced that Adam's condition was "not good." What was wrong? Adam was alone.

The necessity of the horizontal relationship. It is a stunning fact that even with a perfect relationship with God, something was missing. Something in the difference between Creator and creature left a void in the soul of man. Ultimately this resulted in the creation of woman, the sight of whom caused the delighted Adam to shout with joy and anticipation (Gen. 2:23). This scene reveals the importance of human, horizontal relationships.

Relationships are central to everything in human existence. As every counselor instinctively knows, we are broken in relationships, and we are healed in relationships. Health, in large part, is a function of living in a rich and nourishing social web of relationships. Pathology increases as we become more isolated and experience brokenness in our closest relationships. We are in relationship not only with other people but also with ideas, organizations, government, and the planet. Pastors, doctors, and nurses often report that the last words people speak before passing into eternity are seldom about money, career advancement, or hobbies. They almost universally lament or rejoice about their most valued relationships.

Relationship as the ultimate cure. Loving and healing relationships are the ultimate salve to trauma, loss, psychopathology, and the deepest grief we can know. The development of transference, when the client begins to relate to the counselor as he or she does to the most significant relations in life, is triggered by the most painful past relationships in the person's life. By understanding, by avoiding being trapped in those troublesome relationship patterns, and by behaving in more healthy and life-giving ways, the counselor intensifies the significance of the therapeutic relationship to bring healing and increasingly mature interactions in the client's life.

Relationship healing is vitally important. Counseling without a strong focus on relationship healing—the vertical relationship with God and the horizontal with significant others—is seriously flawed in perspective and practice. If the client is avoiding dealing with relationship issues in counseling, the new Christian counselor must gently but firmly raise those fundamental questions and bring relationships back into view.

Part of what we want clients to understand is that in the context of relationships—especially core relations with the person's mother and father early in life—clients begin to develop core relational beliefs about others, about themselves, and about God. Those core beliefs affect intimacy with God and others. Working through these beliefs is a very important part of the counseling process, and coming to terms with them is an essential part of our clients' spiritual, relational, and emotional journey toward health.

Attachment Theory

In recent years we have come to value and adopt some of attachment theory to explain both healthy and unhealthy relationships. The desperate search for safety and significance goes back to attachment, bonding, and relationship lessons we learned from our parents and, in fact, from all the members of our family of origin. Life isn't experienced in isolation. Rather, the self is embedded in both vertical and horizontal relationships that impact each other. Even hell itself is best understood as the ultimate isolation, a person's choice to be separate from God and from others. Hell can be described in part as a maddening process of spending eternity isolated from relationships.

Roots of attachment. In both England and the United States in the last half century, research in attachment theory arose from the study and treatment of severe and complex trauma—especially violent trauma in young children and its pervasive effects throughout life. Understanding the complexity of relationships is, without doubt, one of the most difficult clinical puzzles we face in practice. English psychiatrist John Bowlby was the pioneer in this field. His lab produced a prodigious amount of research on the nature and process of attachment while working with infants and their mothers (Bowlby, 1977–1980).

Safe Havens and Secure Bases

At its most basic level, attachment theory explores the way relationships shape our brain's ability to both participate in close, intimate relationships and to regulate emotion (Schore, 1994). Emotion regulation is the ability to tolerate and manage strong negative emotions, such as anxiety, anger, and sadness, as well as to fully experience a complete range of positive feelings, including hope, joy, contentment, and peace.

Testing a safe or a dangerous world. Attachment begins with a God-given motivation for people to seek others who are stronger, wiser, and usually older for comfort during times of distress. In this relationship, a deep emotional bond is created and nurtured in that "safe haven" relationship. At birth, our brains are not fully capable of self-regulation. We were created for relationship. Our need for connections doesn't show a deficiency—it's a God-given need that must be met for us to survive, let alone thrive. God's first "not good" pronouncement about his creation was attached to the aloneness of man. One definition of an attachment disorder tracks this psycho-spiritual crisis—that of being alone, of being detached and disconnected in a social sea of potential relationships.

In a sense, the infant brain continually asks a key question: "Is the world I'm living in a safe or dangerous place?" (Perry & Pollard, 1996). Depending on its experiences, especially with the mother or primary caregiver, the baby's limbic system (sometimes accurately referred to as the emotional brain) begins to wire itself for either safety or danger.

Internal working models. The brain is also formulating a network of basic assumptions about the self and others. "Am I worthy of love and capable of getting my needs met?" "Are others safe, reliable, and accessible to me during times of distress?" These core assumptions form the basis of what Bowlby (1977–1980) referred to as the *internal working model,* which is encoded as a blueprint in the emotional brain and forms a template for evaluating the world and what to expect and how to interact in future relationships.

This internal working model is at least roughly analogous to the biblical heart or soul of an individual, the mental schema or root belief system of cognitive therapy, the psychodynamic unconscious motivation system, and transactional analysis scripts. Moreover, analyzing our root beliefs about relationships—whether we believe God's truth or the subtle (or sometimes blatant) lies about our self, our social life, marriage, and family life—embeds the entire process into a holistic person-in-environment conception in social work, or ecological system theory. This is where attachment theory is at its bridge-building best in synthesizing systems and cognitive theories.

Changing the emotional brain. Because this model is based on relational experiences and is encoded in the emotional brain, it is nearly impossible for clients to modify these beliefs by simple logic and information. In other words, cognitive therapy alone is rarely a sufficient modality for producing change. These core beliefs were programmed into the brain through emotionally charged relational experiences. They can be accessed and modified only through the same means—repeated and emotionally charged relational experiences that disconfirm these negative, destructive beliefs. Therapy—at least the kind beyond the current "managed care" conception of symptomatic control in a few sessions—eventually must become an intensely emotion-focused venture to produce deep healing and lasting change (Greenberg, 2010).

When secure exploration is possible. The secure base system is the crucible in which all of this is formulated—it is the context for healthy child development and for the reparenting challenge of effective transformational psychotherapy. It begins with the concept of a *secure base*, as the child (or adult in therapy) relies on the caregiver to regulate its strong emotions. From this perspective, security begins with parental and systemic regulation that evolves into healthy self-regulation.

From a secure base, the *exploration system* turns on, and children will begin exploring the world around them. Exploration is the precursor to self-esteem and self-confidence. However, should the child feel threatened or if she is separated from the caregiver, the attachment system turns on (anxiety and anger), and exploration is terminated. *Proximity seeking* and *emotional signaling* are then activated as the child attempts to get close to the safe-haven parent in order to be reassured about their safety and identity, resulting in the emotional security that turns on the exploration system again. A similar process occurs in reparenting a client in therapy.

Cycling between security and exploration. This cycling between security seeking (running to mother for safety) and exploration (going out from mother to search the world) is constant in human development. Security (or proximity seeking and emotional signaling) can utilize any package of behavior (crying, whining, crawling, running, screaming, stomping...even hitting and aggressing) designed to achieve closeness to the caregiver. The parent is alerted to the child's distress by reading and detecting her signaling and proximity-seeking behavior. A safe-haven experience occurs when the child returns to her mother's arms and is comforted. Secure-base attachment is restored, and exploration begins again.

Secure and Insecure Attachment Styles

Early attachment relationships have long-term effects (as Bowlby, 1988, said, "from the cradle to the grave"), affecting people in every relationship for the rest of their lives. Attachment interactions in childhood become internalized (they become an internal working model) and stored in the emotional brain, providing a template for one's core beliefs of self and others and shaping one's adult emotional regulation styles and relationship styles. Based on a positive or negative view of self or others ("Am I worthy of being loved?" and "Are others reliable and trustworthy?"), four attachment styles have been identified (Hazan & Shaver, 1987).

Secure attachment. Security is the very definition of a healthy child or adult, a condition that flows out of relationships that provided a secure attachment base. People who feel confident and secure have a balanced and accurate view of the dangers in this world, and they approach life with a mostly optimistic orientation—"I'm okay, and so are you." This is the resilient person who knows how to manage distress, is well-regulated emotionally, and is able to participate in close and meaningful relations with others. These people also pass these same skills and traits on to their family. Security becomes a valued family legacy.

Avoidant attachment. This person is characterized by the perception,

"I'm okay, but you're not." Because they were not soothed and nurtured by their caregivers when they felt hurt or alone, they taught themselves not to trust others. Instead, they found ways to calm and soothe their own distress. *Avoidants* tend to be aloof in relationships, they are overly self-reliant and self-protecting, and they are often functional abusers of drugs and addictions as adults. In our clinical experience, avoidants often suffer from depressive disorders, sexual control problems, anger control problems, and narcissistic personality disorders.

Anxious attachment. Like the avoidant, those with an anxious style were also unfulfilled in primary caretaker relationships. However, they did not find ways to cope with their loss. They developed an orientation that is opposite or mirror-image of the avoidant's—"I'm not okay, but you are." Clinically, they usually present with an array of anxiety disorders, depressive disorders, problems with enjoying sex, and dependent and histrionic personality disorders. These people are less likely to be content by themselves and usually are clingy and demanding in relationships. They feel they have to be attached to others to feel complete as a person, but their desperate, demanding behavior often drives people away.

Disorganized or disturbed attachment. People with this style tend to be the most psychiatrically disturbed of the four types because they often experienced their primary caregiver as abusers—direct sources of pain and suffering. Their orientation to themselves and others is mostly negative. "I'm not okay, and neither are you." Clinically, they present with the more troubled psychiatric issues: complex traumas, severe posttraumatic stress disorder, schizophrenia, dissociative identity disorder and milder dissociative disorders, psychotic disorders, borderline personality disorder, and the schizotypal (bizarre) spectrum of personality disorders.

Clients' attachment styles offer vital information about their fundamental attitude and their core orientation to self and to others. This knowledge has significant benefits whether doing individual therapy or couples counseling. Tailoring interventions in line with these core characteristics—instead of trying and failing with countervailing tactics—gives therapists a distinct advantage in the development of workable treatment plans.

Trauma Affecting the Secure Base

Attachment and trauma. One of the major mental health problems, early childhood relational and repeated trauma (that is, complex trauma), has been understood in the framework of attachment theory (Williams, 2006). Complex trauma almost always involves two core characteristics: (1) It begins early in development (often within the first five to seven years), and (2) it involves various forms of traumatic relationship experiences (such as physical abuse, sexual abuse, severe neglect, and witnessing family violence), the most destructive of which is known as attachment trauma (Wright, 2003).

Attachment trauma occurs when the person to whom a child looks for comfort and safety becomes the direct source of abuse to the child—the cause of the child's fear and distress. The primary safe-haven parent or caregiver perversely becomes the major source of pain and suffering in the child's life. When attachment trauma occurs repeatedly throughout childhood, the stage is set for a wide array of psychological, emotional, spiritual, and even physical maladies in adults (Van de Kolk, 1994).

Trauma and the secure-base system. In traumatic homes, a number of problems interfere with the operation of the secure-base system. First, the caregiver is often emotionally overwhelmed and self-absorbed, so the child is unable to achieve a secure base. The child, in fact, is often left in a chronic state of hyperarousal. This has an enduring effect on the developing nervous system, priming it to be in a constant state of tension, anxiety, fear, and irritability, and is often the precursor to post-traumatic stress response in adults.

Second, without an effective secure base, the child has difficulty with self-esteem because self-esteem begins with other-esteem. These children lack self-confidence, which may turn into aggressive, acting-out behavior, chronic underachievement in school, or anxious withdrawal and extreme forms of shyness. Some children attempt to compensate through overachievement. They become oppressed by self-imposed perfectionistic standards and/or they frantically attempt to please others. Others turn to escapist modes of coping, such as drugs and illicit sex at an early age, to medicate the chronic anxiety that is already programming them as children for dysfunctional adult living.

Trauma threat is the key. Third, in the unsafe home, trauma and abuse do not occur every moment of every day, but the *threat* of trauma is constant. The traumatized child feels as if she can never let her guard down because she may be ambushed by another traumatic event. This is often manifested in a fear of normality and happiness because the child interprets these experiences as harbingers of bad things to come. Clinton and Sibcy (2006) call this "happy-phobia." It robs the person from ever being able to enjoy love and good times.

The tragic paradox. Finally, in unsafe homes, the child is faced with a relational paradox. Their attachment figures, those responsible for providing a secure base, are often the very source of the child's distress and fear (Main, Goldwyn, & Hesse, 2002). When this happens, the child is left in a state of intense emotion, and she has no organized way to manage her fear. Dissociation and other forms of unhealthy coping behaviors originate in this type of environment.

Unfortunately, because the child's attachment system is overly activated, she may attempt to cling even more intensely to the offending caregiver. This phenomenon is often seen in sexual abuse victims' fierce loyalty to their abusers. Another common outcome is that the child becomes controlling and aggressive toward the parent. Both of these patterns—blind loyalty and angry defiance—can replicate themselves in adult relationships, where the individual finds herself feeling trapped in abusive relationships or where the individual becomes abusive and controlling of others.

Repairing and Restoring Relationships

Today's Christian counselors pursue deeper understanding of the chaos in disruptive family environments, and they are committed to restore perception and health in relationships. With insight, skill, compassion, and tenacity, there is great hope for our clients. Brokenness begs for healing, and sin begs for grace. Our prevailing hope is that God graces us and our clients with all we need to overcome brokenness and restore relationships. In the practice of counseling, nothing is more practical than a profound relationship theory that operates from the premise that we are broken in relationships and healed in relationships.

The antidote to trauma and brokenness is healthy relationship. The Scriptures, the long history of the church, and our own spiritual experiences tell us that the hope for healing and cleansing comes from Jesus Christ. He is the author and perfecter of our faith, the one we look to for forgiveness, purpose, and power. He is the one who has the power to forgive any sin, and he delights to shower sinners with his grace. He is the one who has the power to heal any hurt, and he demonstrated his compassion by healing the sick, touching lepers, freeing people from demons, and giving sight to the blind.

Not all addiction is sin, but all sin is a type of addiction to run our own lives and be the kings and queens of our domain. No one can cure the idolatry of the heart except Christ. Anything else we pursue in the lifelong journey to anesthetize emotional pain eventually becomes an addiction. It is a hopeless journey, but Christ offers another way if people will take his hand.

Brokenness and Attachment

Attachment theory helps address the brokenness of self, the brokenness of others, and our broken relationship with God. A proper analysis begins with this triangle. It is never about curing only the self because the self is inextricably embedded with other people and God. The vertical and horizontal relationships are all connected.

Life is lived in a web of relationships. The journey into grace involves the restoration of shalom, God's peace and well-being. The first Adam's sin created chaos and brokenness, but the last Adam (Christ) came to redeem and restore. From the first Adam, we have received an idolatrous legacy that fails to love God. We've replaced God with our pursuit of counterfeits: pleasure, approval, possessions, and power. These things promise life and meaning, but they cannot deliver. The grace of Christ transforms our hearts, changes our desires and motivations, and gives us the power to begin to fulfill the Great Commandment—to love God with our whole being and to love our neighbor as ourselves.

The heart and purpose of Christian counseling is to effect Christ's enabling reconciliation of relationships in the life of every client. Reconciliation is more than the cessation of conflict. It's the presence of love, the promotion of a feeling of safety derived from my newfound relationship with a loving and securing heavenly Father, and the growing skill to demonstrate empathy for other persons. Research shows that the development of empathy skills are rooted in good parent–child relations (Wallin, 2007). Abused people often lack the core empathic skill to connect in meaningful ways because their marred parent–child relationships caused them to become defensive or aggressive (or both). Imparting love, connecting clients to a loving God, and teaching our clients to love are key components of effective Christian counseling.

The idea that we are broken in relationship and restored in relationship is a foundational premise for Christian counselors, but every Christian leader benefits from this insight. In every aspect of church life and ministry, nothing is more practical than some relationship theory. Understanding the dynamics of attachment is helpful in the framework of counseling, leading teams and groups, and discipling individuals.

Committed relationships. The word *commitment* has multiple meanings and implications for the new Christian counselor. The Bible uses many different concepts and metaphors to describe commitments. A covenant is a solemn vow, signified with a seal of ownership, authority, and protection. God seals his relationship with Abraham and his descendants throughout history with a covenant in Gen. 12. Eph. 1:7-14 explains that God seals believers in a relationship of love by the Holy Spirit of promise, who guarantees our eternal inheritance in Christ. God's commitment to covenantal sealing is meant to signify the unchangeable nature of his relationship to his children. He will never leave us or forsake us. We are safe forever under the umbrella of his love and grace.

Relationships and shalom. In the Bible, God's peace, often called shalom, is never experienced in a vacuum, and it is never the result of financial prosperity or career advancement. We have peace *with* God through the sacrifice of Christ, who paid the just penalty for our sins and took away the righteous wrath of God. We enjoy the peace *of* God when we trust his goodness, wisdom, and greatness in every situation in our lives. On the horizontal level, God made provision for our peace when he "destroyed the barrier, the dividing wall" of suspicion, resentment, and superiority in our human relationships.

Throughout the Bible, we see shalom in the context of relationships. In loving, forgiving, affirming relationships, people experience an exchange of healing and restorative power. Then shalom prevails. Moses was tired, and Aaron and Hur empowered him by holding up his arms (Ex. 17:10-13). Later, when Jethro came to visit, he empowered Moses by telling him, "The work is too heavy for you" (Ex. 18:18). The Bible says that two are better than one and that they have a good reward (Eccl. 4:9). Moreover, the strength of a three-fold cord is not easily or quickly broken (verse 12). When we show compassion, forbearance, forgiveness, and love, the peace of Christ rules in our hearts and relationships (Col. 3:12-16).

Relationships are central to God's plan. Most often, when the enemy of our souls attacks people, he attacks their relationships. Satan's goal is the destruction of relationships—especially our relationship with God. If he can't dislodge that primary bond, he attacks the family and the community, taking a more indirect route of destruction. We don't have to look far to see his schemes in practice. To destroy bonds of love, he uses bitterness, resentment, suspicion, withdrawal, and lies.

Brokenness occurs in community, and healing occurs in biblical community. People can learn a lot from reading books, but they can't be healed in isolation. In effective Christian counseling, the helper must always attend to both the vertical and the horizontal relationships. Relationships are the anchor point. When the anchor is dislodged, the ship of life goes hopelessly adrift. We all desperately need the restoring grace of God.

Relationship Lies Versus the Truth

Before sin and the Fall, Adam and Eve were anchored in God and with one another. In Satan's attack, his lie was designed to break the anchor point. His deception led to sin, which broke the relationship with God. How did the first couple respond to the effects of their sin? They blamed each other and God. Things haven't changed much since then.

Lies and deceit. Adam first blamed Eve for convincing him that sin was good, right, and acceptable. "She made me do it," he whined to God. Suddenly, the first couple was set adrift. They had lived in perfect harmony with God and with each other, but now they felt guilty and ashamed. To cover their sense of shame, they pointed fingers of blame and put on clothes. Those solutions didn't help. They were banished from the Garden, but not before God gave them a provision for their sin. Even at their point of rebellion, God promised love and forgiveness.

Freedom always includes relationship. Deep in the heart of every person are two conflicting desires—to be free and to be connected. The lie of Satan is that we can run our own lives, be completely free of constraints, and have it all. But this false promise of freedom leads to the bondage of sin, hopelessness, alienation, and shame. True freedom is realized only in a relationship with God, a relationship of love and loyalty. When we recognize that he is the true King and he has made us his dear children, everything changes. We don't demand to be free. Instead, we delight to be loyal to the one who proved his love to us in such a dramatic sacrifice. Actually, complete freedom is an illusion. Peter explained, "You are always going to be a servant, whether a bondservant to the good, or a slave to the way of sin" (2 Pet. 2:19 paraphrase). Paul said much the same thing in Rom. 6:16-18.

The lie today is the same as it was in the Garden, and people are just as quick to believe it. Our task as Christian counselors is to recognize the lie in our own lives, turn daily to God's grace, power, and truth, and become channels of his truth and grace to the people who come to us for help. They are both victims and sinners, and we have the privilege to address both problems with skill and kindness.

The human heart is "desperately wicked" (Jer. 17:9 NKJV). We naturally look to anyone or anything other than God to fill our hearts and give us purpose, but they all fail miserably. The counterfeit gods of wealth, beauty, applause, and comfort are suitors who plead with us to love them. Like prostitutes, they take our money and our attention but leave us feeling even more alone, ashamed, and worthless. One of our most important tasks as Christian counselors is exposing the deception and pointing people to the only hope for genuine love and fulfillment—the cross and kingdom of Jesus Christ. The counterfeit gods may excite us for a while, but they produce profound emptiness over time.

Lies of lust. In his first letter, the apostle John distinguished lust from love.

> Do not love the world or anything in the world. If anyone loves the world, the love of the Father is not in them. For everything in the world—the lust of the flesh, the lust of the eyes, and the pride of life—comes not from the Father but from the world. The world and its desires pass away, but whoever does the will of God lives forever (1 Jn. 2:15-17).

Lust is unashamedly self-absorbed. It wants what it wants right now! It's the opposite of love. The lust for beauty, power, prestige, and pleasure leads to heartache and division in relationships. Relationship is the core of meaning in life, but lust is the quest to put self first, which destroys connectedness. It moves us from an "us" pursuit to a "me" obsession. The inherent lie of lust is the idea that self is sufficient unto itself—"You will be free" and "You will be full."

Spiritual disciplines. The desperate and selfish desire to find meaning apart from God ultimately leads to being alone. Beauty, wealth, power, and pleasure aren't inherently evil. They are often good gifts God bestows on us. But we are tempted to evil when we value them more than God. They become idols. If we value good things too much, they become evil influences in our lives. Quite often, people put others in God's rightful place in their lives, so a spouse, a child, a parent, or a friend becomes an idol. The lure of love is captivating.

Dallas Willard (2002) observed that the motivation for change must necessarily be desperation, which forces people to be ruthlessly honest about their pursuits. The dependence on love and approval can be just as addictive as cocaine and just as ruinous. The spiritual disciplines become vital because they help us to become desperate in our pursuit of God. Confession, prayer, Bible reading, service, praise, and other familiar practices refocus our hearts on the one who is worthy of our love and loyalty. We also recommend the practice of fasting. The deprivation of food reminds us how deeply we are attached to food and other physical things. This realization leads us to recognize that our need for God is greater than the need for food.

Control of the will. By participating in one or more of the disciplines, I am pursuing a state of self-denial for a greater good in my life. I am saying to my body, "You do not control me. I want a rich, dynamic, intimate relationship with my God, and I want to make him the controlling dynamic in my life." When this is your goal, you approach the disciplines as helpful, normal ways to develop your relationship with God, not as drudgery or magic formulas for spiritual success.

In spiritual life, we experience a constant battle between willingness and willfulness (Moon, 2004). In order to become willing most of the time, learn to participate with God as his beloved child and his valued partner. To strip away our inordinate desires, he sometimes allows us to experience the deprivation of aloneness, and if needed, the loss of other things we hold dear.

That's what happened when God told Abraham to sacrifice his son Isaac. The old man's love for his son may have pushed God out of the center of his life, and God didn't blink. He told the old father to do the unthinkable—to sacrifice his dear son. Abraham's obedience cleansed his heart and restored his relationship with God. Our willfulness is defiance against God and his will for our lives. Our obsession with being free to control our own lives and clinging to the things we love is incredibly strong and doesn't evaporate when we become believers (see Rom. 7). Still, even when we're in the spiritual desert, God never abandons us. We may feel wretched, but "there is now no condemnation for those who are in Christ Jesus" (Rom. 8:1). God never gives up on us. His commitment is strong even when we don't see it or feel it.

Lies of addiction. Addictions distort thinking and create a web of lies. In the downward cycle of addiction, people become completely absorbed with getting and using. They no longer care for the people they once loved. Eventually, addiction can take its victims to a place where they actually believe that the world is better off without them and they would be better off dead. They can get lost in that dark detour.

As it is with God. Theologically, we need relationships because we are created in the image of God. Because God exists eternally in the context of relationships, vertical and horizontal connections are vitally important in the heart of every person. The drive for relationships comes from the deep core of the self—it comes from the image of God. The core element of human personality is our need for authentic, loving, faithful relationships.

Astoundingly, God created us in his image. God spoke in plurality when he said, "Let us make mankind in our image" (Gen. 1:26). In the Trinity, we find a healthy submissiveness. Speaking of the Father, Jesus said, "I do always what pleases him" (Jn. 8:29), and to the Father he prayed, "Not my will, but yours be done" (Lk. 22:42). The Spirit's role is to show us the truth and to bring honor to Jesus (Jn. 16:5-16). Our own interconnectivity, rooted in the mutual submissiveness of the Trinity, is required for healthy attachment and healthy relationships. Godly transformation happens in the center of our being, and then everything comes from it—from the inside out.

The "one anothers." Many passages in Scripture help us understand our responsibility in the body of Christ. How does God want to see his body function? Many authors, especially Paul, tell us to love one another, forgive one another, accept one another, and so on. These passages remind us that we can't escape our connections with others. They matter, and we have a God-given responsibility to relate to one another in positive, honest, affirming ways.

We like the idea that living well in the context of relationships brings a reward. In many ways, we experience an abundant life as we give and receive support and encouragement in our relationships. We're always in process, and we won't arrive until we see Jesus in glory, but that's no excuse for apathy or selfishness. Paul encourages us, "Strive for full restoration, encourage one another, be of one mind, live in peace. And the God of love and peace will be with you" (2 Cor. 13:11).

Relationship Healing and the Triune God

As we learn to relate to God, we sometimes find that we connect in somewhat different ways with each member of the Trinity. Some charismatic people's relationship with the Holy Spirit is central to their theology, worship, and prayer. It's a power theology, an overcoming theology. Many Christians focus their attention on Jesus, the Son. But others think most deeply and often of the Father—his love and authority and the way he breaks into contemporary history to reveal himself. No matter which one occupies our thoughts at any moment, the common theme is God's majesty and kindness, and our only proper response is grateful trust.

Abuse victims and the Trinity. Those who counsel adults who were sexually abused as children often report their clients' fear and anger toward God the Father, who represents the abusing father. They accuse the heavenly Father of failing to rescue them when they cried out for deliverance. For these victims, one of the goals of Christian counseling is a reconciliation with the Father through Jesus. Christ mediates relations between us and the Father, so sexual abuse victims often embrace Christ while they are angry toward the Father. As they go deeper into Christ's love, sacrifice, and kindness, they gradually form a new perspective of God the Father.

Abuse trauma in relationships. Trauma isolates and destroys. It mars the victims' perception of safety and love in a relationship. Victims accurately conclude, "I am being abused by someone who is supposed to love me." This is terribly confusing. When clients come from abusive backgrounds, they usually come to faith in God through the Son and the Spirit, not the Father. The Father seems harsh or distant, so they have to experience healing and gradually build faith in the Father. They will eventually grow into an awareness and appreciation of the depths of the Father's love for them, but it may take a very long time.

The blessing. In *The Blessing*, John Trent and Gary Smalley (2004) explain that a person who never received words of blessing from a father will not be able to move easily into discussions of the fatherhood of God. The practical effect of the power of the blessing, or the lack of the blessing, is revealed in living color by the person's perception of God. This has to be kept in view in the therapeutic relationship. You can't start everybody in the same place, and you can't have the same expectations for every client.

The lack of a father's blessing causes serious and varied problems. A nationally known pastor and church leader once said, "Do you know how many years I have spent in ministry trying to prove that I was worthy to be my father's son? And I hated my father for it." Another Christian leader relates a father's piercing, bitter words to his child: "Before I ever knew you, I hated you. You were my son, but I never accepted you as my son." Even a casual exploration of a client's parental relationships can be incredibly revealing.

Know yourself. Ultimately, the goal of therapy isn't helping clients know about relationships, but helping them do relationships in new, healthy ways. As a therapist, you will bring everything you have experienced to the challenge of healing hearts and relationships. And if you were abused, if your father was absent, if your mother ran your family...factors like these will shape the way you react to clients and conduct therapy. Therapists' personal histories have affected and even infected their family relationships and practices. For this reason, a growing number of training programs require counseling students to participate in counseling for themselves as a part of their training. It is not just because they need to spend time as clients—itself an important experiential education—but to deal with the abuse, the abandonment, the divorce...the struggle of living in and coming to terms with the family histories that have shaped them.

As a therapist, you must understand yourself—your hurts, drives, and perceptions shaped by your childhood experiences and subsequent relationships. If you do not know yourself, you almost certainly will undermine or even sabotage your therapeutic relationships. Like your clients, you are a great mystery, a montage of good and evil. Surfacing long-buried perceptions and wounds is incredibly challenging and rewarding. We aren't alone, and we aren't without resources. We are stewards of the great mysteries of God—his amazing love and complete forgiveness. When we embrace his grace in our story, we feel relationally connected and safe and free to become effective ambassadors of Christ in this lifelong call to restoration.

WISDOM'S REVIEW

In his social cognitive therapy, Mark McMinn talks about being transformed by meditating on Rembrandt's *The Return of the Prodigal Son* (McMinn & Campbell, 2007). The famous painting is displayed in the State Hermitage Museum in Saint Petersburg, Russia. McMinn argues that that picture is a vision of the heavenly Father. If that is true, it suggests that if you or your client has any other picture of God, it is a sub-Christian view of the Father. Sub-Christian views of God have plagued the church across its history and given rise to a great deal of emotional pain for the people of God.

God the Father of the prodigal son. In Christian counseling, one of the primary goals is to reconcile your client with the picture of the Father of the prodigal son. Jesus's famous parable (Lk. 15) describes a Father who longs for us, runs to meet us, loves us, kisses us, and doesn't care about the rules of the game when we come home to him. This is the vision of God we want to introduce to abused or broken clients. This may be our highest calling.

Outlandish grace. God is ready to pour out outlandish grace on those who seek him. In his book *The Grace of God*, Andy Stanley (2010) develops a similar theme and paints the same picture. The new Christian counselor leads with love and seeks to produce in his clients an accurate perception of the lavish love the heavenly Father wants to bestow on his children. This is the same love that has existed among the three members of the Trinity since eternity past.

God image is so vital. Many people are unaware of how their preconceived image of God impacts the relationship with self, the relationship with God, and the relationship with others. The new Christian counselor needs to be sensitized to this powerful dynamic and to understand that the path to healing starts when a person is reconciled to the God who is unveiled in the story of the prodigal son. Reconciliation of our beliefs and emotions with this view of God sets in motion a process that brings together the different and disunited parts of the self. It allows one to move into a community of believers that can facilitate healing and restoration in broken relationships (Crabb, 2004, pp. 23–30).

The establishment of a relationship with the God who loves and welcomes the prodigal introduces us and our clients to a safe haven and helps us to experience shalom in the deepest parts of our soul and in the most difficult of situations. He doesn't promise to rescue us out of our pain (though he sometimes works this way). Far more often, he rescues us *through* our pain, using difficulties to show us our need for him. When we're tempted to doubt his love and question his intentions, we need to remember the cross. There, Jesus suffered and died to prove his love for us.

> [Let us fix] our eyes on Jesus, the pioneer and perfecter of faith. For the joy set before him he endured the cross, scorning its shame, and sat down at the right hand of the throne of God. Consider him who endured such opposition from sinners, so that you will not grow weary and lose heart (Heb. 12:2-3).

We may not have answers to all our questions in this life, be we can trust that the God who has chosen to relate to us as sons and daughters knows, cares, and will ultimately show us the way out of darkness into a wonderful place of safety and security.

God has chosen to be in relationship with us even though we are still flawed, finite human beings who are slow to grasp the wonder of his mercy, love, and grace. He has fixed his love upon us not because of who we are and what we can do, but because, for reasons known only to him, he has chosen to own us as his sons and daughters. One day, when he renews all things, he will bring us home, and we will plant our feet on the solid ground of the safe haven he has prepared for all his children (Matt. 18). This is the hope that secures us now and brings courage to counselors and clients to endure and enjoy life in the present as his gift to us (Heb. 6).

References

Biebel, D. B., & Koenig, H. G. (2004). *New light on depression: Help, hope and answers for the depressed and those who love them* (ch. 11). Grand Rapids, MI: Zondervan.

Bowlby, J. (1977–1980). *Attachment and loss* (Vols. 1–3). New York, NY: Basic Books.

Bowlby, J. (1988). *A secure base* (p. 62). New York, NY: Basic Books.

Clinton, T., & Sibcy, G. (2006). *Why you do the things you do: The secret to healthy relationships* (p. 62). Nashville, TN: Thomas Nelson.

Crabb, L. (2004). *Connecting: Healing ourselves and our relationships*. Nashville, TN: Thomas Nelson.

Greenberg, L. S. (2010). *Emotion-focused therapy* (p. 63). Washington DC: American Psychological Association.

Hazan, C., & Shaver, P. R. (1987). Romantic love conceptualized as an attachment process. *Journal of Personality and Social Psychology, 52,* 511–524.

Icenogle, G. W. (1994). *Biblical foundations for small group ministry: An integrational approach* (p. 10). Downers Grove, IL: InterVarsity Press.

Main, M., Goldwyn, R., & Hesse, E. (2002). Adult attachment scoring and classification system. Unpublished manual. Berkeley, CA: University of California.

McMinn, M. R., & Campbell, C. D. (2007). *Integrative psychotherapy: Toward a comprehensive Christian approach.* Downers Grove, IL: InterVarsity Press.

Moon, G. (2004). *Falling for God: Saying yes to his extravagant proposal* (p. 97). Colorado Springs, CO: WaterBrook Press.

Perry, B., & Pollard, R. (1996). Childhood trauma, the neurobiology of adaption and use-dependent development of the brain: How states become traits. *Infant Mental Health Journal, 16*(4), 271–291.

Schore, A. N. (1994). *Affect regulation and the repair of the self.* New York, NY: Norton.

Stanley, A. (2010). *The grace of God.* Nashville, TN: Thomas Nelson.

Trent, J., & Smalley, G. (2004). *The blessing: The gift of unconditional love and acceptance.* Nashville, TN: Thomas Nelson.

Van de Kolk, B. (1994). The body keeps the score. *Harvard Review of Psychiatry, 1*(5), 253–265.

Wallin, D. J. (2007). *Attachment in psychotherapy* (p. 146). New York, NY: Guilford Press.

Willard, D. (2002). *Renovation of the heart: Putting on the character of Christ* (pp. 126–127). Colorado Springs, CO: NavPress.

Williams, W. (2006). Complex trauma: Approaches to theory and treatment. *Journal of Loss and Trauma, 11*, 321–335.

Wright, N. (2003). *The new guide to crisis and trauma counseling* (pp. 127–142). Ventura, CA: Regal Books.

5

Addiction and Idolatry

God intended for mankind to enjoy the fullness of shalom. As we have seen, shalom is far more than simply peace. The Hebrew concept of shalom includes the sheer delight of flourishing in the love, power, and wisdom of God. It implies the full development and implementation of our talents and abilities, put to good use to honor God and care for others. It is nothing less than a taste of the new heaven and new earth in the ups and downs of the here and now.

Humans are capable of great good because of their heritage as image bearers and their conscience. Both of these were damaged in the rebellion of Adam and Eve but retain the knowledge of God and the content of his law. Additionally, all humans share the witness of creation to God's existence and goodness and are called to reflect that beauty in their relationships and cultures. A person's potential for good is strengthened or weakened by experiences in the family, church, and culture, and by the person's decisions to receive or suppress the truth.

However, humans are also capable of great evil. Any potential to act on the claims of the law, conscience, or culture in a consistently positive manner are challenged by the presence of sin as a fixed component of the human personality inherited from the Adamic rebellion.

As we have observed, sin has tarnished the image of God in us, disrupted our relationships, and distorted the inner world of our thoughts, motives, feelings, and will. Sin brings death to our bodies, corrupts our cultures, and places us in continual tension with the architect of evil and his demonic horde. We were created to live in God and for God, but we chose to live apart from him, opposing his rightful rule or ignoring him. Sin is much more than breaking moral laws or rejecting God's absolutes. It is a personal offense against God himself and ultimately a decisive blow against freedom and health in the soul, in our relationships, and in our world. Sin wants what it wants when it wants it, regardless of the consequences.

A biblical and transformational model of Christian counseling requires a comprehensive understanding of the nature of sin and its effects so that our clients learn to treasure the freedom, power, and love found in a right relation to God's amazing grace. To understand the powerful dynamics of evil in the human heart, we need to connect the concepts of sin, addiction, and idolatry.

Sin as Addiction

As we mentioned in chapter 3, not all addiction is sin, but all sin has the destructive quality of addiction. Some argue that addictions, such as alcoholism, are at least partially the product of genetic predisposition. Other behaviors, such as sexual abuse, are often triggered by the perpetrators' own victimization as children. Regardless of the various influences, all sin is ultimately self-absorbing, self-deceiving, and self-corrupting, and it numbs the moral senses through tolerance. Christian counselors insist that except for a few instances, people are responsible for their choices, regardless of the contributing circumstances. Personal responsibility is a part of human dignity. Though sin has demonstrable negative effects, the person continues the behavior, thinking, "I don't care who it hurts," or "This time it will be different."

Like addiction, sin is inherently self-corrupting. Manipulation and self-protection are normalized. Lies risk exposure, so liars lie about telling lies. Abusers blame their victims and excuse their own destructive behavior. Those who harbor dreams of revenge have hearts like a desert, unable to absorb love and kindness from others, and they become more hateful each day. All addictions contain an element of irrationality for the onlooker, they ruin valuable relationships, and they poison the will. But the addict cannot fathom life without the escape and enjoyment of his addiction.

Like addiction, sin is also irrational. It ruins the sinner's most valuable relationships and poisons his heart, but he keeps sinning in the same way again and again because it seems to make perfect sense to him. In fact, he can't think of any other way to live.

In his explanation of sin's parallel with the dynamics of addiction, Cornelius Plantinga (2002, p. 50) asserts that both lead to a form of slavery.

> The real human predicament, as Scripture reveals, is that inexplicably, irrationally, we all keep living our lives against what's good for us. In what can only be called the mystery of iniquity, human beings from the time of Adam and Eve (and, before them a certain number of angelic beings) have so often chosen to live against God, against each other, and against God's world. We live even against ourselves. An addict, for example,

partakes of a substance or practice that he knows might kill him. For a time he does so freely. He has a choice. He freely starts a "conversion unto death," and, for reasons he can't fully explain, he doesn't stop until he crashes. He starts out with a choice. He ends up with a habit. And the habit slowly converts to a kind of slavery that can be broken only by God or, as they say in the twelve-step literature, "a higher power."

Sin as Idolatry

The addiction of sin is inherently idolatrous. It removes God from the center of people's lives and replaces him with a habit, a substance, or another person. These idols aren't necessarily sinful objects, but people engage in sinful and destructive behavior when they make these things more important than God. Pastor Tim Keller (2009, p. xiv) offers this explanation in his book *Counterfeit Gods*:

> The human heart takes good things like a successful career, love, material possessions, even family, and turns them into ultimate things. Our hearts deify them as the center of our lives, because, we think, they can give us significance and security, safety and fulfillment, if we attain them.

Idols aren't abstract, optional issues. They become the central, defining, essential, compelling thing in people's lives. Without them, people feel that they can't be happy and might not even be able to exist. Like an addiction, the sin of functional idolatry drives people to invest everything to possess, cherish, and use the idols.

Idols can be many things. God's greatest blessings can become addictive idols. Abraham waited for 25 years for God to fulfill the promise of a son. The birth of Isaac was a dream come true for the old man and his wife, Sarah. After a few years, the old father's love for his son evidently may have surpassed his love for God. God tested Abraham to provide him with an opportunity to demonstrate that no other in his life came before his devotion to God. Simply put, Abraham was without idols. And Christians are not immune to the allure of these idols.

We might think of idols as little statues worshipped in a thicket by half-naked savages, but they are all around us—and in us. The lie of idolatry is that a created thing can adequately replace the Creator and give us the joy, fulfillment, purpose, love, and strength only God can give.

Several simple tests reveal our deepest values.

- What do I daydream about?
- What are my greatest worries and fears?
- Where do I invest my time, money, and talents?
- What threatens me? What gives me joy and relief?

|||||||||||

Idolatry and the addictive nature of sin are central issues in the work of Christian counseling. In an article titled "Idols of the Heart and 'Vanity Fair,'" David Powlison observed, "That idols are both generated from within and insinuated from without has provocative implications for contemporary counseling questions" (Powlison, 1995, p. 36). He concludes that the gospel of grace is the only hope for our clients—and for us.

> The biblical Gospel delivers from both personal sin and situational tyrannies. The biblical notion of inner idolatries allows people to see their need for Christ as a merciful savior from large sins of both heart and behavior. The notion of socio-cultural-familial-ethnic idolatries allows people to see Christ

as a powerful deliverer from false masters and false value systems which we tend to absorb automatically. *Christ*-ian counseling is counseling which exposes our motives—our hearts and our world—in such a way that the authentic Gospel is the only possible answer (Powlison, 1995, p. 50).

The long, sad saga of sin in human history is one of unparalleled tragedy. We were created for much more—for the beauty and glory of shalom, for the richness of our God-ordained purpose in his plan for humanity, and for deep relatedness to him and others. Apart from God, we still have a master, but not a kind and noble one. When we turn our backs on God, we seek to make ourselves the master of our own private universe, but even then, as in *The Wizard of Oz*, another player is behind the screen. But this is no harmless trickster. Paul describes the enemy of our souls as "the ruler of the kingdom of the air." Without God's grace and shalom, the picture of the human condition could not be more bleak:

> As for you, you were dead in your transgressions and sins, in which you used to live when you followed the ways of this world and of the ruler of the kingdom of the air, the spirit who is now at work in those who are disobedient. All of us also lived among them at one time, gratifying the cravings of our flesh and following its desires and thoughts. Like the rest, we were by nature deserving of wrath (Eph. 2:1-3).

Under the deceptive influence of the enemy, people have tried to take control of their own destinies and goals to fulfill their desires. The original temptation in the Garden was to be like God, that is, to be independent and self-possessed. That's still sin's goal and drive.

Of course, most people would never say their primary aim in life is to become their own God. Spoken out loud, this claim sounds too arrogant. After all, if by some chance there is a real God, this brashness might offend him and cause real problems. However, most people have no problem ignoring God and the question of his existence, being consumed with the pursuit of power, prestige, and pleasure. Everywhere they turn, they hear promises that this product, that service, or another experience will give them the fulfillment they long to enjoy—and they believe every word. These promises are so pervasive, they are the water we swim in each day. Thoughts of God and his truth rarely if ever invade most people's minds. If they do, they are summarily dismissed. Without God's wisdom and strength, people are left to their own devices and to the false promises trumpeted by the media—with disastrous results.

As counselors we see clients who have believed the lie or have been victimized by those who believe the lie. We see the ruined people who believed more money, more power, more alcohol or drugs, more sex, more cosmetic surgery, or more approval would fill the gaping hole in their souls. Like the fish fooled by the worm dangling on the hook, these people have pursued idols with all their hearts, thinking these things would bring them true happiness and the control over their lives they longed for, only to end up enduring intense unhappiness, broken relationships, and bondage. They come to our offices perplexed. They don't understand the powerful forces and the lie that has driven them to despair.

Idolatry makes powerful but empty promises of complete freedom, thrills, and shalom. In the addictive cycle of sin and idolatry, the person first found delight and perhaps welcome relief from pain, but soon the substance or behavior became a cruel master over the person's thoughts, attitudes, desires, relationships, resources, and goals. He has become an addict. The person no longer uses the behavior or substance. Rather, *the idol now owns him.* Breaking free requires a new, powerful way of perceiving life and a rigorous commitment to spiritual, psychological, and physical warfare. Addiction and idolatry have taken possession of the entire soul. Freedom will come only through the Spirit's grace and power in concert with the person's courage to overcome the devastating impact in all of the modalities that constitute personhood and contribute to their individual ways to the imprisonment of the soul.

New Variables of Addiction

Our understanding of counterfeit gods and the addictive nature of sin applies to every client, but especially to those who struggle with the behaviors we traditionally define as addictions. In their lives we see the effects of these forces writ large. It is estimated that 22.6 million Americans (about 9.2% of the population) ages 12 or older have struggled with substance dependence or abuse in the last year (Substance Abuse and Mental Health Services Administration Press Office, 2006).

The good news is that the rates of addiction among teens and twenty-somethings have leveled off and have remained nearly steady over the past decade. However, the bad news is that addiction rates among boomers, the 50- and 60-year-old age group that has recently experienced a large demographic bulge in the US population, has nearly doubled during that same time period (Substance Abuse and Mental Health Services Administration, 2010). Though people 65 and older make up only 13% of the population, they account for one-third of all medications prescribed.

Two specific variables are important in addressing this new reality in treating addictions. First, the fastest-growing addiction is to narcotic painkillers (Maxwell, 2006). The National Survey on Drug Use and Health found the use of pain relievers increased from 530,000 initiates in 1990 to more than 2.5 million initiates in 2000. Second, this addiction is happening to older people with aging bodies—bodies less able to avoid the harmful effects of narcotics. If this trend continues—and there is nothing on the horizon to suggest it will abate among boomers—three troubling outcomes are likely to arise.

Corruption of medicine. First, increased rates of addiction to narcotics threaten to corrupt modern medicine. Increased abuse of prescription drugs often leads to an increase in illicit narcotic use as well because addicts become desensitized and seek out more potent narcotics (Brizer & Castaneda, 2010). Many desperate, gray-haired addicts turn to heroin, which can be snorted or injected for a powerful daylong, pain-controlling high. The natural progression from pain medications to prescription drug addiction to illegal drug use is a slippery slope for aged abusers.

Death by overdose. Second, especially among those who combine two or more psychoactive drugs, overdose and unintended death are becoming significant issues. People who mix alcohol and narcotics—who cannot accurately judge dosage levels and the limits of their aging bodies—are especially at risk (Loue & Sajatovic, 2008). Family members often are embarrassed and try to cover up the reality of death by overdose with more socially acceptable stories.

Drug-induced suicide. Third, based on current conditions and the drastic increase in prescription drug addiction, authorities project a spike in suicides by drug abuse. Intentional deaths by these narcotic substances will increase significantly. The onset of cancer, Alzheimer's disease, debilitating neuromuscular diseases, and sustained chronic pain are projected to push many elderly abusers to swallow triple or quadruple the number of pills they normally take, end it all, and leave their family members to assumed they died peacefully in their sleep. Accurate statistics on elderly suicides by drug abuse are difficult to obtain because many families fear the shame (and the loss of insurance proceeds), so they cover up any evidence of suicide (Ross, 2001).

What Is Addiction?

The *Diagnostic and Statistical Manual of Mental Disorders* (American Psychiatric Association, 2000) has perhaps the most comprehensive definition of substance dependence, or addiction. Three or more of the following symptoms must have been present at some time during a 12-month period.

1. *Tolerance effect.* The person needs increased dosages or mixes addictions in order to produce the same intoxicating effects. The user experiences significantly diminished effect when the same amount of the substance or behavior is used. This factor is often behind drug overdoses.

2. *Withdrawal symptoms.* When the addiction is quickly stopped, the person suffers significant physiological or psychological withdrawal. The substance or behavior is often used to manage and relieve withdrawal symptoms.

3. *Increasing dosage.* The addictive substance or behavior is used in larger amounts and over a longer period of time than was originally planned.

4. *Compulsive use and lack of control.* After the initial stages (which are bypassed by some drugs so the person proceeds to addiction from the first use), the person experiences a strong and overriding desire, "being driven" to use and abuse the substance or behavior. The person is unable to control or reduce substance-taking or behavioral addiction patterns.

Attempts at controlling use are quickly overcome by an
insatiable desire.

5. *Increasing time commitment.* The person experiences increased
   levels of obsessive thinking and time spent in addictive
   pursuits. The process of seeking, finding, preparing, using,
   and then experiencing the high becomes highly ritualized.

6. *Increasingly exclusive focus.* Other pleasures and self-care
   are progressively reduced. Previously enjoyable social,
   recreational, and occupational activities become
   unimportant.

7. *Continuing denial of harm.* The person persists in addictive,
   self-destructive behaviors even when negative consequences
   increase. In fact, denial of harm increases even when the
   person faces direct physical or psychological consequences.

The most prevalent and studied addictions are alcohol, drugs, sex,
gambling, and food, including the impact on family members. However, many other variations of addictive substances and behaviors are part
of the story. Beyond the individual differences is one unerring reality—
addiction is a downward spiral that produces dissolution, despair, dis-
ease, and if not stopped, death.

Types of Addictions

People can turn any good or bad thing into an addiction. Literally
anything—behavior, pursuit, or substance—can be corrupted. They try
to find something that will give them relief from the pain of living and
perhaps provide a biochemical buzz.

Alcohol and drugs. Many people use legal and illegal substances to medicate the body and brain. They may use cocaine, alcohol, or narcotics—including narcotics increasingly prescribed by physicians—which temporarily bind with the pain receptors in the brain. The user is lulled into a few idyllic hours of somnolent denial. These drugs temporarily cause the person to feel good, relieved, even ecstatic...for a while. However, when the drugs wear off, the pain comes roaring back, even more incessant in its life-draining demands. The progression from use to misuse to abuse to addiction may take months or even years for some people and their drug of choice, but some drugs hook people into virulent addictions almost instantly.

Food. Today, many people obsess over food and body image, which often leads to compulsive behaviors and disorders. Anorexics starve themselves to feel and appear thin, and even when they are far below their recommended body weight, they still perceive themselves as fat. This drive is often fueled by deep insecurity, perfectionism, and the fear of losing control. Bulimics binge on high-calorie, fat-filled, or sweet foods (often gorging on them in secret) and then purge through self-induced vomiting or the use of laxatives. They are often of normal weight, but they, too, are plagued with self-doubt and driven to control at least one element of their lives. Compulsive overeaters binge, but they don't purge. Their motives may vary. Many view food as a friendly companion, and some become obese as a self-protective mechanism to keep people and risks at bay.

Gambling. Compulsive gamblers are always looking for the big win. They win enough to keep them hopeful, but they lose so often that they get into trouble. Like other addictions, the habit may start innocently. These people may begin betting casually with friends, but it spirals out of control. Soon they are obsessing about winning, studying poker plays or horses (or whatever type of gambling they've chosen), worrying about past losses, lying about their financial problems, and hiding their losses and behavior from family members. To keep their habit going, many of them resort to stealing from family and friends. In the addictive cycle, they have to place increasingly larger bets to get the same rush of excitement.

Twisted sex. God's gift of sex is one of the most wonderful, pleasurable, exciting aspects of human relationships. It's attraction and power, however, can cause it to be terribly misused. Sexual addiction comes in many forms, from occasional, seemingly innocent pornography to rape or child sexual abuse. In *False Intimacy*, Dr. Harry Shaumburg (1997, p. 22) defines sexual addiction:

> Sexual addiction exists when a person practices sexual activity to the point of negatively affecting his or her ability to deal with other aspects of life, becomes involved in other relationships—whether real or through fantasy—and becomes dependent on sexual experiences as his or her primary source of fulfillment...regardless of the consequences to health, family, and/or career.

Pornography is based on the illusion of never-ending, thrilling, perfect sex with a beautiful mate who never complains, never talks back, and never ever says no to kinky, perverse, and painful sexual practices. For many, pornography is only a first step. After a while, it no longer satisfies. The gnawing emptiness pushes the sex addict deeper. He or she turns to prostitutes, child porn, date rape, and increasingly risky criminal behavior. The bottomless pit and downward, destructive spiral of addiction in general may be most clearly seen in the world of sex addiction and perversion.

Approval. In families that exist in chaos, people feel the daily effects of insecurity, despair, and fear. They long for love and justice. Some of them try to cope with the chaos by desperately trying to control those who are out of control. They fix people's problems, plead with them to act responsibly, try to argue them into healthy choices...but nothing works. These people hope they can do enough to win the love they want to experience. They live on the false hope they can do just one more thing that will make others love them. Their minds are consumed with pleasing, fixing, and earning love—just as much as an addict's thoughts are consumed with acquiring and using a drug.

Money. In our nation, which consumes 25% of the world's goods and services with only 4% of the world's population, many people are obviously materialistic. People who are addicted to wealth cocoon themselves in the illusion they need more and finer cars, clothes, houses, boats, and pleasures. The lust behind this full-on, consuming pursuit may be the power and prestige that come from wealth, the pleasure money can buy, or the perceived popularity that comes from the adulation of jealous observers. These perceptions are reinforced by virtually every media advertisement and conversation, so they seem completely normal.

Education and learning. Some people are on a lifelong quest of learning and education, which is highly valued in America. They believe advanced degrees and academic awards will give them the security and respect they long to enjoy. When they look back years later, they may realize they've sacrificed the things that really matter to the vain pursuit of false security and applause.

Technology and video games. Some people are obsessed with the latest advancements in technology. They live for the introduction of the latest phone, tablet, website, or app. When a new product comes on the market, they sacrifice everything to have it. Similarly, many people—adults as well as teenagers—are hooked on video games. They spend hours every day learning techniques to play better, interacting with competitors and friends across town or around the world. Like other addicts, they are obsessed with their behavior, and they neglect relationships, responsibilities, and other important aspects of life.

A million other things. Almost any desire or pursuit can become addictive. We can fixate and obsess on cooking, fly fishing, cleaning the house, travel, or anything else. These are not necessarily evil things. In fact, they are sometimes very good things. But when they become the most important things in life, the person has entered into the realm of idolatry and addiction.

Increased User Tolerance

User tolerance is insidious. Gradually—almost imperceptibly in most cases—the person becomes desensitized, requiring more of the substance or behavior to receive the same effect. When that level doesn't work any longer, the person may switch to more extreme behaviors and more powerful drugs to achieve a sense of relief or thrills. The ugly truth about tolerance is that it is inherently progressive. Unless the cycle is arrested, the user becomes an abuser and then an addict.

Not surprisingly, the devastating impact of increasing tolerance sneaks up on people who are progressing deeper into the cycle of addiction. The tolerance effect eventually becomes stronger than the addict's willpower. When the progression from use to addiction began, the activity may have been fun and benign. After a while, however, the effect of tolerance causes the addiction to consume the person's thoughts, desires, and pursuits. The brain chemistry and wiring change to an addictive pattern, so choices to change become even harder. Eventually, addicts can't get out of their addiction. No matter how hard they try—and eventually they either stop trying, are arrested, or die—they can't escape it without the help of others. They are in bondage, slaves to their drug or behavior of choice.

Sin and Addiction

Sin is the universal enslaving power that delights in sponsoring any form of addiction. The heartbreak that inevitably flows from saying yes to sin's sponsorship of a promising addiction is that once a person buys in they can barely free themselves on their own. In his insightful little book *Sin and Grace in Christian Counseling: An Integrative Paradigm*, Mark McMinn assesses the pervasive impact of sin from the triple perspective of psychology, theology, and spirituality.

Psychology and human defensiveness. Psychology contributes to our understanding of sin and addiction by delineating the ways we lie to others and deceive ourselves when the truth about life is too hard to accept. "We live behind armor, protecting ourselves from painful realities with selective forms of self-deception. When bad things happen, we explain them to ourselves. Most often, we explain things in ways that take blame off ourselves, and place it onto others" (McMinn, 2008, p. 78).

A theology of sin and grace. An astute biblical theology speaks about the depth and depravity of sin and the damaging effects of addictions in our own lives and in the contamination of every relationship and the entire creation. But it also reveals the depth of God's gracious love, the only power able to set us free from the insatiable grip of sin and addiction.

> Freedom can come through repentance. When we sin, we need to go through the humbling process of confessing, repenting, receiving forgiveness, and also experiencing grace. We must continually pray for a deeper awareness of our sin, the necessity of repentance, and the wonderful gift of grace that is never-ending. God does not desire us to wallow in

shame, but to turn from our self-deceived ways and to seek a new and better way of living (McMinn, 2008, p. 83).

A spirituality of loneliness. The paradox of modern loneliness is that in spite of the worldwide impact of social media, telephonic technology, and a crowded planet, loneliness is increasing. If we do not admit our utter sinfulness and inability to be fulfilled this side of heaven, we will never appreciate the painful but accurate assessment that sin, pain, failure, and deficiency are normative. And without this perspective about the pervasive and powerful impact of sin, we won't truly grasp the wonder of God's amazing grace.

When a jeweler wants to show the brilliance of a diamond, he puts it on the backdrop of black velvet. God's grace is the diamond that is most clearly seen against the dark, dismal backdrop of human depravity. We may not be as bad as we can be, but we're as bad off as we can be—apart from God's grace.

The endless search. The text of history books and today's newspapers tells stories of man's search for meaning. People have tried to fill the emptiness of their souls with power, profit, pleasure, and applause. But regardless of how hard they have tried to fill the void, the emptiness remains. God has made us with a deep yearning for our lives to matter, for a connection to something filled with purpose. When we look to other people or to things to fill the yawning hole in our hearts, we remain dissatisfied. We keep searching until we find God, or we die with the hole unfilled and the ache unhealed.

Linking sin and grace. McMinn (2008, p. 90) makes this conclusion:

> Awareness of sin is a good thing. Pleading guilty, admitting our fallen, broken state opens the possibility of a grace that is greater than all of our sin and all our accomplishments. James Bryan Smith (1995), an author and spiritual leader, writes,

"Now we can stop lying to ourselves. We are saved from our own self-deception the moment we say with the tax collector, 'God be merciful to me, a sinner' (Lk. 18:13). We no longer need to apply cosmetics to make ourselves more acceptable to God. We have been accepted by God; therefore we can accept our selves" (p. 36).

One day when I was particularly sensitized to my own sin and inadequacies, I said to God, "If our relationship depends on my getting all of the stuff right, we might as well call it quits right now."

In a flash, God spoke to my inner soul. "Where did you ever get the idea that your relationship with me was about your ability to perform well? This has always been about my decision to love you and have a relationship with you. It's always been about my free choice to love you with all of your frailty and failures. It's always been more about who I am than who you are."

Christian counselors understand that, as McMinn has said, awareness of sin is a good thing. When that awareness is joined to the kind of true repentance Paul outlines in 2 Cor. 7, counselors and then clients are led into an experience of God's grace and love that transforms our view of how relationship need to be done. Experiencing God's grace not only delivers us into a safe haven of relationships—often for the first time in our lives—but also shows us in a powerful way the direction in which our client must go to find their way to their own safe haven.

The causes for and types of addiction vary, and the treatment of addictions requires attention to many of the modalities contributing to the life of the soul. *Caring for People God's Way* (Clinton, Hart, & Ohlschlager, 2005) describes an array of effective interventions. These range across the biological, psychological, social, and spiritual spectra.

Physical Stabilization and Self-Care

Addicts often damage their bodies. Many alcoholics suffer neurological, gastrointestinal, or liver complications. Food addicts may starve themselves to death, ruin their teeth from repetitive vomiting, or suffer multiple effects of chronic obesity. Sex addicts run the risk of sexually transmitted diseases and a variety of sexual dysfunctions. All addicts also risk significant stress resulting from chronic fear and anxiety, often due to the consequences of the addiction.

Medical and psychiatric evaluations. At the beginning of treatment, addicts need a complete medical evaluation. Alcoholics and some drug addicts may need to be hospitalized and supervised during detoxification. Anorexics may also need to be stabilized in the hospital to address the effects of chronic malnutrition.

When stabilization has been achieved, addicts then need a thorough neuropsychiatric evaluation. The presence and severity of depression must be determined. In some patients, assessment is appropriate for a variety of forms of attention deficit disorder. Some addicts require pharmacological help for depression, and others need medications to manage the brain's need for constant stimulation. Counselors should develop a relationship with a competent psychiatrist who can perform these evaluations and services.

The role of abstinence. Abstinence from the drug or behavior of choice will, over time, change the level of neurochemical tolerance the addict has developed. With support and accountability, alcoholics and drug users are able to achieve total abstinence from a substance. Food addicts may be able to abstain from certain kinds of food. Process addicts often have a harder time abstaining because secrecy is easier to maintain and accountability is more difficult. In some cases, temporary abstinence is recommended for addictions to good things that have become addictions. Some addicts, such as gamblers, can stop certain behaviors altogether. Sex addicts, however, can arouse themselves by fantasizing about sexual behavior. One common protocol with sex addicts is to have them abstain from all forms of sexual activity for a period of time in order to achieve a detoxification effect from sinful sexual activity.

Finally, addicts need to learn the skills of self-care. Paul explained that our bodies are temples of the Holy Spirit (1 Cor. 6:19-20), but addicts have been treating their bodies more like the city dump than God's holy temple. Being tired, hungry, angry, or lonely makes any addict more vulnerable to destructive behavior.

Behavioral Change

Addicts have developed strong, highly ritualized, even automatic behavior patterns in order to maintain their addictions. They go to extraordinary lengths to deny, minimize, or rationalize their destructive behavior. Counselors play an important role in challenging, correcting, and replacing old patterns. The idols of addiction can't simply be suppressed—they must be supplanted by the grace, love, wisdom, and power of God. It's not enough to attend church or groups, and it's not enough to go to counseling or read the Bible. People need a genuine, heart-changing, life-transforming encounter with Jesus Christ, accompanied by the motivation and resources to put off old patterns of behavior and put on new, healthy, productive ones that please God.

Honesty and behavior change. As the old dictum goes, all addicts are liars. Therapists need to look beneath the client's words, be suspicious of promises and explanations, and insist on raw honesty about behavior. When the addict seeks to divert discussion to family, emotional, or financial concerns, the therapist needs to redirect attention back to behavior. Effective treatment may eventually address a wide range of important issues, but the clinician can't let the habitual (but often convincing) lies of the addict take therapy off course.

A productive tactic is to link the tangential topics the client raises with the central issue of his addiction. For example, if an addict complains about his wife, the counselor might refocus his response toward the addictive behavior by asking, "So how is the way you approach your anger toward your wife similar to the way you act out your anger in your sex addiction?" Or "How is your tendency to denigrate yourself reflected in your addiction ritual?" Clients often assume their addiction has a life of its own and operates apart from other concerns. That's not true. It's always integrally connected with every other aspect of the person's life. Unlike many other diseases and clinical issues, addiction is both symptom and disease.

Changing ritual behavior patterns. Addicts need to find the courage to change certain behavior patterns that trigger or maintain their addiction. These behaviors are referred to in the addiction community as rituals. Many different authorities describe this cycle, which usually includes dissatisfaction, craving, fantasizing, obsessing, acquiring, using, shame, and dissatisfaction again.

The competent Christian counselor helps an addict assess the cycle of ritualistic behavior and how he or she acts out. Taking detailed histories of usage and behavioral patterns is essential. When this information has been sorted out, addicts must be trained to identify triggers, make good choices (for instance, to call a sponsor or leave the area), and establish boundaries against those behaviors in the future. Alcoholics need to avoid friends who are drinking and drugging, particular areas of town, or stressful situations that led them to drink and use. Food addicts may need to avoid going to the grocery store in the early days of recovery, or they may need to schedule meals at regular times and find someone to encourage them and hold them accountable to eat at those times. Sex addicts need to avoid people and places that trigger them into their fantasies or "connecting" rituals. For example, sex addicts who use the computer to connect need to become accountable for every minute of online access.

Intervention. In most cases, family members have begged and threatened the addict for years, but the lack of enforceable consequences has sent clear signals that these were empty threats. The addict saw no reason to change. At some point, however, the family should choose a formal, structured intervention under the guidance of a professional trained in this important arena. The professional will meet with the family to determine the goal of intervention, the consequences of refusal to comply, the process, and the role of each person. In the encounter with the addict, the professional takes the lead, explains the purpose of the meeting, and asks those present to communicate their stories of hurt, betrayal, and loss. When they've finished, a clear step of treatment is demanded, and significant consequences are outlined. If the consequences aren't enforced, the intervention will fail. Even if they are enforced, there are no guarantees even the finest treatment center will be effective. Still, intervention is one of the most powerful tools in the therapist's toolbox.

Twelve-step programs. Many kinds of 12-step groups serve as essential support and accountability for addicts. Increasingly, believers are establishing Christ-centered support groups in local churches. For example, several ministries are creating materials for the field of sexual addiction. Consult such websites as faithfulandtrueministries.com for useful information. One Christian group, Overcomers Outreach (Bartosch & Bartosch, 1994), has created Christian materials for general addiction support groups.

The Nehemiah principle. When Nehemiah was building the walls of Jerusalem after the long years of captivity, he learned an attack could come at any time at the weakest spot in the wall. He prepared for the enemy by carefully supplying his men and giving them orders. He didn't close his eyes and hope an attack wouldn't happen. He did everything possible to be ready and strong. His attitude was, "Whatever it takes, we'll be ready to fight and win!"

In a similar way, addicts need to prepare in their times of strength and renew their determination to change their thinking and behavior in times of weakness. If they wait until the attack comes, they won't be ready. For example, addicts should talk with sponsors daily and attend support groups regularly—even when they don't feel as if they need to. These are some of the common principles of relationships in recovery:

1. Never try to recover alone.

2. Fellowship is essential to promote freedom from addiction.

3. Prepare in times of strength and resolve to stay connected to others in recovery during times of attack and weakness.

4. Be in intimate accountability with at least four people.

Be alert to relapse. It is not unusual for an addict to relapse a number of times and to take a year or more to establish a consistent path toward mature Christian living. Temptations threaten progress, and small setbacks can trigger urges to use again. But relapses are not tragic. The tragedy occurs when the addict refuses to repent and come back. Staying free of any addiction is a lifelong challenge that requires addicts to keep their guard up over the course of their lifetime.

Emotional and Cognitive Restructuring

Addicts tend to come from family environments that have wounded them emotionally, physically, sexually, and spiritually. They experience deep anger, pervasive fear, feelings of shame, nagging sorrow, and loneliness. They replicate these wounds in harming their spouse and children, so the destruction is passed on to the next generation. The destructive pattern of behavior, however, may not be identical from one generation to the next. For example, one child of an alcoholic may become a substance abuser. Another child may religiously avoid alcohol and drugs but become addicted to approval and the desperate desire to please others.

Healing family-of-origin wounds. Family stress and emotional wounds deriving from this stress need to be addressed early in counseling addicts. Unhealed wounds are time bombs waiting to explode. Unresolved painful feelings often are contributing factors in relapse. Stimuli that trigger addicts' ungrieved wounds and unhealed anger often cause them to retreat to the familiar, destructive answers and activities they used to medicate and change those feelings. These rationalizations are referred to as stinkin' thinkin' in the AA vernacular.

Cognitive restructuring involves identification, confrontation, and correction of erroneous thinking, which requires a psycho-educational approach. Pastors and friends may think they are offering good advice when they give simplistic answers to an addict's dilemma, but it is irresponsible to suggest that a person should just forgive and forget. Healing of life's hurt can be a rewarding, lifetime journey, but there are many detours that get people stuck in sadness and anger. The process of healing requires several factors, including...

1. understanding the nature of the harm that caused the wounds

2. providing support

3. addressing anger or bitterness

4. allowing the person to grieve the losses

5. helping the person find meaning in suffering

6. guiding the person in the process of forgiveness of those who caused the harm

7. adopting healthy, new, biblical thinking and self-talk

Relationship Repair

People who live with addicts know how painfully difficult it can be to sort out truth from lies and distinguish authentic love from manipulation. Sometimes the spouses of addicts are referred to as co-addicts or codependents. Addiction is a family problem. Everybody is affected, and everybody needs help. Competent counseling assesses the emotional and spiritual health of people living with addicts. In therapy, some hard questions commonly surface: Is it safe to continue to live with the addict if he doesn't get help? How have other family members suffered from the betrayal of lies, the untrustworthy and irresponsible behavior, and the anger and control? Often, the spouse and children also have drinking or other addiction problems. Mark Laaser's research has shown that about one third of spouses who live with sex addicts are also sex addicts.

Old scripts cycle in new generations. Counselors should assess factors that brought spouses together. New theories are being developed which suggest that people find each other to resolve painful, destructive patterns of family trauma. Sex abuse survivors may, even unconsciously, find another sex abuse survivor—or even a sex addict—for a relationship. Authorities theorize that addicts may be trying to replay old patterns in order to create a different result. A corollary theory is that addicts replay old family patterns, trying to become the one who controls the situation rather than remaining the victim. The attempt to find healing in a marriage relationship for early life wounds is called "trauma bonding." Both parties, the addict and spouse, together or individually, need concentrated, skilled, therapeutic intervention to restore the marriage. Simple communication strategies or intimacy-building exercises will not work in these situations. Work on the deep wounds with both partners is essential to help them heal and rebuild.

Suffer little children. Invariably, the children of addicts are deeply wounded, confused, and angry. Counselors need to address these issues and support the entire family. The most common (and understandable) tactic in these families is to blame the addict for every imaginable problem. There is, however, enough culpability and responsibility for everyone. Gentle forms of education and support can be helpful. Support groups, books, seminars, and therapy may be utilized to provide insights, encouragement, and steps to new ways of relating to one another.

Victim empathy. Multifaceted addiction treatment encourages addicts to develop empathy for loved ones they've hurt by their destructive behavior. The addict is taught to understand and empathize with their victims. Genuine empathy gradually tears down walls of shame, hatred, and distrust, and it begins to rebuild relationships based on trust and respect. However, when addicts develop empathy and consider the consequences of their actions, they may present with suicidal ideation, shame, and guilt. The road to recovery in relationships is long and difficult, but the possibility of profound intimacy is worth the effort.

Spiritual Renewal

Addicts are spiritually immature, so they often search for childish, black-and-white answers to their problems. If addicts have developmental problems, they will also have faulty, immature beliefs about God. Christian counselors, pastors, and lay helpers who work with addicts have several spiritual challenges.

Letting go. Addicts must address their craving for control. Many of them have made professions of faith in Christ, but their hearts, minds, emotions, and wills were not transformed. They may be angry with God for not "delivering" them from their cravings and the consequences of their foolish, selfish choices. In addition, they have a hard time letting go of the high and the mood alteration of their addictive activities. Addicts have become accustomed to getting their way regardless of the cost. They demand control. Being enslaved to addiction is what they know, and turning back to what they know is a temptation for a long time. One of the first principles of AA is to "let go and let God." This statement reflects the need for addicts to admit they're not God, not in control, and not the center of the universe. It sounds like a simple statement, but it has profound implications for recovery.

Learning new habits. Addicts almost universally tend to drift back to familiar people, places, and practices even if those things have wreaked devastation on them and their families. They have lived out of control, but they thought they were totally in control of themselves, their addiction, their families, and their finances. In therapy, they need to learn new ways of thinking, believing, relating, and acting.

When Jesus met a paralyzed man lying by a pool, he asked the man, "Do you want to get well?" It seems like an absurd question for a man who had been paralyzed for 38 years. The man, however, didn't answer affirmatively, but instead gave excuses why he hadn't been able to get into the pool.

Christian counselors also have to ask this hard question. When we ask, "Do you want to get well?" we implicitly also ask, "And are you willing to take the risks, surrender control to God, cooperate with the counselor and do the hard work that is necessary?" Regardless of how much we want them to change, and regardless of how much their family members plead with them, addicts have to answer for themselves.

New habits are established the same way Nehemiah built the wall around Jerusalem: one brick at a time. In the first few weeks of therapy and treatment, the old cravings may threaten progress every day. With renewed faith and support and the acquisition of new skills, people begin to climb out of the hole they've been digging for years. Gradually, they begin to develop a wide range of new habits of reflection, truth, trust, communication, and responsibility. During this time, the hard work of forming new ways of thinking and acting courageously begins to rewire the brain.

In the first months and up to a year, family members should be suspicious. The addicts have undoubtedly made plenty of promises in the past and broken every one. But after a while, healing, trust, and love can become the new normal in the family.

Do it for others. In the grip of their addiction, addicts were motivated by a poisonous blend of arrogance, anger, fear, and anxiety. At all costs, they avoided consequences for their behavior by blaming everyone else—especially those closest to them. They have been totally self-absorbed. In recovery they learn the value of humility, and they begin to care for others. The 12th step of Alcoholics Anonymous states, "Having had a spiritual awakening as the result of these Steps, we tried to carry this message to alcoholics, and to practice these principles in all our affairs." Serving others is an important part of maturing spiritually and is vital to getting well emotionally and physically. Paul encourages believers to "follow God's example, therefore, as dearly loved children and walk in the way of love, just as Christ loved us and gave himself up for us as a fragrant offering and sacrifice to God" (Eph. 5:1-2). In a 180-degree turnaround made possible through real repentance, addicts learn to sacrifice, giving their lusts and cravings to God, surrendering to accountability, appropriately fearing their addiction of choice, and giving themselves to love and care for others.

Getting to spiritual roots. Addiction is, at its root, a spiritual issue. Alcohol is called "spirits" for a good reason. A spiritual awakening is essential for someone to leave the clutches of addiction and find meaning, forgiveness, joy, and power in a new life of sacrifice and service. Discipleship never happens in a vacuum. We need the support, correction, love, and acceptance of others who love us enough to share with us the wonderful truth of God's grace and the hard truth about our sin.

In initially assessing clients, note their spiritual perception and attitude toward God. "By examining the patient's religious views in the context of his or her personality dysfunctions, the clinician can differentiate between valid expression of spirituality and defensive religiosity" (Earle, Earle, & Osborn, 1995, p. 12).

WISDOM'S REVIEW

Life hurts at times! As Hemmingway wrote in *Farewell to Arms*, "The world breaks everyone."

Solomon concluded that the hurt we experience sends us in pursuit of anesthetics. We search for pain killers, but we are forced to confess that our quest is like trying to catch mist in a bottle, and we cry out, "Everything is meaningless" (Eccl. 1:2). This accurate and painful assessment of life under the sun leads multitudes into idolatry and addiction.

By this analysis, we can surmise that everyone is addicted to something and flirts with idolatry. Addiction and idolatry are the natural outcomes for someone who doesn't value the wisdom and love of God as the primary treasures of life. All of us can sing with hymn writer Robert Robinson, "Prone to wander, Lord, I feel it; prone to leave the God I love." The lure of wealth, the thrill of sex, the joy of approval, the relief of feeling no pain...these pleasures and more drive us to pursue things that cannot possibly satisfy us. We're all fools at times, and the best thing we can do is admit it.

Hope for a Way Out

We often think of repentance as something people have to do only occasionally and only after really big mistakes. That's not the picture we have of repentance in the Bible. People with a tender heart toward God are sensitive to the Spirit's whisper when they're drifting as well as when they've completely gone off the tracks. When Martin Luther nailed the 95 Theses to the church door in Wittenberg, this was first on his list: "When our Lord and Master Jesus Christ said, 'Repent,' he willed the entire life of believers to be one of repentance."

That's the message of God to addicts, to people who have put their hopes in the wrong things, and to all of us who are serious about knowing, loving, and following Jesus. Repentance becomes a way of life. When we admit our sin, we don't grovel in self-blame and shame. Instead, we rejoice in the love and delight of God, who has graciously forgiven us. True repentance always produces joy, love, and gladness. This kind of repentance is essential for transformational change to begin and to continue for the rest of our lives.

Make no mistake. Sin, idolatry, and addiction are not trivial matters. The choice to go our own way apart from God led to death in the Garden, and it leads to death today. People often say an addict needs to hit bottom, but even that doesn't guarantee he will come to his senses and repent. Some insist on remaining in the cesspool of resentment, self-absorption, and the corruption of everything God has promised.

We are, as Gary Moon (1997) has written, homesick for Eden. Every person's behavior and choices can be analyzed as attempts to find the peace and thrill of Eden or numb the pain of failing to find it. We instinctively know things have gone terribly wrong. We long for something else, something more, an opportunity to find our true home of joy, meaning, and shalom. Even the most basic, crass behavior can be understood in this way.

A person who masturbates creates a moment of euphoria. A few hours later, he does it again—not for the behavior, but for the euphoria. Euphoria is a comforting high, a brief but false sense that everything is right with the world. For the moment, endorphins circulate in the brain, and life seems good.

Or in another situation, a woman buys a new car, sits in the driver's seat, and takes a deep breath. The smell of the leather is wonderful! And for a moment, she's back in Eden. It's not the addiction, but an Eden experience that people really want. The addiction is merely the means to an end. But apart from God, it's a destructive means to an illusory end.

Spiritual life is a long journey. It's not a quick helicopter ride to the top of a mountain—it's more like a long hike up a trail to the summit. Sometimes we look out on beautiful vistas of trees, mountains, and sunsets, but often we have our heads down, looking at the next place we put our boots. Through it all, God is cheering us on, inviting us to trust in him, and providing the resources we need. He doesn't protect us from all trouble, but he promises to use every situation for good in our lives— even our sin and the sins others commit against us.

In his letter to the Romans, Paul asked some piercing questions that have implicit answers:

> What, then, shall we say in response to these things? If God is for us, who can be against us? He who did not spare his own Son, but gave him up for us all—how will he not also, along with him, graciously give us all things? (Rom. 8:31-32).

When we look at the cross, we never need to wonder if God cares, if he loves us, or if he is invested in our lives. The Father demonstrated the immensity of his love by sending his Son to die for us. Paul concludes,

> For I am convinced that neither death nor life, neither angels nor demons, neither the present nor the future, nor any powers, neither height nor depth, nor anything else in all creation, will be able to separate us from the love of God that is in Christ Jesus our Lord (Rom. 8:38-39).

In earlier chapters, we have seen that a biblical and transformational approach to Christian counseling occurs from the inside out. Genuine and lasting change doesn't happen by following rules or wishing change would occur. God melts our hearts with his love and empowers us to walk in a way that honors him and produces spiritual fruit.

This kind of transformation is also upside down. In Jesus's day, people assumed the insiders were the rule-keeping Pharisees, the wealthy Sadducees, or the politically powerful Herodians. They saw prostitutes, tax collectors, foreigners, and the blind, lame, and sick as outsiders. Jesus turned this concept upside down. The outcasts flocked to him and became insiders in God's new kingdom, while the religious, rich, and powerful chose to remain outside, angry and self-righteous.

The good news for addicts and their families is that even though people may have thought of them as second-class, outsiders, and unfit for God or church, Jesus opens his arms wide to embrace all who are humble enough to admit their need for him.

Because of God's grace, there's hope for all of us—including addicts, idolaters, and sinners of every stripe. Some of the people who come into our counseling offices have ruined their own lives and the lives of those they were supposed to love. No matter how badly they've sinned, no matter how far they've fallen, no matter how much bitterness and hopelessness clouds their hearts, God's love is deeper, higher, and wider. God delights in dramatic stories of rescue and restoration—stories like yours and ours.

References

American Psychiatric Association. (2000). *Diagnostic and statistical manual of mental disorders* (4th ed., text rev.). Washington, DC: Author.

Bartosch, B., & Bartosch, P. (1994). *Overcomers outreach: A bridge to recovery.* Enumclaw, WA: Pleasant Word.

Brizer, D., & Castaneda, R. (2010). *Clinical addiction psychiatry* (p. 167). New York, NY: Cambridge University Press.

Clinton, T., Hart, A., & Ohlschlager, G. (Eds.). (2005). *Caring for people God's way: Personal and emotional issues, addictions, grief, and trauma.* Nashville, TN: Thomas Nelson.

Earle, R. H., Earle, M. R., & Osborn, K. (1995). *Sex addiction: Case studies and management.* New York, NY: Brunner/Mazel.

Keller, T. (2009). *Counterfeit gods.* New York, NY: Penguin Group.

Laaser, M. (2009). *Healing the wounds of sexual addiction.* Grand Rapids, MI: Zondervan.

Loue, S., & Sajatovic, M. (2008). *Encyclopedia of aging and public health* (p. 72). New York, NY: Springer.

Maxwell, J. C. (2006). Trends in the abuse of prescription drugs. Retrieved from http://asi.nattc.org/userfiles/file/GulfCoast/PrescriptionTrends_Web.pdf

McMinn, M. (2008). *Sin and grace in Christian counseling: An integrative paradigm.* Downers Grove, IL: IVP Academic.

Moon, G. (1997). *Homesick for Eden.* Ann Arbor, MI: Vine Books.

Plantinga, C. (2002). *Engaging God's world: A Christian vision of faith, learning, and living.* Grand Rapids, MI: Eerdmans.

Powlison, D. (1995). Idols of the heart and "Vanity Fair." *The Journal of Biblical Counseling, 13*(2), 35–50.

Ross, B. (2001). *After suicide: A ray of hope for those left behind* (pp. 134–135). Cambridge, MA: Perseus.

Shaumburg, H. (1997) *False intimacy.* Colorado Springs, CO: NavPress.

Smith, J. B. (1995). *Embracing the love of God: The path and promise of Christian life.* San Francisco, CA: HarperSanFrancisco.

Substance Abuse and Mental Health Services Administration Press Office. (2006). *New national survey reveals drug use down among adolescents in U.S.—successes in substance abuse recovery highlighted.* U.S. Department of Health and Human Services.

Substance Abuse and Mental Health Services Administration. (2010). *Results from the 2009 national survey on drug use and health: Volume II. Technical appendices and selected prevalence tables.* Office of Applied Studies , NSDUH Series H-38B, HHS Publication No. SMA 10-4856 Appendices. Rockville, MD. Retrieved from http://www.oas .samhsa.gov/NSDUH/2k9NSDUH/2k9ResultsApps.htm#AppG

6

Authority and Armor

In a postmodern world, *authority* has almost become a dirty word. Social Darwinism has taken root in many academic circles, and scholars emphasize the supremacy of individual rights and liberties. A recent edition of the *Chronicle of Higher Education*, the greatly respected voice for most contemporary higher education in America, featured an article titled "The Task of the American University." The thrust of the article was that the university must separate its students from the belief system of their parents. Contemporary culture promotes at every turn the "sovereignty of the self."

In stark contrast, early academic institutions in America viewed the educational process within the context of what was called *in loco parentis*. Teachers viewed themselves as functioning in place of the parents and promoting views and values that supported the views and values that the parents had taught their children.

The Scriptures are not silent on the issue of authority, providing a lofty and expansive concept of the authority of God as well as a rich and balanced perspective on the use and abuse of authority by people created in his image. God's authority is absolute and is embedded in his nature, whereas human authority is only and always derivative—it comes from God to us, and it must always be exercised for God in ways that are consistent with his character and bring honor to him and his purposes.

The Authority of God

As the Creator, God has all authority throughout his creation. The early chapters of Genesis proclaim God's delight in creating everything that exists in all its varieties, colors, complexities, and idiosyncrasies. (They also reveal the richness of his imagination and love for diversity, for he created giraffes, hippos, ladybugs, and us!)

When Job asked God for answers to the enigma of his suffering, God didn't give him specific answers to his particular dilemma. Instead, God provided a catalog of his vast and wondrous creation, from stars to sea monsters. The implication to Job was crystal clear: We may not understand what God is doing, but there is no doubt that he is sovereign over all things. King David wrote eloquently about the wonder of God's omniscience, omnipresence, and omnipotence (Ps. 139). To the children of Israel who complained about the difficulties they faced, God spoke through Isaiah, "I form the light and create darkness, I bring prosperity and create disaster; I, the LORD, do all these things" (Isa. 45:7). Like us, the Israelites sometimes wondered if God was even aware of their predicament. God corrected their misconceptions.

> Why do you complain, Jacob?
>   Why do you say, Israel,
> "My way is hidden from the LORD;
>   my cause is disregarded by my God"?
> Do you not know?
>   Have you not heard?

The LORD is the everlasting God,
  the Creator of the ends of the earth.
He will not grow tired or weary,
  and his understanding no one can fathom.
He gives strength to the weary
  and increases the power of the weak.
Even youths grow tired and weary,
  and young men stumble and fall;
but those who hope in the LORD
  will renew their strength.
They will soar on wings like eagles;
  they will run and not grow weary,
  they will walk and not be faint (Isa. 40:27-31).

As the Word, the very expression of God, Jesus embodied the fullness of God's authority. As he walked the earth, he laid aside some aspects of his authority and "emptied Himself" (Phil. 2:7 NASB), but the Gospel writers describe many scenes that demonstrate Christ's supreme majesty and might. Matthew gives us three glimpses into the authority of Jesus.

The power of his words. The teaching of Jesus about the nature, purposes, and grace of God was astounding to those who heard him. "When Jesus had finished saying these things, the crowds were amazed at his teaching, because he taught as one who had authority, and not as their teachers of the law" (Mt. 7:28-29).

His power over the physical world. Jesus healed many people, even from a distance.

When Jesus had entered Capernaum, a centurion came to him, asking for help. "Lord," he said, "my servant lies at home paralyzed, suffering terribly."

Jesus said to him, "Shall I come and heal him?"

The centurion replied, "Lord, I do not deserve to have you come under my roof. But just say the word, and my servant will be healed. For I myself am a man under authority, with soldiers under me. I tell this one, 'Go,' and he goes; and that one, 'Come,' and he comes. I say to my servant, 'Do this,' and he does it."

When Jesus heard this, he was amazed and said to those following him, "Truly I tell you, I have not found anyone in Israel with such great faith. I say to you that many will come from the east and the west, and will take their places at the feast with Abraham, Isaac and Jacob in the kingdom of heaven. But the subjects of the kingdom will be thrown outside, into the darkness, where there will be weeping and gnashing of teeth."

Then Jesus said to the centurion, "Go! Let it be done just as you believed it would." And his servant was healed at that moment (Mt. 8:5-13).

His power over death. The resurrection showed Christ's authority over death. Before he ascended, he reminded the disciples where they would get their authority to reach the world with the gospel of grace.

Then Jesus came to them and said, "All authority in heaven and on earth has been given to me. Therefore go and make disciples of all nations, baptizing them in the name of the Father and of the Son and of the Holy Spirit, and teaching them to obey everything I have commanded you. And surely I am with you always, to the very end of the age" (Mt. 28:18-20).

Derivative Authority

All that we are, all that we have, and all that we can be comes from the hand of God. In the opening chapters of the Bible, God gave Adam and Eve a crucial role—to multiply, fill the earth, and have dominion over it by caring for the plants and animals God entrusted to them. King David reflected on the delegated authority given to man, a role and responsibility we still have today. As he thought about the role of human beings, he marveled at God's grace to include us in his plans.

> When I consider your heavens,
>> the work of your fingers,
> the moon and the stars,
>> which you have set in place,
> what is mankind that you are mindful of them,
>> human beings that you care for them?
> You have made them a little lower than the angels
>> and crowned them with glory and honor.
> You made them rulers over the works of your hands;
>> you put everything under their feet:
> all flocks and herds,
>> and the animals of the wild,
> the birds in the sky,
>> and the fish in the sea,
> all that swim the paths of the seas.
> LORD, our Lord,
>> how majestic is your name in all the earth! (Ps. 8:3-9).

Centuries later, Paul wrote a circular letter that was initially sent to the Christians in Ephesus. His prayers give us insight into God's purpose for us. He asked that God would open the eyes of our hearts so we'd know Christ more intimately, follow his leading more fully, delight in his love more deeply, and experience the fullness of his power. Paul described Christ's power in terms designed to stimulate our faith and deepen our humility.

> That power is the same as the mighty strength he exerted when
> he raised Christ from the dead and seated him at his right

hand in the heavenly realms, far above all rule and authority, power and dominion, and every title that is invoked, not
only in the present age but also in the one to come. And God
placed all things under his feet and appointed him to be head
over everything for the church, which is his body, the fullness
of him who fills everything in every way (Eph. 1:19-23).

All people are recipients of *common grace*. God has given insights,
resources, and blessings to every person who draws breath. Rain falls on
both the just and the unjust. However, those who know, love, and follow him have received the *special grace* of the forgiveness of Jesus Christ
and adoption into the family of God. We have rights and responsibilities as his children and as his partners in the grand enterprise of reclaim-
ing the world with the gospel.

Many passages in the Scriptures describe our role as God's children
and partners. One of the most familiar is found in Peter's first letter.

You are a chosen people, a royal priesthood, a holy nation,
God's special possession, that you may declare the praises of
him who called you out of darkness into his wonderful light.
Once you were not a people, but now you are the people of
God; once you had not received mercy, but now you have
received mercy (1 Pet. 2:9-10).

Christ fulfilled the roles of prophet, priest, and king.

In his threefold office as prophet, priest, and king, Jesus cures
our ignorance, he removes our guilt, and he delivers us from
our corruption. It is here that we find some of the specifics of
what it means for Jesus to be the only mediator of the covenant of grace (Riddlebarger, 2012).

As his followers, he entrusts those roles to us, so we become his hands, feet, and voice. Counselors meet people at their point of need. Christian counselors derive their authority from Christ in these three responsibilities.

- As prophets, we speak the Word of God to people, point them to his grace, and warn them to avoid the consequences of a wayward life.

- As priests, we intercede with God for our clients, caring for them with tender hearts, empathizing with their pain, and providing comfort in their suffering.

- As kings, we give direction to clients, speak with authority, point out the way for them to walk with God, and support them as they make progress.

Of course, counselors express these roles in very different ways depending on their training, counseling models, experiences, personalities, and spiritual gifts. We often feel most comfortable in the role of a comforting priest, but we serve as prophets when we ask diagnostic questions, and we're kings as we make gentle suggestions and issue directives. The point is that the most important, powerful, spiritual role we play in the lives of our clients wasn't bestowed by the state licensing committee. It was delegated to us by the authority of God himself.

Strength From Strength, Strength From Weakness

God has given us many resources to use in the exercise of spiritual authority. We have the message of hope, forgiveness, and eternal life. We have the power of the Spirit and the spiritual gifts he has entrusted to us. We also have our training and experience. When someone steps into our counseling offices, we offer them our help from a position of strength. Yet our role is paradoxical. We exercise this strength by admitting its source is outside us, and we confess our inherent flaws and weakness. We are able to empathize because we, too, have experienced pain. Regardless of how talented and experienced we are, we always need to rely on God to accomplish his purposes in the lives of people we counsel. We are cracked pots (2 Cor. 4:7), and we are strong only when we admit we're weak (2 Cor. 12:9). When we are full of pride, God has little room to work in and through us.

Natural talents are wonderful, God-given resources. The finest academic training adds to our abilities and understanding. But humility is a vital trait for Christian counselors. In a chapter on the shepherd-counselor in *Competent Christian Counseling*, Diane Langberg (2002) instructs counselors to deliberately step down in order to be raised up and made useful by God. In God's upside-down kingdom, a position of weakness makes us depend on God's power to accomplish his purposes in our clients' lives.

Jesus exemplified humility. He stepped out of the glory and riches of heaven and became poor to make us rich in grace. In him, omnipotence became weak, and omnipresence became a baby, a boy, a man, and then a victim of brutal injustice. Augustine beautifully described Christ's humility.

> Man's maker was made man, that He, Ruler of the stars, might nurse at His mother's breasts; that the Bread might be hungry, the Fountain thirst, the Light sleep, the Way be tired from the journey; that the Truth might be accused by false witnesses, the Judge of the living and the dead be judged by a mortal judge, Justice be sentenced by the unjust, the Teacher be beaten with whips, the Vine be crowned with thorns, the Foundation be suspended on wood; that Strength might be

made weak; that He who makes well might be wounded; that Life might die (cited in Lawler, 1978, p. 107).

As Christian counselors, we depend on God's wisdom and strength, we use every resource he has given us, and we humbly represent Christ as his prophets, priests, and kings on our clients' behalf. Christ's authority is delegated to us, and we learn to use it with humility, grace, and skill. We exercise our spiritual gifts, such as leading, comforting, discerning, serving, and teaching. Our anchor is the greatness, goodness, and grace of God. Jesus depended on the Father, spent long seasons of prayer, and always devoted himself to do what the Father wanted him to do regardless of the cost (Jn. 8:29). He is our example. We are committed to the possession of our souls through the power of the Holy Spirit under the authority of the Word of God within a community of accountability and encouragement for the express purpose of the imitation of the Christ.

In counseling, the requirement of informed consent challenges us to be explicit about our sources of authority and to create a safe relationship in which clients can learn and grow. Authority, as Jesus exemplified it in his relationships, provides a safe place and leads to a successful path forward. In the transformational model of biblical counseling, our effectiveness is rooted in Christ's authority, and we are protected by the spiritual armor we have chosen to put on piece by piece.

Sadly, scandals in the Christian world have eroded trust. The recent sexual abuse scandals in the church are some of the worst abuses of religious authority since the sexual exploits of the Borgia popes in the Middle Ages. Some clients come to us with suspicions that we don't have their best interests at heart. We have always had to to earn their trust and vulnerability. We now have to work even harder to win their respect and confidence.

Authority and Revelation

A proper understanding of delegated authority is integrally connected to the concept of revelation—both general and special revelation. God has revealed his existence and aspects of his character through all he has created. David looked up at the night sky and exclaimed, "The heavens declare the glory of God; the skies proclaim the work of his hands" (Ps. 19:1). Paul was less poetic and more pointed.

> The wrath of God is being revealed from heaven against all the godlessness and wickedness of people, who suppress the truth by their wickedness, since what may be known about God is plain to them, because God has made it plain to them. For since the creation of the world God's invisible qualities— his eternal power and divine nature—have been clearly seen, being understood from what has been made, so that people are without excuse (Rom. 1:18-20).

God gives general revelation through the amazing vastness and complexity of creation. We see his good and beautiful work whenever we look through a telescope or a microscope.

God gives special revelation through the presence, person, and purpose of Jesus Christ, through the inspired Scriptures and through the work and guidance of the Holy Spirit. The writer to the Hebrews explains that this was always God's plan.

> In the past God spoke to our ancestors through the prophets at many times and in various ways, but in these last days he has spoken to us by his Son, whom he appointed heir of all things, and through whom also he made the universe. The Son is the radiance of God's glory and the exact representation of his being, sustaining all things by his powerful word.

After he had provided purification for sins, he sat down at the right hand of the Majesty in heaven (Heb. 1:1-3).

The Word of God, the revealed Scriptures, articulate the majesty, holiness, grace, and purposes of God. In Psalm 119, David describes literally hundreds of ways God uses the Bible in our lives. Paul summarized his view of the power and beauty of God's truth in his letter to Timothy: "All Scripture is God-breathed and is useful for teaching, rebuking, correcting and training in righteousness, so that the servant of God may be thoroughly equipped for every good work" (2 Tim. 3:16-17).

> Built into Christianity is a principle of authority. This is because Christianity is revealed religion. It claims that God our creator has acted to make known his mind and will, and that his revelation has authority for our lives. Biblical religion is marked by certainty about beliefs and duties. The diffidence and indefiniteness of conviction that thinks of itself as becoming humility has no place or warrant in Scripture, where humility begins with taking God's word about things. All through the Bible, God's servants appear as folk who know what God has told them and are living by that knowledge. This is true of patriarchs, prophets, psalmists, apostles and other lesser lights, and is supremely true of the Lord Jesus Christ himself (Packer, 1995, pp. 22–23).

The Holy Spirit awakens our hearts so we can respond in faith, and he illuminates our minds so we can grasp spiritual truth as we read and study God's Word. Special revelation becomes operative and alive in us when we trust Jesus Christ as Lord. When we begin this relationship, we enjoy the blessings of adoption, we grow in our faith, we use the gifts of the Spirit, and we serve God by caring for people. Then, as groups of people love and honor God, he reveals himself through the community of the people of God.

As students of the Scriptures, human nature, and our culture, we have a high calling and privilege to step into people's lives at their point of need. To provide effective care, we need insight and discernment. We use every resource available to us, including valuable insights of psychology filtered through biblical truth. In fact, if we look through the lens of the Scriptures, we gain greater insights into family systems, addictive behaviors, personality disorders, and other problems our clients face.

We close this portion of our discussion of authority by referencing again the words of J. I. Packer.

> True freedom is found only under God's authority. What we are seeing now is that it is found only under the authority of Scripture. Through Scripture, God's authority is mediated to people, and Christ by his Spirit rules his people's lives. Biblical authority is often expounded in opposition to lax views of truth. Not so often, however, is it presented as the liberating, integrating, invigorating principle that it really is. The common idea is that unqualified confidence in the Bible leads to narrow-minded inhibitions and crippling restraints on what you may think and do. The truth is that such confidence produces liberated living—living, that is, which is free from uncertainty, doubt and despair—that otherwise is not found anywhere. The one who trusts the Bible knows what God did, does and will do, what God commands and what God promises. With the Colossians, the Bible believer understands "God's grace in all its truth" (Col. 1:6), for the Christ of Scripture has become his or her Savior, master and friend (Packer, 1995, pp. 36–37).

The Armor of God

As God's children and his partners in advancing his kingdom, we are in a spiritual battle with the dark forces of Satan as well as the blindness and evil of human nature. Some Christian counselors seldom think about this dynamic as they work with clients because their training has omitted this crucial, unseen factor. We don't want to overemphasize the reality of spiritual conflict, but we don't want to minimize it either. In Paul's letter to the Ephesians, he paints a grand, sweeping picture of God's desire and design. In three places in the letter, he refers to authorities and powers opposed to Christ and his people (Eph. 1:21; 3:10; 6:10-12). For Paul, the eminent theologian and church leader, the reality of spiritual conflict was undeniable.

In Ephesians, Paul beautifully describes the wondrous grace of God, the magnificent purposes of God, and the specific ways Christians can repent, trust, and follow Christ in humility, love, and strength. At the end of the letter, Paul finishes with his final admonition.

> Finally, be strong in the Lord and in his mighty power. Put on the full armor of God, so that you can take your stand against the devil's schemes. For our struggle is not against flesh and blood, but against the rulers, against the authorities, against the powers of this dark world and against the spiritual forces of evil in the heavenly realms (Eph. 6:10-12).

People who come to our offices often feel weak, angry, confused, and out of control. Their expectations of love and fulfillment have been shattered. They may have made many attempts to improve themselves, but all their attempts have ended in failure. They feel more ashamed than ever. Or they may have become consumed by the substances or behaviors they have used to numb their pain. Those they love have betrayed them, or they have betrayed those who have counted on them. They have often failed to realize that we are all in the midst of a conflict that goes beyond family, finances, and anything else in the tangible world.

Many of those who seek our help have a small, narrow, flawed view of God. Some see him as a vending machine. They're convinced that if they do the right thing, they can expect blessings and safety. Some view God as a traffic cop who is waiting to catch them doing something wrong, or a fierce judge who delights in meting out punishment. Still others drift away from these dark views of God and think of him as a kind but senile grandfather who overlooks their flaws, or a Santa Claus who gives lots of gifts with no questions asked. Eventually, all of these faulty concepts of God leave people confused, angry, and desperate. Gently pointing them to the truth of God's provision for battle, majesty, grace, and sometimes inscrutable purposes is part of our task to help them be strong.

Difficulties, the Bible clearly explains, aren't aberrations in God's plan for his people. They are the curriculum God uses to teach us lessons of humility and dependence. They are classrooms where we learn the most important principles about the meaning of life. Whatever the source of problems may be—the sin inside us, the sin inflicted by others, or tragic, unforeseen circumstances—God will use everything to weave our lives into a beautiful fabric...if we trust him. Part of our task as Christian counselors is to help our clients gain new insights about their struggles so they can trust God with them. Only then can they follow Paul's directive to "be strong in the Lord."

As a loving Father and powerful commander, God has given us, his soldiers, the necessary equipment to fight effectively. Paul uses an image that was familiar to his readers—the armor of a Roman infantry soldier—to explain the resources God makes available to each of his children to achieve victory over Satan and sin. Each piece of equipment parallels truths we can count on in fighting the forces of darkness.

Therefore put on the full armor of God, so that when the day
of evil comes, you may be able to stand your ground, and after
you have done everything, to stand. Stand firm then, with the
belt of truth buckled around your waist, with the breastplate
of righteousness in place, and with your feet fitted with the
readiness that comes from the gospel of peace. In addition to
all this, take up the shield of faith, with which you can extin-
guish all the flaming arrows of the evil one. Take the helmet
of salvation and the sword of the Spirit, which is the word of
God.

And pray in the Spirit on all occasions with all kinds of prayers
and requests. With this in mind, be alert and always keep on
praying for all the Lord's people. Pray also for me, that whenever I speak, words may be given me so that I will fearlessly
make known the mystery of the gospel, for which I am an
ambassador in chains. Pray that I may declare it fearlessly, as
I should (Eph. 6:13-20).

Let's examine the components of our armor.

The belt of truth. The Roman soldier's belt held everything together.
His pouch and sword hung on it, and it held his tunic in place. Our belt
is the truth given to us in the Scriptures. In the Bible we find a full and
truthful account of God's power, creativity, compassion, and forgiveness.
Life is confusing—counselors and their clients need the truth of God's
inspired Word to guide our thoughts and actions. Some people think
the Bible is outdated because it was written thousands of years ago, but
its pages describe human nature, family dynamics, and the complexities
of motivations in vivid and relevant terms.

The breastplate of righteousness. A soldier's breastplate covered his chest
and primarily his heart. In the Bible, the heart is the seat of reflection,
feelings, and desires. Apart from the redeeming power of the gospel, our

hearts are desperately wicked. Even as believers, we are easily deceived and discouraged. We can be arrogant when we're doing well and ashamed when we're failing miserably. One of the glorious truths of the gospel is that we can't earn a right standing with God on our own merits, but God graciously gave us the righteousness of Christ when we first trusted in him. We are declared righteous, with the merit of Christ instead of our own. Jesus is our substitute. He lived the life we should have lived, and he died the death we should have died. He took our sins on himself, and he gave us his righteousness. Paul described this great exchange this way: "God made him who had no sin to be sin for us, so that in him we might become the righteousness of God" (2 Cor. 5:21).

The boots of the gospel of peace. A soldier in the first century wore hobnail sandals, much like today's golf shoes. The spikes gave the soldier firm footing when climbing slippery hillsides, trudging through mud, and making sudden movements to defend himself or attack his enemy. For believers, stability and inner calm are the results of a deep, profound grasp of the gospel of grace. The more grace penetrates the recesses of our hearts, the more we feel profound relief that we don't have to measure up by trying harder to earn God's acceptance. The Bible says God has chosen us, adopted us, forgiven us by the sacrifice of Christ, and sealed us in this relationship by the Holy Spirit (Eph. 1:3-14). In all this, God "lavished" his love on us. When our clients (or we) feel insecure and lacking in peace, we need to go back to the incredible, life-giving, heart-transforming truth of the gospel.

The shield of faith. Roman soldiers often carried leather-covered shields into battle. They sometimes wet the leather as protection against the enemy's flaming arrows. If an enemy appeared on the flank or in the rear, the Roman infantry soldier turned his shield to face the attack. Similarly, we need the mobile defenses of finely honed spiritual disciplines so our faith can shield us from the effects of deception, accusation, temptation, false thoughts about God, and the manipulation or abandonment of those we trusted. Our faith must always be on guard because we never know where or when the enemy will attack.

The helmet of salvation. A soldier's helmet protected his head from arrows and blows. God's salvation protects our thoughts from the many lies of the enemy (and the enemy's partners in the visible world). Believers are often deceived and easily manipulated. Satan sometimes appears as "an angel of light" (2 Cor. 11:14) so his foolish suggestions seem reasonable and his sinful choices feel right. When we wear the helmet of salvation, we study God's truth, trust in his grace, and live by his promises.

The sword of the Spirit. The sword of the Spirit is God's truth, which reveals God's nature and exposes our sins. It cuts deep into our hearts and reveals our deepest secrets (Heb. 4:12-13), and we wield it to protect ourselves and those we love. God invites us into a relationship so that we know and love him. But we are finite, and he is infinite. We will never fully grasp the wonder and majesty of God, but it is our delight to keep pursuing him, so we are continually amazed.

Prayer. Soldiers can't fight effectively if they aren't communicating with their commander. In the same way, prayer is our two-way connection with God. We pray "in the Spirit" (Eph. 6:18). Believers have various conceptions of this phrase, but we can all agree that it means that we rely on the Holy Spirit to focus our attention on the grace of Christ, we trust him for wisdom, and we depend on him for the courage to carry out his will. Sometimes, we don't know how to pray for ourselves or our clients, but the Spirit "intercedes for God's people in accordance with the will of God" (Rom. 8:27).

||||||||||||

Paul directed believers to "put on the full armor of God" (Eph. 6:11). A Roman soldier wouldn't go into battle with only part of his equipment. Omitting one or two pieces would be foolish and perhaps deadly. Similarly, the Christian counselor must never engage with a client without bathing the upcoming encounter in prayer and submitting to the need to put on each piece of the armor so we are equipped and ready to face every challenge. For centuries, believers have put on their armor by practicing spiritual disciplines of prayer, Bible study, confession, fellowship, fasting, and service. These don't earn points with God. Instead, they focus our minds and hearts on God so we grow stronger in grace, more humble in attitude, more loving toward God and the people around us, and better prepared to engage the spiritual battles that await us around every corner in our ministry to souls.

Establishing Authority as a Counselor

We don't establish our authority in the counseling office by demanding compliance or impressing people with our knowledge of psychology or the Bible. We establish it by letting the grace and power we experience in a relationship with Christ pour out from us into the lives of others. For authority to be authentic, it has to come from the inside out.

Through the American Psychological Association, counselors are held responsible for their profound influence on clients (Strong, 1968). Genuine authority makes an impact, for good or for ill, and counselors must be able to control and stop ill effects while maximizing the beneficial effects of influence in the life of those being helped.

Perhaps counterintuitively, true authority is the source of true freedom. As we work and serve under the authority of God and exercise derivative authority, we realize we aren't the final source and resource for our clients. We are simply God's messengers, God's mouthpiece, and

God's servants to care for the brokenhearted. Actually, we hold the seemingly counterintuitive roles of being God's prophets, priests, and kings, but at the same time, we are servants of God.

Every person, the apostle Paul asserts, is a slave of something or someone. Believers have chosen (and must continue to choose) to make God our master. "Now that you have been set free from sin and have become slaves to God, the benefit you reap leads to holiness, and the result is eternal life" (Rom. 6:22). It is a paradox: Freedom of heart comes from being the slave of a loving, wise, and powerful Master. In counseling, our task is to help our clients transfer their allegiance from other gods (their addiction, children, spouse, past wounds, and so on) to the true God.

How do we impart this lesson to our clients? The powerful blend of God's Word, God's Spirit, and God's people convinces minds and transforms hearts. Faith—initially in salvation and then throughout the process of growth and change—is a gift that must be received to be experienced. Rational argument alone is insufficient. As Christian counselors we must remind ourselves often that the love of God must melt hearts, the Spirit of God must redirect choices, and the power of God must provide the strength and courage to take steps leading to lasting change.

As God's servants, we follow the example of Christ when we speak truth in love and depend on the Spirit to do a work in the heart of the client producing real repentance and opening the path to change. We never coerce and manipulate. We don't demand compliance or obedience. We may ask, "Do you want to get well?" And we respect the person's reply. We always give people the freedom to choose, and we are well aware that patience is necessary. God is supremely patient with us, so we model his kindness and patience by giving people time to choose change or to choose to continue on a familiar path.

Some people claim Christian counselors are demanding and manipulative. That accusation may be true in isolated instances, but this is a grossly inaccurate and false caricature of our engagement in the counseling profession. Jesus spoke the truth—both the glorious truth about grace and the hard truth about sin. He offered the gift of eternal life but he frequently watched and allowed people to walk away when they chose to. When the rich young ruler walked away from Christ, Jesus didn't yell condemnation and didn't call him back. His heart broke for him as he allowed him the right to make his own choices and shape his own destiny.

Authority without the wisdom to allow others the freedom of choice results in the abuse of that authority and a dominance of others that is a gross abuse of power. Wisdom without the courage to properly use authority is sentimental and directionless. To exercise good and godly authority with the insight and balance required, we must rely on God's wisdom. Together with our clients, we collaborate to agree upon goals and the process to be followed in achieving them. As part of our therapeutic model, we see the necessity of imparting truth to clients. We can teach the truth in many different ways. In *Teaching as Treatment*, Robert Carkhuff and Bernard Berenson (1976) made the persuasive case that counseling is a unique form of psycho-education. We believe counseling is a collaborative, educative approach to reaching agreed-upon goals to better the client's life for the ultimate glory of God.

To establish this collaborative process and exercise derivative authority, we practice the skills of our counseling model infused with God's wisdom, love, and power. In our pursuit of God's wisdom, we dig deeper into the Scriptures. Simplistic answers aren't good enough. We seek to understand the four grand aspects of the Bible's message: creation, Fall, redemption, and restoration. We develop a theology of suffering in tandem with the wonderful promises of God. There is, we discover, a dynamic tension between the "already" (promises that are fulfilled in our lives today) and the "not yet" (promises that will be consummated in the new heavens and new earth). Our exploration of God's truth helps us to better understand sanctification, or the process through which God's children grow to maturity. God has given us three major resources to support and resource his children as they seek to reach higher levels of health across all the modalities that contribute to the defining and shaping of their souls.

- *The Holy Spirit's indwelling presence, power, and fruit (Acts 1:8; Gal. 5:22-25).* Through the indwelling of the Holy Spirit, which takes place at the time of regeneration, children of God begin a personal relationship with the same Holy Spirit, who quickened Jesus's body and brought him back from the dead. This resurrection power indwells believers and sponsors the growth of their character by producing his fruit in them.

- *The Word of God (2 Tim. 3:15-17).* Scripture gives insight into God, human nature, relationships, and the purpose of life. Scripture is also more powerful than a two-edged sword. When the child of God memorizes Scripture, the Spirit of God provides what God needs to begin an inside-out transformation of the soul of the child of God, leading in the direction of the imitation of the Christ (Eph. 3; Col. 3).

- *The church, the community of faith, the family of God (Eccl. 4:9-12; Eph. 4:15-16; Heb. 10:24-25).* Through intimate, powerful relationships with other believers, we find the necessary encouragement, exhortation, and accountability required for growing to full maturity in Christ.

The Opposition of Atheistic Secularists

In some corners of our nation, our faith is under the strain of ridicule or is ignored as irrelevant. The First Amendment to the United States Constitution bars a national church but not faith's influence of God on public policy. The Constitution *has never barred* God's influence on the affairs of state, even from the birth of our republic. Even though many of the founders were deists, they believed in a deity similar to the God of the Bible. The words on our currency state, "In God We Trust." Our country was founded with reverence for God and trust in his goodness and sovereignty.

Christian counseling is under attack from some political and academic sources today. Ironically, this comes at a time when faith-based counseling, spiritual identity, religious freedom and diversity, and the explicit incorporation of spiritual assessments and practices in all forms of counseling and psychotherapy are increasingly popular and respected (Clinton & Hawkins, 2011; Tan, 1996, 2011; Taylor, 1994). Christian counseling, in fact, is in the center of the developing Fifth Force of religious faith and spirituality in psychotherapy (Keltner & Haidt, 2003; Koenig, 2004; Sandhu, 2007), following the assent of the psychodynamic, behavioral, humanistic, and multicultural forces.

Christian counseling has enjoyed more than half a century of robust and global development. Represented by the American Association of Christian Counselors, with membership that has pushed as high as 50,000 members in all 50 states and in more than 50 foreign countries, faithful professionals, ministers, and lay leaders make a vibrant public commitment to the faith and to Christian counseling (American Association of Christian Counselors, 2009; Clinton & Ohlschlager, 2002).

However, a distinct and distressing faith gap is growing between American citizens and America's mental health professionals. More than

90% of Americans profess some form of belief in God, depending on how he is defined and how the faithful are counted (Gallup & Jones, 2000). As we saw in chapter 1, most Americans claim that belief in God gives their lives meaning and helps them cope with the pressures and stresses of life (Oman, Flinders, & Thoresen, 2008; Oman & Thoresen, 2003). In spite of this, less than half of the mental health professionals in America express similar belief in God (Clinton & Hawkins, 2011, p. 23). Moreover, psychology and psychiatry, the two leading mental health professions, have the least affinity for God. For example, Shafranske (2000) reports that only 33% of psychologists had any religious faith tradition, and 51% said that religion is not important to them.

Against the backdrop of the unbelieving majority of mental health professionals in America, an assertive majority of Christians prefer counselors who actively use their faith in the practice of their craft. A Gallup poll on mental health delivery to believers found that more than 60% of those polled wanted to be able to choose a counselor with like-minded spiritual beliefs and values, and 80% wanted their own beliefs and values respected, even assuming a central role in counseling (Bergin & Jensen, 1990; Gallup & Jones, 2000; Worthington, 1988).

Dr. Gerald Corey, a respected clinician, teacher, ethicist, and writer, made this comment about the significance of spirituality in counseling.

> Spiritual and religious matters are therapeutically relevant, ethically appropriate, and potentially significant topics for the practice of counseling in secular settings. Counselors must be prepared to deal with their client's issues of the human spirit. Religion and spirituality are often part of the client's problem, but can also be part of the client's solution. Because spiritual and religious values can play a major part in human life, spiritual values should be viewed as a potential resource in

therapy rather than as something to be ignored (cited in Sherman, 2009, p. 521).

The size and stubborn endurance of this faith gap is the subject of clients' complaints about members of the various counseling professions who are unbelieving and even hostile to faith. It is no wonder that so many Christians—especially among evangelical and conservative faiths—express so much distrust toward psychology and counseling. Many believers are discouraged by this distrust and don't seek help from competent, professional Christian counselors.

The ethical obligations—the intersection of informed consent and religious diversity values—of all licensed clinicians and the organizations supporting them must honor the call to therapist-client matching that also includes matching of religious beliefs. The record of many secular therapists and secular mental health associations is very spotty in this regard.

WISDOM'S REVIEW

The Bible clearly communicates that neither moralism nor relativism is the path for Christian counselors and that the right path isn't a delicate balance between the two. Christian counselors are committed to a third way—devotion to both justice and mercy, grace and truth, and the necessity of responding to both the tender invitation of God and his demanding summons.

> He has shown you, O mortal, what is good.
>   And what does the LORD require of you?
> To act justly and to love mercy
>   and to walk humbly with your God (Mic. 6:8).

The God of the Bible requires that we who give counsel on his behalf exercise spiritual authority and wear the armor of God. His counselors do not drift to extremes, becoming right-wing fanatics who demand compliance with truth, or left-wing adherents who espouse love without cost or expectations. Counselors working in the context of the upside-down kingdom of Jesus hold tightly to justice *and* mercy while exercising both with humility. We are as powerful and confident as soldiers in full battle armor but as devoted and humble as the lowest servants. We follow the example of Jesus in full devotion and submission to the Father and in willing sacrifice and service for others. The source of our commitment isn't rules or vapid relativism. As the marvelous grace and truth of God's presence fills our hearts, we want to honor him, and we do that best when we imitate Christ and serve as channels of his grace and truth in the lives of those around us.

> Therefore, as God's chosen people, holy and dearly loved, clothe yourselves with compassion, kindness, humility, gentleness and patience. Bear with each other and forgive one another if any of you has a grievance against someone. Forgive as the Lord forgave you. And over all these virtues put on love, which binds them all together in perfect unity (Col. 3:12-14).

That's our calling. That's our challenge. That's our privilege.

References

American Association of Christian Counselors. (2009). Letter from President Tim Clinton to the worldwide membership of the AACC. Forest, VA: Author.

Bergin, A. E., & Jensen, J. P. (1990). Religiosity of psychotherapists: A national survey. *Psychotherapy, 27,* 3–7.

Carkhuff, R. R., & Berenson, B. G. (1976). *Teaching as treatment.* Amherst, MA: HRD Press.

Clinton, T., & Hawkins, R. (Eds.). (2011). *The popular encyclopedia of Christian counseling: An indispensable tool for helping people with their problems.* Eugene, OR: Harvest House.

Clinton, T., & Ohlschlager, G. (Eds.). (2002). *Competent Christian counseling: Foundations and practice of compassionate soul care* (p. 15). Colorado Springs, CO: WaterBrook Press.

Gallup, G., & Jones, T. (2000). *The next American spirituality: Finding God in the twenty-first century.* Colorado Springs, CO: Victor/Cook Communications.

Keltner, D., & Haidt, J. (2003). Approaching awe, a moral, spiritual, and aesthetic emotion. *Cognition and Emotion, 17,* 297–314. doi:10.1080/02699930302297

Koenig, H. G. (2004). Religion, spirituality, and medicine: Research findings and implications for clinical practice. *Southern Medical Journal, 97,* 1194–1200.

Langberg, D. (2002). Profile of a shepherd-counselor: Lessons learned from the good shepherd. In T. Clinton & G. Ohlschlager (Eds.), *Competent Christian counseling: Foundations and practice of compassionate soul care* (pp. 712–724). Colorado Springs, CO: WaterBrook Press.

Lawler, T. C. (1978). *St. Augustine: Sermons for Christmas and Epiphany.* Ancient Christian writers (Vol. 15). Mahwah, NJ: Paulist Press.

Oman, D., Flinders, T., & Thoresen, C. E. (2008). Integrating spiritual modeling into education: A college course for stress management and spiritual growth. *International Journal for the Psychology of Religion, 18*(2), 79–107. doi:10.1080/10508610701879316

Oman, D., & Thoresen, C. E. (2003). Spiritual modeling: A key to spiritual and religious growth? *The International Journal for the Psychology of Religion, 13,* 149–165.

Packer, J. I. (1995) *Knowing Christianity.* Wheaton, IL: Harold Shaw.

Plante, T. G. (2009). *Spiritual practices in psychotherapy.* Washington DC: American Psychological Association.

Riddlebarger, K. (2012, January 24). Basics of the Reformed faith: Jesus as prophet, priest, and king [Web log post]. Retrieved from http://wscal.edu/ blog/entry/basics-of-the-reformed-faith-jesus-as-prophet-priest-and-king

Sandhu, D. S. (2007). Seven stages of spiritual development: A framework to solve psycho-spiritual problems. In O. J. Morgan (Ed.), *Counseling and spirituality: Views from the profession* (pp. 64–92). New York, NY: Houghton Mifflin.

Shafranske, E. P. (2000). Religious involvement and professional practices of psychiatrists and other mental health professionals. *Psychiatric Annals, 30,* 525–532.

Sherman, J. (2009). Spirituality and counseling. In American Counseling Association, *The ACA encyclopedia of counseling* (pp. 520–521). Alexandria, VA: Author.

Strong, S. R. (1968). Counseling: An interpersonal influence process. *Journal of Counseling Psychology, 15*(3), 215–224.

Tan, S.-Y. (1996). Religion in clinical practice: Implicit and explicit integration. In E. Shafranske (Ed.), *Religion and the clinical practice of psychology* (pp. 365–387). Washington, DC: American Psychological Association.

Tan, S.-Y. (2011). *Counseling and psychotherapy: A Christian perspective* (p. 368). Grand Rapids, MI: Baker Books.

Taylor, E. (1994). Desperately seeking spirituality. *Psychology Today, 27*(6), 54. Retrieved from http://www.psychologytoday.com/articles/200910/ desperately-seeking-spirituality

Worthington, E. L., Jr. (1988). Understanding the values of religious clients: A model and its application to counseling. *Journal of Counseling Psychology, 35,* 166–174.

7

Atmosphere and Alignment

Advocating for Clarity on the Importance of
Counselor Presence and Alignment
for Building a Powerful Therapeutic Alliance

Communication, as we know, is far more than the words people say. Studies show that only 7% of meaning is found in the actual verbiage. The remaining 93% of meaning in verbal communication is found in the tone of voice, gestures, and body language. In our counseling offices, some clients are so emotionally numb, they don't pick up on social cues from us. Many others are hypervigilant, reading every raised eyebrow, glance, and intonation. They suffer from radical insecurity and the fear of being inconsequential. They desperately want to know they are loved and they matter to someone. They have come to us to receive assistance with moving forward with their lives. They come believing that we are trained and invested in helping them achieve an outcome they value. The old saying is a trusted adage because it is true: People don't care how much you know until they know how much you care.

At the heart of the biblical and transformational model of Christian counseling is a powerful partnership that facilitates genuine change and encourages clients to explain and explore their needs.

Most clients—believers and unbelievers—come to our offices with secrets and high walls of self-protection (see Sexton & Whiston, 1994). These are some of the most common conditions:

- The client is coming from a very hurting place.

- The client is coming from a very unsafe place.

- The client is coming from a place of brokenness, of impotence and failure. They will likely feel ashamed and reluctant to admit their failure to change or grow.

The building of a working alliance requires counselor attention to the development of a positive therapeutic atmosphere. The client is coming to you—a person they may neither know nor initially trust—for help because their attempts at applying God's grace and power to their problem issues have not worked.

Success in forming a collaborative engagement directed toward the achievement of goals that will be perceived as beneficial to the client depends on the counselor's ability to create a particular kind of environment, or atmosphere. This environment is characterized by several valuable elements, including a commitment to positive presence and successful alignment with client preferences. We use the word *atmosphere* to describe the all-encompassing environment in which the interaction between the counselor and the client takes place. It is the sum of the counseling processes as they unfold and in which the counselor-client relationship dynamics are contained.

An atmosphere includes visible, physical aspects, such as the counseling office setting, and nonvisible aspects, such as the intellectual, spiritual, relational, and emotional context and tone of the counseling sessions. In this book, we advocate that the counselor pay strict attention to the development of an atmosphere that is permeated with the presence of God, evidences a commitment to the faithful incarnation and communication of the loving heart of God, and generates hope in the heart and mind of the care seeker. The creation of such an atmosphere will contribute greatly toward the establishment of a safe place where clients can be intentionally vulnerable and take necessary risks for healing.

Attending to alignment issues focuses the attention of the new Christian counselor on the task of adapting to the particular preferences of the client as the challenges related to change and interaction are encountered. Alignment requires attention to the preferred "firing order" of the client (Lazarus, 1981). The new Christian counselor appreciates the value of attending to client modal preferences in order to efficiently and effectively join with the client to establish a working alliance. Alignment requires that the counselor first assess the modalities through which this specific client prefers to engage the challenges he is facing.

This alignment with modal preferences is critical to successfully joining with the client to establish a therapeutic alliance. Some prefer to be approached with attention to thoughts, others with attention to feelings, others with attention to behaviors, others with attention to spirituality, and still others with attention to management of relational issues. These preferences or commitments to certain styles of problem management and information processing require that as counselors we engage with clients cautiously and with due attention to alignment with their modal preferences. Equally important to the success of the counseling encounter is the counselor's appreciation for the necessity of ordering the exploration of client modalities at a pace and in keeping with the prioritization established by the client. To ignore these necessities is to abandon the spirit of collaboration that is essential for effective intervention and to create an environment that feels unsafe for the client.

This attention to alignment does much to develop mutual understanding and trust, which are at the heart of a powerful therapeutic alliance. When this happens, the impossible becomes possible. When it doesn't happen, the counseling dynamic is significantly hindered. This level of human connection invites clients to feel and respond honestly to the brokenness, confusion, loss, abuse, and failure in their lives. Beyond empathy, the authentic presence of a caring counselor allows an authentic trust to be built so the client believes, "My counselor really understands me and listens to me without judgment. For this reason, I'm going to take the risk of revealing more of my heart." Counselors who fail to establish this kind of relationship with clients suffer a consistent pattern of premature terminations, failed appointments, and adversarial relationships with clients.

Unique Resources Available to the Christian Counselor That Contribute to the Development of a Therapeutic Atmosphere

The new Christian counselor is humbled by the triadic nature of the counseling and healing process. She believes that the Creator God who has revealed himself in Christ desires to be fully present in the counseling event. Additionally, she is convinced that the God who has revealed himself in the person of Jesus Christ is more concerned and invested in the welfare and healing of the client than she can ever be. God's primary posture as he interacts with humanity is as the Healer attempting

Illustration 2
Elements Contribu"ring to the Defining and Shaping of the Soul and
Resources Unique to the Christian Counseling Experience

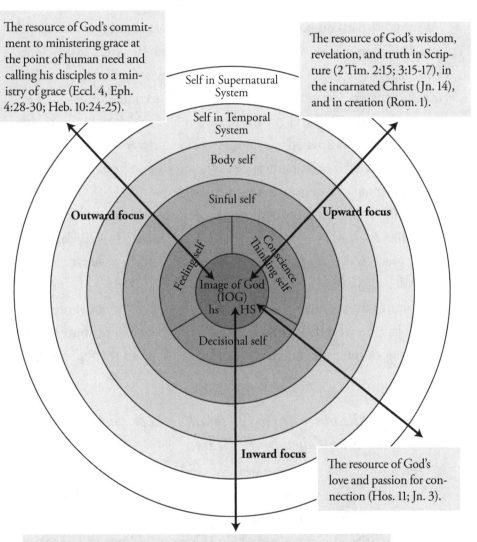

The resource of God's commitment to ministering grace at
the point of human need and
calling his disciples to a ministry of grace (Eccl. 4, Eph.
4:28-30; Heb. 10:24-25).

The resource of God's wisdom,
revelation, and truth in Scripture (2 Tim. 2:15; 3:15-17), in
the incarnated Christ (Jn. 14),
and in creation (Rom. 1).

Self in Supernatural System

Self in Temporal System

Body self

Sinful self

Outward focus

Upward focus

Conscience
Thinking self

Feeling self

Image of God
(IOG)

hs   HS

Decisional self

Inward focus

The resource of God's
love and passion for con-
nection (Hos. 11; Jn. 3).

The resource of the Holy Spirit generating wisdom, patience, power for
change, and shalom in the core self. The Holy Spirit contributes to the
restoration of the image of God in the core self and makes Christ visible
in the words and works of the disciple (Gal. 5:16-26; Eph. 4–6).

the healing of broken and wounded souls. The new Christian counselor is honored to sit at the feet of this veteran Healer as he prays, "Lead us, Lord, into the path of healing as we jointly confess our need for instruction and grace in this moment of our journey."

The Christian counselor is honored to serve as a conduit of God's love and God's passion to connect with those who bear God's image. The Christian counselor serves as conduit of words wrapped in a disposition that incarnates God's glory, love, and grace. The counselor becomes in the encounter with the client the outshining of the glory of God. The grace and truth incarnated in a unique way in Christ are incarnated again in the moment of meeting between two minds and hearts for the purpose of healing and personal transformation.

In this setting, God often shows up, and we see his grace and truth in the life, eyes, and words of the Christian caregiver. This revelation of God's grace and truth is uniquely present in a heart-to-heart encounter under the umbrella of the divine presence. Illustration 2 helps identify some of the unique resources that are present in the encounter that takes place between helper and care seeker and that contribute to the reshaping of the elements that in turn contribute to the reshaping of the soul.

The Unique Resource of God's Unfailing Love and Passion for Connecting With Fallen Image Bearers

Foremost in the mind and heart of God is the unveiling of his persistent love for those who, though fallen away from him, bear his divine image. We see this persistent commitment to loving in the works and words of Christ. When we read of God's love in the book of Hosea, we gain insight into what this love looks like when it is incarnated in the life and work of the counselor.

God calls the prophet Hosea into service when Israel has forgotten God, has ceased obeying the Lord, has played the harlot against their God and has joined herself to idols and asks counsel from them (Hos. 2:13; 4:12,17; 8:14). Israel is away from God in what the NKJV calls a backslidden condition (11:7). God's faithfulness to Israel had resulted in the building of a wealthy and prosperous nation—a nation that God had chosen to bless all the nations of the world and reveal His glory (Gen. 12:1-3). Israel became the luxuriant vine God foretold, but then God observed, Israel "brings forth fruit for himself," and "their heart is divided." He says to Israel, "You trusted in your own way" (Hos. 10:1-2,13 NKJV).

This raises an issue of great importance to the Christian counselor and client: Where is God's heart in all of this? How engaged is God in helping us achieve healthy outcomes in our sessions? How does he respond in his heart to a people chosen for his glory and purposes who have prostituted his gifts and abandoned their appointed mission?

Some will find the answer to this question shocking. The sovereign Creator God of the Old and New Testaments is in agony. He is troubled.

How can I give you up, Ephraim?
How can I hand you over, Israel?
How can I make you like Admah?
How can I set you like Zeboiim?
My heart churns within Me;
My sympathy is stirred.
I will not execute the fierceness of My anger;
I will not again destroy Ephraim.
For I am God, and not man,
The Holy One in your midst;
And I will not come with terror (Hos. 11:8-9 NKJV).

Hosea speaks of a God whose love for those who bear his image is relentless; it is a love that refuses to surrender its object. This is the same loving God who refused to surrender Adam and who, motivated by love, cried out, "Adam, where are you?"

We see the full blossoming of God's passion for intimate connection in the incarnation of Jesus Christ. Jesus is the supreme witness to this undying love, and in him, God demonstrates the extent to which his unfathomable and unparalleled love will go to reconcile those who are away in idolatry and who have forgotten their God and Creator. This is the standard for the kind of love to which the new Christian counselor is called to bear witness and incarnate in the sacred event we call counseling. Not a love of our own invention, but a love we have experienced and attempt to pass on in our broken and faltering humanity. This incarnated love, delivered in the context of encouragement and accountability, when received, opens a door of hope in in the midst of the most profound human suffering (Eccl. 4; Hos. 4; Eph. 4:28-30; Heb. 10:24-25).

I (Ron) remember so well my first encounter with a person who communicated love to me and the power of that encounter. I was 17, had left an abusive, alcohol-saturated environment in my family of origin, and had started attending a small, rural church. I had great respect for my pastor. One night after an evening service, we had a conversation that became very personal. He spoke to me of the love of God, but I remember remonstrating, "No one loves me." His reply was believable and transformational for me: "You're wrong, Ron. God loves you, and I do too." I heard the God part, but I *felt* the "I do too" part. That rocked me to the very core. Something inside me broke, and I could feel tears welling up. I was deeply embarrassed and quickly went out into the night. I was now weeping uncontrollably. A person loved me and spoke to me of a God who loved. I wept for what seemed like forever, and with the tears I could feel a process of transformation beginning in me that would change the entire orientation of my inner world and change forever the story of my life.

In my interaction with Glenn that night, I not only experienced love, but at the same time I experienced grace. I don't know if Glenn understood the power of what he said to me, but his words spoke to the deepest need of my life. I needed to know that a man for whom I had respect could actually value me and love me. I needed to know that I was lovable for me.

Glenn not only loved me that night, he also graced me. Grace is operative when a person who has what I need determines to know me well enough to discover my need and then willfully commits the use of his resources to meet that need. Love is the motivation behind the action, but grace is the volitional commitment to bless another. Love and grace are companions. God so loved that he gave. To love is to give. To grace is to give with laser focus to the deepest need of the heart next to yours.

Such deep knowing is possible only when we are under the umbrella of a wisdom that opens our minds to the truth about ourselves and others. This wisdom is given freely by God to all who seek it. Through the development of the counselor's personal relationship with God and her personal pursuit of the truth revealed in Scripture, the counselor finds her acquaintance with the ways of wisdom expanding across the trajectory of her personal story.

The Holy Spirit was present and involved in inspiring the conversation between Glenn and me all those many years ago. Glenn may not have known of the presence of the Spirit in that moment, and I surely did not. However, as I experienced the melting down of strongholds of anger and fear in my inner world and a strange witness to a new kind of faith, hope, and love, I was experiencing the power of the Holy Spirit to change and transform my inner world and, to my surprise, my relationships with others as well.

As Christian counselors, we listen carefully and lovingly to the stories of those who come to us for assistance. We listen carefully, praying for wisdom to know what cannot be seen but is nonetheless controlling the inner world of the person before us. We want to know where grace must touch down or be tucked in if healing is to begin, and wisdom can point us with laser-like focus to the area in need of grace. We listen with dependence, knowing that what wisdom informs can be transformed only by the presence and power of the Holy Spirit and by a decision on the part of the client to partner with the one giving counsel and with the Spirit directing that counsel.

The Unique Resource of God's Grace Evidenced in Counselor Presence and Commitment to a Grace-Based Relationship With the Client

Grace is another resource that is uniquely present in a counseling encounter anchored in Christian theology. Grace is love focused and committed in laser-like fashion on the meeting of a need discovered in the life of a person (Eph. 2:8-9). Grace provided the covering of skin to address Adam's and Eve's shame in the garden. Grace provided for humanity's redemption in the one who, in his sacrificial atonement, positioned himself as the sole mediator between man and God. Encouragement and edification are provided to the discouraged person through the ministry of words that convey grace and healing (Eph. 4:28-30). This ministry of grace through carefully chosen words addresses real human needs as opposed to wounding with callously delivered words. As a result, hurting peers in the body of Christ are encouraged and edified. Love motivated God in his pursuit of fallen man, but God in his grace provided Hosea, Jesus, and helpers as messengers of that love and equipped us with words and plans for the deliverance of the offender. Grace is love with feet and hands working for the deliverance and enrichment of people living in an upside-down world where the number of things wrong is so great they cannot be added up and the crooked cannot be made straight (Eccl. 1:15).

The Unique Resource of the Holy Spirit for Empowering Transformation in the Core Self

The Holy Spirit is the third person of the biblical Godhead. His presence in the counseling encounter is of special significance because of the unique power for change and transformation of persons that is his alone to provide. This is the Holy Spirit who brought order out of chaos (Gen. 1), life into the valley of dry bones (Ez. 37), and Jesus out of the tomb of his death. The Spirit bestows power for the new birth promised to all who believe in Jesus Christ (Jn. 3). The Holy Spirit, in his indwelling of the believing sinner, brings the power to make all things new. He brings the power to restore the damaged image of God in the core self. The Spirit works to form Christ's character in the core self so that the regenerated Christian across time looks and sounds more and more like Jesus. He brings in his indwelling presence the power to make all things new and enables the believer to live a life filled with good fruit that holds great power for the restoration and enrichment of human relationships (Gal. 5:16-26; Eph. 4–6).

The Unique Resource of Scriptural Wisdom and Truth

Another resource unique to the Christian counseling encounter is the guidance received through Scripture regarding the way of wisdom and truth. This resource, when properly engaged, does much to lead us to the experience of inner peace and profit in the life we are designed by the Creator God to live out in time and eternity. God, who created humans for intimate relationship with himself and one another, has provided a road map for our achievement of meaning and peace in this world and the world to come. That road map is found in the wisdom and truth revealed in the Bible.

The apostle Paul bears witness to the Bible's unique authority and power to guide when he writes, "All Scripture is given by inspiration of God" (2 Tim. 3:16 NKJV). Scripture is God's gift for us to place us in connection with a wisdom grounded in him, a wisdom designed to point us to the way of lasting profit in a world where the number of things that are broken are so great they cannot be added up (Eccl. 1:15). In this world of brokenness, the Scriptures provide counselors and clients with a sure or certain word from our Creator God that says, "This is the way; walk in it" (Isa. 30:21; see also Ps. 119:105). This special revelation of his wisdom and truth is profitable for instruction on all the critical issues pertaining to living well in this world and in the kingdom of God that is to come. The new Christian counselor believes that when the Holy Spirit, who resides in the core of the regenerated Christian, is provided with the Word of God in the mind of the child of God, the stage is set for the commencement of a journey into personal transformation directed at the imitation of the Christ.

Summary Thoughts on Resources Unique to Christian Counselors

In summary, illustration 2 (p. 205) has pictured for us the reality that the Christian counselor is blessed with a unique arsenal of powerful resources as he engages in the ministry of soul care. We are carried along in the arms of the powerful, life-giving Holy Spirit of God. We possess great peace and confidence as we struggle for the souls and hearts of the broken of this world because the Holy Spirit is present, reviving and assisting us in every moment of our work. As counselors we are anchored. Our feet are firmly planted in the Scriptures. In that body of revealed truth we have discovered the God who never leaves us or forsakes us. We can count on him for guidance, and we can count on him to do things in our lives and the lives of those we seek to help that are beyond the means of mere humans.

We move forward in our words and manner consistently under the influence of his grace and love. Truth never precedes grace, and truth is not spoken until grace has given permission. Then, when truth is spoken, it is spoken softly and with unbending confidence that the truth of God has an inherent power and that the word of truth given in the Word of Scripture never returns void, but always accomplishes the purpose God has for it. As disciples of the risen Christ, we believe that! We are therefore, of all counselors, filled with a sense of expectancy that through him, human problems are solvable. People can and have overcome every addiction and malady known to mankind through faith in Christ, submission to the Word of God, dependence on the Spirit of God, and submission to accountability coupled with encouragement received from the family of God.

Christian counselors have an additional motivation for being hopeful in all they do with clients. God is alive. Easter is not just a historical event, but is occurring every day in the life of someone somewhere because the God who is the same yesterday, today, and forever is at work in our world in every minute of every day. This faith gives rise to a spirit of hopefulness that permeates every encounter the Christian counselor has.

Counselor Behaviors That Add to the Counselor Presence and Development of a Positive Therapeutic Environment

Attending demonstrated through nonverbals. SOLER is an acronym that defines a group of nonverbal behaviors that communicate to the client your interest and readiness to help.

- **S**quaring up to face the client directly (attention elsewhere is disrespectful).

- Maintaining an **O**pen posture (a closed and rigid posture shuts down communication).

- **L**eaning toward your client occasionally (too much distance makes relationships cold).

- Maintaining **E**ye contact (lack of eye contact means lack of emotional contact).

- Staying **R**elaxed (a rigid and uptight demeanor is off-putting to the client) (Egan, 2010).

Attending demonstrated through facilitative responsiveness. We are looking to create an atmosphere in which clients feel safe and sense that they can trust us. Counselors must be committed to facilitative responsiveness—a delicate attunement with our clients that facilitates further exploration and the development of goal-directed behaviors. Clients must be able to say to themselves, "I trust this person. They understand me and know what they are doing. They are leading me to some answers that have escaped me." Kottler and Brown (1992, p. 69) have summarized the research of others to list counselor behaviors that either facilitate or inhibit this essential challenge of safety and trustworthiness.

Facilitative Behaviors	Inhibiting Behaviors
acceptance	exclamation of overconcern
open-mindedness	expressions of overconcern
reflection of feelings	moralistic judgments
open-ended questioning	punitive responses
physical closeness	probing of traumatic material
self-disclosures	self-indulgent disclosures
sympathetic remarks	criticisms
demonstrations of warmth	false promises
supportive statements	threats
expertness	rejection
consistency	displays of impatience
diplomatic honesty	political or religious discussions*
structuring	ridicule or sarcasm
respect	belittling
patience	blaming
genuineness	intolerance
paraphrasing of content	dogmatic statements
positive reinforcement	premature deep interpretations

* As Christian counselors, we distinguish edifying spiritual discussions—those that build up and strengthen the client—from religious discussions that only reinforce the client's efforts to dodge important issues.

Attending demonstrated through the use of empathy. To empathize means to "feel with" or "be with" another at both an intellectual and emotional level. From the broader perspective of emotional intelligence, empathy is the ability to deeply understand another person by getting into the other's emotional state (Hughes, Patterson, & Terrell, 2005) and communicating or reflecting back that emotion to the person experiencing it (Burns, 2008; Egan, 2010). Counselors are called to come alongside clients who come from unsafe places where they have experienced pain and shame. Accurate empathy creates in the mind of the client the idea that "I am in a safe place with someone I can trust to lead me to a better place even when I have unpacked all my darkest secrets."

Empathy that facilitates client change contains three essential forms of being.

- *Being in.* This is the ability to get into the client's world, to understand it emotionally, cognitively, and behaviorally, and to clearly communicate that understanding back to the client.

- *Being with.* This connotes the ability to understand your client at a deeper emotional level while also maintaining your perspective as a therapist. This level of empathy involves being intimate with your client with clear boundaries and without client enmeshment.

- *Being for.* Like the value of love, this refers to the ability to communicate to the client that you are unconditionally for that person even when you are challenging sin and misperceptions in their life (Moustakas, 1997). This is the ability to give grace to the client and is useful in communicating your respect and validation of the person.

Empathy as the emotional glue of counseling. Empathy facilitates the building of an emotional bond between counselor and client (Tryon, 2002). It assists the client with overcoming their fears and embracing the challenge of significant life change—it is the foundation that facilitates ongoing exploration of alignment with client and counselor adaptation.

Empathy is also important in overcoming resistance to change at any point in the ongoing counseling process. A client will manifest reluctance for change or lack of motivation, largely because change is scary (Egan, 2010). Especially when clients are defensive, accurate empathy is one of the most potent skills that challenge clients to drop their defensiveness and resistance (Burns, 2008).

Grace is unveiled differently in the life of each of the members of the Trinity. The gracious Father provides the safety and gives warm encouragement. The gracious Savior provides redemption and forgiveness. The gracious Spirit provides empowerment and keeps regenerating hope.

Building a Positive Environment for Counseling Through Alignment

Successful counselor alignment with clients is an additional skill that when paired with empathy will contribute significantly to the efficiency and effectiveness of the interventions created for a specific client. The ability to align with the client's preferred firing order is crucial to advancing the core mission of transformational change. It is not enough to merely empathize with your clients—to feel and respond as they do to the loss, abuse, and failure in their lives. The new Christian counselor understands clients' need for a counselor who can demonstrate that she is paying attention to the patterns they feel most comfortable with for communication and the management of behaviors. Lazarus uses the acrostic BASIC ID to summarize this view on the pillars of human temperament and personality (Lazarus, 2008). Lazarus charges counselors to bridge to clients' preferred modality before gently moving them into other channels. We have outlined the modalities we believe will require attention from the new Christian counselor in illustration 3 (page 240).

The careful assessment of client firing order, or an appreciation and ability to assess what modalities the client feels most comfortable functioning in as they tell their story and envision a new beginning, is absolutely critical to the establishment of a working alliance with a client. For example, a client who is highly cognitive will not do well with a counselor who insists on a feeling- or action-oriented path toward change. The new Christian counselor will be sensitive to the need for discerning these preferences and their critical importance to the development of an initial therapeutic alliance and ongoing best-fit intervention strategies for collaboratively assisting clients with the initiation and continuance of action plans leading to a preferred future.

Hutchins accomplished the goal of creating alignment by calling counselors to adapt to client preferences for thinking, feeling, and acting utilizing the TFA/Matrix System (Hutchins, 1982). By limiting behavioral preferences to thinking, feeling, and acting, Hutchins could assess a client's preferences by using his Hutchins Behavior Inventory and then tailor his interventions to fit the client preferences. This strategy also assists with joining clients and fostering a strong therapeutic alliance. In simple terms, if a client prefers feeling over thinking and the counselor is committed to using cognitive strategies for joining and designing interventions, the chances of effective joining and intervention are dramatically reduced.

Arnold Lazarus created his BASIC ID strategy for assessing client preferences and guiding counselor approaches to clients. We agree with him that this strategy can facilitate successful joining and management of client-specific interventions. Lazarus insists, "Multimodal therapy is personalized and individualistic....Clinical effectiveness is predicated on the therapist's flexibility, versatility, and technical eclecticism" (Lazarus, 2008, p. 369). The question of what works best for this particular person at this particular time should always be uppermost on the mind of the counselor. Lazarus believes "by assessing clients across the BASIC ID, one is less apt to overlook subtle but important problems that call for correction, and the overall problem identification process is significantly expedited" (Lazarus, 2011, p. 474). We advance in this book a model similar to the BASIC ID but with the important difference that our metamodel makes explicit additional elements in the human persona that are of great importance to a biblical and theological view of the etiology and resolution of human challenges.

Central to Lazarus's multimodal model are two other concepts: *bridging* and *tracking*. *Bridging* refers to the fact that clients have modalities they feel more comfortable operating in. These preferences differ from client to client. Managing the therapeutic process well demands that the therapist pay attention to these preferences and style their interaction with clients in a manner that is congruent with clients' preferences. For example, a client who is highly cognitive or looking for an action plan will not do well with a therapist who is simply reflecting feelings. The client wants and needs a therapist who is alongside or bridging to the client across the cognitive domain to build action plans.

"The term *tracking* refers to a careful examination of the 'firing order' of the different modalities" (Lazarus, 2008, p. 371) for a particular client facing a specific situation. For example, a specific client might start with cognition and then move to action, then to feeling, then to sensation, then to body, and so on. Other clients start with feeling, go to sensation, then to body, then to thought, etc. The new Christian counselor is grateful for these contributions from Lazarus and sees them as helpful in creating the therapeutic alliance, developing best-fit strategies for change, and developing long-term maintenance strategies.

In practical terms, I like to think of alignment as a skill that is required of any successful quarterback. A good quarterback of a successful football team has a series of plays that he calls against the opposition. These plays have a proven record of success for him with this particular team. However, he will occasionally come to the line ready to follow through with a strategy that was agreed on in the huddle, but based on his experience, he sees that the defense is structured in such a manner that if he goes with the play he had planned, the end will be disastrous. He therefore calls an audible at the line of scrimmage. He changes the plan based on the feedback he received by a careful examination of the defense and his perception of the needed response.

Good counselors do this all the time. They might have their favorite approaches to clients, and their approaches and strategies may work most of the time. But the new Christian counselor's commitment to collaborating with clients and recognition of the clients' right to self-determination creates the awareness that staying alongside this client in this moment requires a change in approach. The client who usually operates from cognition has shifted his ground and wants to operate from the action side of his soul. Like the successful quarterback, the successful counselor is highly empathic, intuitive, and analytical. She is ready to change the play and fit interactions and interventions with client modal preferences. The new Christian counselor is client-centered, flexible, and highly adaptive.

Alignment Demonstrated in the Interaction of the Father and Son With People

In the ultimate example of alignment, "God so loved the world that He gave his only begotten Son, that whoever believes in Him should not perish but have everlasting life" (Jn. 3:16 NKJV). God is love, and he chose to move near to humanity. But we humans can't receive his love because we are in bondage to self and sin, and like Adam, we are hiding. In a great mystery, God made a decision to meet man's need. God chooses alignment with human need and gives his Son. The decision is rooted in both the response of God and the need of humanity. God's passion for connection drives him to align, and his decision to align makes it possible for humanity to experience his love and receive his grace. Alignment is a decision and an action rooted in concern and garbed in grace. God's decision to align creates a grace environment that provides the necessary conditions for the human person to participate in a collaborative process of change. Two conditions are provided for that change: God's commitment and provision, and human self-determination—a mystery anchored in collaboration.

Jesus Christ is the incarnation of God's commitment to alignment and adaptation. God's passion for connection and intimacy is embedded in his character. The God of Christianity is a triune God. He exists in the mystery of an intimacy of persons we call the Trinity. This commitment to intimacy extends from the persons in the Godhead to the relationship between God and the humans he created in his image. This commitment is revealed in the covering of Adam and Eve with animal skins, the incarnation of Jesus Christ, and the redemption that is made possible through the death and resurrection of Christ. Everything about Jesus Christ and the Holy Spirit is centered in the willingness of the God of the Bible to adapt to human need.

This adaptation to human need is at the core of the biblical definition of grace. Grace is God flexing to wrap himself around human needs without the compromise of his character. God so loved the fallen human family that he gave his only Son to meet man's need for redemption and reconciliation. This is God moving in grace toward humans. Paul will therefore say, "For...by grace you have been saved, through faith—and this is not from yourselves, it is the gift of God" (Eph. 2:8).

The new Christian counselor is humbled by the reality that God has called her to share in his troubled heart, to participate in real suffering related to real-life situations. This calling is as real for us as it was for Hosea and exposes us to great personal suffering. The troubling of God results in the issuing of a call to us to share in that troubling and to faithfully position ourselves in the life of clients as channels through whom God's love can freely flow. God in His love is ever the pursuer of the wounded and fallen. We are called to nothing less than the incarnation of his love in our witness and presence alongside the clients we serve.

Alignment Demonstrated in the Ministry of the Apostle Paul

The apostle Paul models the spirit of alignment in his work and witness.

> To the Jews I became like a Jew, to win the Jews. To those under the law I became like one under the law (though I myself am not under the law), so as to win those under the law. To those not having the law I became like one not having the law (though I am not free from God's law but am under Christ's law), so as to win those not having the law. To the weak I became weak, to win the weak. I have become all things to all people so that by all possible means I might save some (1 Cor. 9:20-22).

Paul demonstrated this commitment to adaptation in the strategy he used to connect with the Athenians. He wisely chose to honor the Athenians' preference for intellectual discussion, and he bridged to their orientation to a cognitive platform. Luke reports, "All the Athenians...spent their time doing nothing but talking about and listening to the latest ideas" (Acts 17:21). Paul is adaptive in his approach to the Athenians because he wants to successfully engage them. He starts where they are by saying, "As I passed by, and beheld your devotions, I found an altar with this inscription, To THE Unknown GOD" (verse 23 KJV). Paul then continues to honor their preference for the cognitive modality by engaging them through their poetic literature. He uses their love for communicating cognitively, and he attempts to engage them in meaningful discussion that he hopes will lead them to change.

We find another example of the Pauline concern for adaptation and alignment in the advice he gave to the Thessalonian elders in 1 Thess. 5:14. Paul is greatly concerned that these elders appreciate the need for approaching different types of church members with different strategies. One approach does not fit all! In this passage Paul cites three different types of persons who will need to be cared for in the church and who will require highly divergent approaches to the care of their souls. There are the little-souled persons, the unruly, and the weak.

The little-souled are the timid (NLT), or disheartened (NIV). These are persons who operate out of a preference for feeling and have a difficult time moving forward on the basis of facts, truth, and rationality. Paul advises engaging the little-souled person with a heavy emphasis on encouragement and support designed to generate an environment filled with strong positive affect. In 2 Timothy, Paul illustrates this commitment to adaptation in his interaction with Timothy. Paul approaches him as a loving father dealing with his son and is consistently attentive to Timothy's feelings as he moves Timothy toward truths or realities that are chosen for their power to encourage the timid disciple.

Paul employs and advises a different approach when dealing with an unruly person. The unruly person is one who has little respect for self-discipline and conformity with laws and governance. The thoughts of the unruly are dominated by their self-designed intellectual constructs of reality and truth, and they are committed to them to the exclusion of input from others. They are right in their reasoning, and all others are wrong. These persons need to be warned, and the truth must be spoken and presented in a reasonable manner that is permeated with grace but designed to undo the pride that has taken possession of their souls. This pride is dangerous and will lead a person to ruin in his relationship with God and with all who are around him and are the victims of his love affair with his own cognitions. Paul models this approach in his relationship and interaction with the Corinthians. In 2 Cor. 10:8 and 13:9-10, Paul illustrates the challenging use of authority in the counseling context, referring to "the authority the Lord gave us for building you up rather than tearing you down....Our prayer is that you may be fully restored." Adaptation and alignment with the prideful demand a confrontive style permeated with grace in the service of edification, not destruction.

When dealing with a person who is weak, Paul advises yet another approach. The weak are persons struggling with a life-dominating sin, such as an addiction. These are persons in bondage to some form of idolatry that has wrapped them up in its chains. Paul advises that we come alongside such persons with a commitment to providing the necessary interventions and supports for the long haul that will be required to set them free. Some persons will be set free miraculously by the power of the Holy Spirit and the interventions of believing and prayerful counselors. Others—and their number is large—will find themselves in a struggle across time that will eventually result, through the support of others, in their being made free. Support implies getting under them with a reinforcement system similar to the pillars or arches under a bridge. Support requires that we patiently surround them with ongoing accountability and encouragement from faithful believers who will stay with them throughout their unique journey.

In these verses, Paul mentions one last requirement for people helping. Christian counselors are required to be adaptive while dealing with different types of clients. But one attribute must always characterize the counselor who is faithful to the Pauline witness. Christian counselors must exercise "humility and gentleness" (2 Cor. 10:1) and be "patient with everyone" (1 Thess. 5:14). Christian counselors are always and forever living vessels through whom God purposes first and foremost to share his unwavering love and patience for the wounded and broken in our profoundly fallen world.

Alignment and Atmosphere Boiled Down to Counselor Presence

Belief in and ultimate reliance on the unique resources available to us as Christian counselors contributes to a presence in the counseling context that holds great promise for healing in the life of our clients. I remember listening to a chaplain who was presenting his final paper for his doctor of ministry degree. His paper was entitled, "The Role of Presence in the Ministry of the Chaplain." He shared with us an experience he had with a group of soldiers he was accompanying into a dangerous area. One of the soldiers said, "I like it when you travel with us, Chaplain. I always feel safer." As counselors, we need to remember that sometimes just being there with a person matters.

However, we need to actually *be* there. We need to be fully engaged, fully for the client, and fully bringing on line all our training, unique resources, and experiences for this person as needed in this moment, because he deserves that from us. As Christian counselors we are uniquely resourced for the work of soul care, but the full power of our resources can be experienced only by those who find us fully present and experience us as fully open, available, and prepared to step into their world as partners with them or support for them in their quest for healing and shalom. Counselors who are fully present with their clients demonstrate that presence in a number of ways but chiefly through skillfully attending to their client's adaption preference and thus building an environment that is rich in its potential for producing the change desired. Counselors demonstrate presence through the practice of good attending behaviors.

The Personal Cost of Christian Counseling

There is a price to be paid for this work—it can be frustrating and exhausting. Attending to others, listening to them, and caring for them are often thankless tasks, and then we go home to a host of other needs, demands, and pressures. If we don't replenish our drained emotional tanks, our passion for our profession can evaporate and our energies can become depleted. Many counselors face the specter of burnout. Jesus knew the price of serving others. One day he was in a crowd of people serving and teaching them. A woman with an issue of blood touched him, and he said, "Who touched me?...I know that power has gone out from me." Jesus knew the exhaustion and fatigue that accompanied serving people.

Counselor burnout is one of the dirty little secrets of the counseling profession. The pressures are enormous. Daily and hourly, we face problems most people avoid at all costs. We try to maintain professional distance, but we are deeply concerned for people who suffer a marriage gone awry, a prodigal's suicide, a drug addiction, the hundredth relapse, financial ruin, the debilitating impact of chronic depression, and a host of other crushing problems. It's difficult to close the door at the end of the day and leave those problems at the office. We may be unable to free ourselves from the emotional triggers. The burden grows, and soon, exhaustion overrides resilience. We become touchy and sullen, we lose sleep, we don't have any energy left for boundary maintenance, and we can't turn the switches off.

To stay centered and healthy, we need to drink deeply of spiritual waters. We need regular, daily soul care, and we need periods of prolonged relaxation. It's not wrong to get tired in doing good work for God and for people, but we drift into pathology when we can't stop and take care of ourselves.

WISDOM'S REVIEW

Alignment is a valued skill we find in the psychological literature and also in the Scriptures. Alignment must be practiced to be well-developed. If God and his servants were not deeply invested in aligning themselves with human need, we would be left in our sin and human misery.

Part of our relationship with Christ rests on the reality that he is uniquely aligned with our life, our story—that he is "touched with the feeling of our infirmities" (Heb. 4:15 KJV). He understands our temptation and knows our brokenness and our loss. We have a High Priest who was tested in every way, just as we are, yet without sin. He is uniquely aligned with us. This High Priest is the preeminent practitioner of *parakaleo* in all its forms and variations. He is our faithful High Priest, who has established a grace place in heaven and bids us to seek him out and bring our needs to him. He is still approachable and tenderhearted with those who come to him in openness and humility.

Jesus often went beyond what was customary in order to align with individuals and meet their needs. To touch a leper was unthinkable, but he touched and healed a leper (Mt. 8:3; Mk. 1:40-42). He held a conversation with a Samaritan woman at the well (Jn. 4:4-30). He interfered with the attempt to stone a woman found in the act of adultery (Jn. 8:1-11). The atmosphere around Jesus was charged with love, compassion, and the willingness to adapt to whatever situation and person he found in front of him. He could be confrontive with the truth, and he could weep at the death of his friend. He could feed thousands when his disciples wanted to send them away hungry. In every way, Jesus was the incarnation of God's willingness to stretch himself over the raw human need around him. We are called to imitate this tenderhearted truth teller.

What About You?

Jesus displayed the entire range of alignment to the need of the moment, whether he was angry and thunderous at the corruption of the world, or tender and caring at the death of a friend. Do you naturally tend toward confrontation and challenge? If so, imitate him so that you do that well, yet wrap the truth in gentleness when the situation demands it. Are you gentle and caring? If you are, imitate him so you can be at your best when comfort is needed and so you can challenge sin and confront lies when that is needed.

References

Burns, D. (2008). *Feeling good together: The secret to making troubled relationships work.* New York, NY: Crown Publishing.

Egan, G. (2010). *The skilled helper: A problem-management and opportunity-development approach to helping.* (9th ed.). Belmont, CA: Books/Cole.

Hughes, M., Patterson, B. L., & Terrell, J. B. (2005). *Emotional intelligence in action: Training and coaching activities for leaders and managers.* San Francisco, CA: Pfeiffer.

Hutchins, D. E. (1982). Ranking major counseling strategies with the TFA/Matrix system. *Personnel & Guidance Journal, 60*(7), 427.

Kottler, K. B., & Brown, R. W. (1992). *Introduction to therapeutic counseling.* Belmont, CA: Books/Cole.

Lazarus, A. A. (1981). *The practice of multimodal therapy: Systematic, comprehensive and effective psychotherapy.* New York, NY: McGraw-Hill.

Lazarus, A. A. (2008). Multimodal therapy. In R. Corsini, & D. Wedding (Eds.), *Current psychotherapies* (8th ed.). Belmont, CA: Brooks/Cole.

Lazarus, A. A. (2011). Multimodal therapy. In T. Clinton & R. Hawkins (Eds.), *The popular encyclopedia of Christian counseling.* Eugene, OR: Harvest House.

Moustakas, C. E. (1997). *Phenomenological research methods.* Thousand Oaks, CA: SAGE Publications.

Sexton, T. L., & Whiston, S. C. (1994). The status of the counseling relationship: An empirical review, theoretical implications, and research directions. *The Counseling Psychologist, 22*(1), 6–78.

Tryon, G. S. (2002). *Counseling based on process research: Applying what we know.* Needham Heights, MA: Allyn and Bacon.

8

Analysis and Assessment

We have offered a definition for Christian counseling that places the emphasis on a collaborative undertaking involving a caregiver and care seeker working together to establish possession of modalities contributing to the shaping of the soul. The goal in soul possession is the achievement of higher levels of emotional, psychological, and spiritual health for the care seeker. What distinguishes the new Christian counselor from his peers in the secular arena is that the process envisioned is carried out under the authority of the Word of God, empowered and enabled by the Holy Spirit of God within a community of accountability and encouragement we call the church, with the overarching purpose of forward movement in the imitation of the Christ.

While guiding the exploration of the modalities outlined in chapter 3 ("Anthropology and Identity"), the new Christian counselor places high value on client self-determination, collaboration, right to informed consent regarding the values and theoretical orientation of the counselor, and assurance of confidentiality. These are a few of the rights of clients that are essential elements in our approach to Christian counseling. Collaboration between counselor and client is a critical necessity for the defining and cementing of a counseling relationship. The absence of a commitment to collaboration is not only a violation of the ethics of our profession but also the negation of all that should be most valued in the counseling relationship. The attempt to push the care seeker into a commitment to a course of action he does not perceive to be freely chosen will never contribute to the long-term attainment of shalom for the care seeker. Only when the value of an action is believed to be helpful for the attainment of a goal freely owned by the client is it reasonable to assume that it will have a chance of making a contribution to change owned as a value added by the client. Beyond the issue of ethics, clients simply will not continue to implement plans for change unless they are fully owned and unless they have an investment in the collaborative creation of the desired outcome. Collaboration is closely tied to client self-determination. Only when the client is free to truly collaborate in the counseling process is the client free to determine the course of action most highly valued by himself. Counselors must be up-front with their values and their commitments to particular theoretical orientations. Informed consent instruments should be signed by the client before the beginning of the counseling process so that any potential value conflicts can be dealt with. When appropriate, these conflicts may require a referral.

Clinical Analysis

The new Christian counselor appreciates the significance of the term *analysis* for the process we call counseling. Counseling is not simply a didactic process in which a healthier person tells a fellow struggler how to perform in a manner that will make him healthier. Counseling is an interactive, collaborative process in which a caregiver and a care seeker establish a relationship focused on exploration and resolution of issues of importance in the life of the care seeker. These are generally issues that have in some way compromised his perceived ability to manage in a satisfying manner elements of the personal self or the self in relationships.

The caregiver is expected to be in possession of a skill set that will enable him to create an environment in which the client feels safe sharing his issues. The counselor is a nonintimidating listener who is skilled in drawing the story from the client. We will delineate some of the elements that contribute to that skill set shortly. Additionally, the new Christian counselor functions at his best when he has a plan for organizing the elements of the client's story in a manner that will allow for an efficient analysis of the critical dimensions of the problem. This efficient analysis will also contribute to the counselor's ability to tease out the relationship between the various modalities contributing to the distress being experienced by the care seeker. Additionally, the analysis will contribute to the counselor's ability to specify the modal preferences of the client for addressing the dis-ease and suggest a "firing order" for bringing on line the remaining modalities to achieve an optimal working environment filled with the greatest potential for a successful outcome. This approach to analysis and assessment is critical for the development of a strategy for change that will be owned by the client and will allow the counselor to achieve the level of efficiency and effectiveness that is of great importance in short-term therapy. We believe that a planful approach to analysis and assessment, such as the one we suggest in this chapter, when combined with good listening and collaboration, does much to increase client confidence and trust in the counseling relationship.

Counselors must be skilled analysts. To analyze well is to be able to take apart the various threads of the story and arrange the parts in a way that produces a coherent story. The coherent story can then be arranged in a manner that places matters of importance into connection with each other in ways that may not be readily apparent to the client. The counselor performs this process as a guide by the side of the client rather than a sage on a stage. Sometimes the ability to see relationships between dissembled parts is the result of years of counseling experience, and sometimes it is the outcome of training and learning. At other times it is the product of the application of a wisdom that has been received as a gift from God.

The counselor's ability to work intraceptively, moving the client from a lack of clarity over the disconnected elements of the story to an understanding of the complex interplay of modalities shaping particular behaviors, does much to strengthen the client's confidence and trust in the caregiver. This trust forms the nexus for the development of a strong working alliance that bodes well for moving to other elements that are central to the counseling process. These include such elements as hope for the development of a better future and commitment to accountability for fulfilling the commitments to a plan of action that is necessary for moving the client from the unsatisfactory present to a valued future.

There are many words that take on special significance for the Christian counselor during the initial phase of the counseling process. Words like *listening, connecting, encouraging, empathizing, modeling, self-disclosing, aligning, teaching*, and a host of others are important for counselors to value as they move through the initial encounter with the client. In this day of managed care, it is imperative that we never lose sight of the important meanings behind these terms. Counseling is first and foremost always about a relationship. However, it is also about efficiency and effectiveness. The counselor needs a plan that moves from initial encounter to accountability for ongoing implementation of changes valued by the client that actually hold significance for heightened effectiveness in the management of the personal self and the self in relationships.

Over the decades we have trained literally thousands of counselors. As a generalization, most of them were scared to death when it came to sitting down with a real client and owning a measure of responsibility for the success or failure of the counseling encounter. We applaud that anxiety. What we came to realize was that the majority of the anxiety was attributable to the lack of a well-conceived plan for conducting the counseling process. Here we offer a plan for guiding the counseling process from beginning to end.

Our plan is both original to us and not original to us. We are indebted to many for helping us to structure our concentric circles (illustration 2, p. 205) as well as our analysis grid, to which we now call your attention (illustration 3, p. 240). We remind you here that we have no desire to contribute to the development of a wooden approach to the counseling process. The template we have designed is an effective tool only when it is in the heart and mind of a person who appreciates the primacy of presence and a heart that is open to and inclined in the direction of the story teller. However, to listen with no strategy for the collection of data making up the stories and analysis of the complex interplay of the modalities requiring attention is not, in our view, the best way to proceed. The development of an intervention plan can be a frightening experience for beginning counselors. Following a template like the one presented here can help to reduce anxiety, assure the collection of all the relevant information, and greatly enhance the potential for developing a plan of intervention that will hold greater attractiveness for the client.

Like Arnold Lazarus, we believe it is highly beneficial when the counselor has come to a clear commitment to the articulation of the modalities that contribute to the defining and shaping of human personalities and behaviors. This articulation allows the counselor to construct a framework into which elements of the story can be placed and reflected upon. The reflection leads the counselor to heightened understanding regarding the origins of the client's problem, the relationship or ordering of the priority given to modalities by this particular client, and the ordering of priority in modalities that must trump any preferences the counselor may have that would not be given the same value by the client.

The collaborative engagement of the client requires that the Christian counselor learn to accurately obtain and evaluate both the readily available and less available elements in the client's story.

Lazarus's BASIC ID, which forms the heart of his multimodal approach to counseling, is of great value for the beginning as well as the experienced counselor. As you examine our development of anthropology in chapter 3, you see that like Lazarus, we believe that it is of critical importance that we spell out our assumptions with regard to what defines and contributes to the shaping of persons and other behaviors. Our model differs at some crucial points from that of Lazarus because we believe in the primacy of Scripture for defining these modalities. In chapter 3, we specified these modalities and developed the importance of each modality for defining and shaping the human personality. We attempted to explain the power of each of the modalities for the creation of strengths and weaknesses in the lives of persons. Understanding that clients place differing values on these modalities for ordering their personal behaviors is of critical importance for the new Christian counselor. Absent that understanding and assessment, the counselor's strategies for producing change with this particular client at this particular time in this particular context are not likely to be accepted and embraced by the client.

Let's turn now to the template in illustration 3 (p. 240). We have set up a column on the left side of the template that lays out vertically each of the modalities that we believe contributes to the defining and shaping of the soul. Jesus has commanded us to take possession of these modalities. Jesus was speaking with a high degree of psychological and spiritual sophistication as he spoke these words to his disciples. The context reveals that his disciples are to experience a great deal of oppression after his departure. In the midst of that suffering, they are to take responsibility for cultivating a relationship with patience that will allow them to manage their thoughts, emotions, wills, sin, bodies, and relationships at a level that is frankly extraordinary.

This self-management, I believe, is in the service of heightening their ability to fulfill the first and greatest commandment in the New Testament, which is that humans are to love the Lord our God with all our minds, souls, hearts, and strength and our neighbor as ourselves. For those under the authority of the Word of God, therein lies the overarching goal for all counseling. Men and women whose value and dignity reside in the reality that they have been created in the image of the divine Creator and Lord of the universe are to pursue a commonly defined purpose in their lives. They live to love God, love others, and love themselves. In that order.

The left column of our analysis template (illustration 3, p. 240) contains the elements and modalities that must be taken possession of in the attempt to fulfill the directive issued by Jesus for the overarching purpose of achieving the love of God, neighbor, and the self. The counselor discovers in each of these modalities content that both serves and detracts from the individual client's ability to live out that love and freedom that Jesus envisions for the image bearer. The new Christian counselor listens to the client narrative with an ear attuned to hearing how the elements in the story fit into each of the modalities we have specified. The counselor segments the unfolding story with its positives and negatives, placing the various elements of the story into the appropriate modality. The counselor works diligently to organize the client's perception of his/her present story into a cohesive narrative, linking past experiences to the present challenges the client is facing where that is helpful.

While listening to the client's story, the counselor seeks to ascertain and align with the client's modal preferences for engagement. The counselor utilizes the structure provided by the vertical listing of the modalities in the "Alignment" column to record elements revealed in the client's story that contribute to understanding the challenges the client is facing. These notes can be placed in the appropriate P1 boxes. Attention to the ordering of the elements of the client story, assigning importance to them, and noting relationships between them is the important first step in the collaborative engagement of the client for the construction of P2. In this phase, the counselor and care seeker collaborate to envision a preferred future. This includes preferred ways of thinking, feeling, acting, and so on. When P2 has been constructed, the counselor will work with the client on the development of a plan of action (P3) that possesses potential for the building of the better and preferred future. This better future is more open to the love of God, neighbor, and the self. Paul sees the pursuit of this goal as the pursuit of the imitation of the Christ, who was the only person who ever loved God, neighbor, and the self in perfect balance (Eph. 5:1). These are the modalities in the vertical column with a brief explanation of each:

- *Spiritual core*, containing the human spirit, the image of God, and the Holy Spirit in the regenerated soul
- *Thinking* in multiple dimensions, such as imagination, metacognitions, conscience as ally or enemy, and conscious thought
- *Decisioning*—human will in its freedom to act or in bondage to something restricting the client's freedom to choose positive action
- *Feelings* as indicators and motivators for health or un-health
- *Sin* as ally in contructing behaviors damaging the self and relationships
- *Body*—appetites residing in the body managed well or out of control
- *Temporal systems*—relational patterns in life contributing to or detracting from overall physical, social, or spiritual health
- *Supernatural systems*—relationship with God and supernatural evil contributing to or detracting from overall well-being

Clarity on the role and importance of each of the above modalities is vital for the new Christian counselor. The need for this clarity drives us to study all available literature (regardless of its source) that speaks to the processes connected to the human soul. The ability to work effectively in each modality and move from modality to modality, mindful of firing order and the relative strength of each modality for contributing to an action plan leading to heightened levels of well-being, is a matter of great importance to the new Christian counselor.

We have carefully specified all modalities contributing to the defining and shaping of the soul because what is not specified is in danger of getting little or no consideration in the counseling process. I call this the danger of the parenthesis. Once you have specified matters of importance in your chosen theory, you tend to ignore other "unimportant" modalities. For instance, let's say that our model is Hutchins's TFA/Matrix system. We examine carefully thoughts, feelings, and behaviors. However, body, social systems, or spirituality may or may not get much attention since they are not specified in our model. Lazarus is committed to the evaluation of many of the components in the model we advance, but he does not focus on spirituality or sin. They are not critical in his theoretical orientation, and he is fiercely non-eclectic when it comes to the construction of his theory. We insist that if a modality is not explicit in our model, we cannot simply say that it is implicit. Hence we have attempted the development of a model that makes explicit all modalities that are critical for the love of God, neighbor, and the self. We believe only then will these elements, which from a biblical frame of reference contribute significantly to the defining and shaping of the soul, receive the attention they deserve. These modalities are set in the larger template, which is designed for collection of data in a manner similar to the one established by Gerard Egan in his problem-management model.

Illustration 3: Grid to Guide Analysis

Alignment Counselor worldview and understanding of the role of empathy and alignment in structuring a therapeutic alliance	P1: Analysis Assessing realities contributing to the present story
Spiritual Core (human spirit, Holy Spirit, image of God, sin)	
Thoughts (conscience, imagination, metacognitions)	
Choices	
Feelings	
Body	
Temporal Systems (ACL) (family of origin, spiritual family, marriage, work...) TM, AS, IG, II, IC, II, GS, ID *	
Supernatural Systems spiritual warfare	
	Adaptation
Atmosphere and Authority	

---

* Erikson's eight stages of psychosocial development:

trust vs. mistrust	identity vs. role confusion
autonomy vs. shame and doubt	intimacy vs. isolation
initiative vs. guilt	generativity vs. stagnation
industry vs. inferiority	ego integrity vs. despair

Illustration 3: Grid to Guide Analysis

P2: Shaping Preferences	P3: Action	P4: Accountability
Developing a new story rooted in truth and serving psychological and spiritual health	Structuring best-fit action plans to produce psychological and spiritual health	Securing accountability and encouragement of ongoing dehabituation of unhealthful behaviors and rehabituation of behaviors contributing to spiritual, psychological, and relational health
Adaptation		
Atmosphere and Authority		

Efficiency in the Management of the Counseling Process

Gerard Egan (2013) has long described counseling as a process similar to drama, to literature, and to storytelling. All of these are inherently three-stage sequential processes with a beginning, a middle, and an end. We advocate a model expanding and adapting his three stages with a specification of the modalities we believe require strategic assessment and expanding to a fourth scenario of community for encouragement and accountability. Egan's adapted stages with the addition of our fourth stage looks like this:

- *Phase 1*—analysis and assessment of realities contributing to the present story across specified modalities contributing to the defining and shaping of the soul

- *Phase 2*—shaping preferences/collaboratively developing a better story anchored in truth and in the service of higher levels of psychological and spiritual health

- *Phase 3*—collaboratively structuring best-fit action plans directed at the production of higher levels of psychological and spiritual health

- *Phase 4*—securing commitment to a community of accountability that will be encouraging, affirming, and confrontive for the reinforcement of habituation and dehabituation action plans leading to higher levels of psychological and spiritual health

Phase 1 (P1): Analysis and Assessment of Realities Contributing to the Present Story

We believe the approach presented by Egan advances when we specify the modalities that we proposed in chapter 2, add a fourth scenario, and embed the counseling analysis in the seven A's (anthropological assumptions, atmosphere, authority, adaptaion, alignment, action, and accountability). Like Lazarus, we believe that stating our assumptions regarding the modalities critical to personal and relational health can only serve to bring greater clarity, effectiveness, and efficiency to the counseling process. We also believe that what is not stated as an explicit assumption may well be ignored in the counseling process. Hence we have given a prominent place in our enumeration of the modalities to such elements as spirituality, supernatural systems, and sin. These modalities are often ignored in contemporary counseling theories even though issues of faith figure largely in the present and past stories of religious clients from all traditions.

We envision that in phase 1 (P1—exploring the present story of the client), the counselor will use the grid provided in illustration 3 to guide the taking of notes as the client tells his story. The notes will focus primarily on what the client is saying regarding the present status of the client's spiritual life, cognitive life, decisional life, emotional life, somatic life, experience with sin, and relational life in both the temporal and supernatural spheres (the modalities specified in illustration 3 in the column at the left and in illustration 2, p. 205). The counselor must remind herself that as she moves through the four phases, she must also pay attention to the client's affect and nonverbal communication. While supporting affect and building the working alliance, the counselor is listening analytically, gathering information on the client's modal behaviors, adapting to the preferred modalities of the client, carefully crafting her responses in support of strengthening the therapeutic alliance, channeling grace through verbal and nonverbal communication, testing the client's narrative against the standard of truth and rationality, and assessing best-fit strategies for bringing on line collaboratively agreed-on action plans. All of these counselor activities are in play to ultimately discern changes desired by both the client and the counselor. Looking beyond the commitment to action, the counselor is able to connect the client with a community of persons for purposes of accountability and encouragement.

Our goal in the P1 stage is to create an environment in which the client feels safe to story his past and present, his struggles, and his dreams and aspirations for a better future. We have discussed at length the conditions that facilitate client self-exploration in chapter 7 ("Atmosphere and Alignment"). Using the analysis grid, we can gather the elements in the story that are relevant for painting a picture of the client's perception of himself, his relationships, his God, and his world. As the client's story unfolds, we can use the modalities to trace the important elements in the story and determine their firing order as well as the best modality to utilize in bridging to the client for the establishing of connection and building of a therapeutic alliance.

Before we move deeper into an exploration of P2, P3, and P4 in our suggested grid for analysis, we want to consider in greater detail the topic of assessment, its contribution to the counseling process, and some strategies for carrying out good assessment as a component of the counseling process.

Clinical Assessment

Counseling, like medicine, begins with accurate assessment. Assessment that is part of a refined sense of clinical judgment is invaluable because you can't treat what you don't see, and can't treat properly what you don't see accurately. Furthermore, the work done to create a therapeutic alliance between counselor and client—to align with the client so he/she believes that you understand them and are *for* them—is not an end in itself. Like a good doctor-patient relationship in medicine, the purpose of a good assessment strategy is to...

- facilitate an accurate and comprehensive evaluation of the problem(s) and the resources available in each modality to "cure" or manage it properly.

- devise an effective treatment plan that is understood, owned, and doable by this client. The plan will build on client strengths, past successes, and collaboratively identified best-fit strategies for moving the client forward in the accomplishment of valued goals.

- assist the client with the identification and engagement of a community of persons where accountability and encouragement may be united to assist the client with the maintenance of newly acquired behaviors.

More to the point, clinical assessment is done in order to accomplish these six things in counseling:

- identify and understand the client's complaints and problem issues

- gather data on and understand the client's world and way of seeing things

- learn about family history, developmental events, and relationship issues

- identify client strengths and weaknesses across the bio-psycho-social-spiritual spectrum

- begin the process that leads to goal definition and treatment planning

- determine what social systems are present to support the client in the accomplishment of his desired change

Subjective and Objective Assessment

On a broad scale, clinical assessment is divided into objective and subjective forms. Subjective assessment is the process of making evaluative inferences—educated hunches based on experience. This subjective assessment is based on interview and observational data about the client gathered in P1 and P2. The new Christian counselor appreciates that someone else is at work with her, guiding the birthing of these subjective hunches. Training is very important, but the Holy Spirit is an empowering presence in the Christian counselor's view of the counseling encounter. The Holy Spirit provides insight and ability beyond the natural to discern the right time and procedure for moving forward (Eccl. 7:12). The words that a counselor uses and the timing for the use of those words can be directed by the Holy Spirit through the gift of wisdom that comes from God alone. The issues of timing and strategies to be employed, which are so central to the counseling process, can also be sharpened and executed to greater client benefit under the direction of the Holy Spirit.

The new Christian counselor sees the counseling process through a triadic prism. God in the person of the Holy Spirit is present to provide wisdom and direction to all who are humble enough to recognize the need for such an anointing. The Holy Spirit is present to provide and create in counselor and client alike the patience and power required for the collaborative creation of a plan of action owned by the client and filled with the potential for meaningful change.

Objective assessment is a more formal process that usually involves standardized tests. All counselors use subjective methods of assessments—especially direct interviewing procedures—but not all use more objective and standardized tests and measures. The competent clinician usually has a variety of assessment tools and uses many of them with each client to get a more complete and individually unique portrait of the client. This specificity can serve to strengthen subjective hunches and provide meaningful data and means for interpreting various patterns of soul behavior that are healthy or unhealthy for the client. Objective assessment can strengthen the counselor's confidence when offering explanations of client strengths and weaknesses.

Test results must be accepted with caution. We must balance their power to reveal with the knowledge that tests do not always reveal a complete or consistently accurate picture of a person. The *AACC Christian Counseling Code of Ethics* (2014) states this regarding assessment and testing:

ES3-200: Testing, Assessment, and Clinical Evaluation
3-210: General Parameters

Christian counselors conduct clinical evaluations only in the context of professional relations, in the best interests of clients, and with the proper training and supervision. Christian counselors avoid: (1) incompetent and inaccurate evaluations; (2) clinically unnecessary and excessively expensive testing; and (3) unauthorized practice of testing and evaluation that is the province of another clinical or counseling discipline. Referral and consultation are used when evaluation is desired or necessary beyond the competence and/or role of the counselor.

3-210-a: Use of Appropriate Assessments

Christian counselors use tests and assessment techniques that are appropriate to the needs, resources, capabilities, and understanding of the client. They...apply tests skillfully, administer tests properly and safely and substantiate findings with knowledge of the reliability, validity, outcome results, and limits of the tests used. They avoid both the misuse of testing procedures and the creation of confusion or misunderstanding by clients about testing purposes, procedures, and findings.

3-210-b: Reporting and Interpreting Assessment Results

Christian counselors report testing results in a fair, understandable, and objective manner. Counselors avoid undue testing bias and honor the limits of test results, ensuring verifiable means to substantiate conclusions and recommendations. They recognize the limits of test interpretation, and avoid exaggeration and absolute statements about the certainty of client diagnoses, behavior predictions, clinical judgments, and recommendations. Due regard is given to the unique history, values, family dynamics, sociocultural influences, economic realities, and spiritual maturity of the client. Counselors also state any and all reservations about the validity of test results and present reports and recommendations in tentative language and with alternative possibilities.

Testing abuse. Maybe you or someone you know has been a victim of testing abuse. You have seen someone discriminated against because of their IQ score or a personality profile. Christian counselors should never confuse the person in front of them with their test score. Tests can reveal important clues about personality, giftings, and preferred relational styles, but they can never fully reveal an accurate composite of the entire person. So watch out for...

> labeling others
> assuming the absolute accuracy of any test
> racial, ethnic, and gender bias
> the "tunneling" effect of testing
> violations of client privacy
> (Clinton & Ohlschlager, 2002, p. 313)

Some Types of Assessment

Clinical interview. The baseline assessment tool used by nearly all counselors with all clients is the clinical interview. Whether done in a formal office setting or over a cup of coffee, the interview is "a conversation with a purpose" (Shaeffer, 1991). Clinical interviewing involves asking a logical train of systematic questions designed to elicit as much information about the client as possible. Our proposed guide for analysis can help counselors structure the clinical interview in P1 by moving through a series of questions designed to address each of the modalities that contribute to the client's present story. We believe attending to the modalities specified in P1 will prove highly valuable for a systematic structuring of these questions and for moving through the hearing of the story with a sharpened ability to garner the information vital to understanding the story. Observing what modalities the client has utilized most frequently in the telling of the story, and what his professional firing order is, the counselor is better prepared to collaborate with the client on the creation of a preferred healing path and a plan of action to achieve success.

Client observation. This is an ongoing clinical process whereby the counselor observes and assesses client behavior in context. Most often this is in context of the client's own storytelling behavior—both verbal and nonverbal cues—but it is also observing the client interpersonally. Sometimes what a counselor sees in context is quite different from what the client describes in session about that context.

Secondhand reports. These are useful corollaries to client observation. They are the reports about the client given by those closest to the client—family, friends, employers, and colleagues. These reports can provide valuable insights about the client's behavior and confirm or disconfirm client reports.

Self-assessment. This is done by teaching your client to journal, write autobiographies and self-coding reports, fill out self-report questionnaires, and create narrative reports. The key difference between self-assessed descriptions and client reports gained by interview is that in self-assessment the client is trained to write down events and self-evaluations soon after they take place. The client is trained to maintain a log of their life experience around problem events or people in a way that produces insights and resources for change that aren't often recalled in an interview. Self-monitoring is a critical part of this type of assessment.

Acted-out and expressive tools. Some clients are so angry, so withdrawn, so regressed and afraid, or so young and nonverbal that you will not get good data using verbal and sit-down assessments. The best way to connect with these clients is to have them draw pictures, paint with hand and brush, play in a sand tray, use the house-tree-person assessment, play with toys, run through a ropes and obstacle course, or use a variety of other active modes of expression. These assessment methods are often preferred courses of interaction with many children and adolescents, with highly regressed and fearful trauma victims, and with certain psychotic patients.

Checklists and questionnaires. These are nonstandardized question-and-answer tools that can give quick and often useful information about a client in a particular area.

Genograms. These are family-systems assessment tools that indicate the interactive web of family relations and indicate the strengths and weaknesses of those interactions and the person being studied.

Multimodal inventories. These are global assessment inventories that reflect a comprehensive and technical eclecticism, such as the BASIC ID meta-model that Arnold Lazarus developed for multimodal therapy.

Standardized psychological tests. These are considered the cream of assessment tools because they have been refined to measure behavior, aptitude, ability, or personality with a high degree of objectivity and consistency (Anastasi & Urbina, 1997).

Objective assessment inventories are valuable in that they provide windows into the soul of the client. No one instrument should be viewed as *the* window. When used collectively, the various objective and subjective assessment strategies we have listed above can provide valuable insight into the strengths and weaknesses that the client brings to life and the counseling process. Armed with these insights, the counselor is better able to generate strategies for change building on the strengths of the client.

Phase 2 (P2): The Preferred Scenario

In P2, the counselor moves with the client from the present, with its trouble and its pain, to a prepared future, where pain and trouble are lessened (but used to motivate the client to action in P3). During the preferred scenario, the counselor works with the client to develop preferred ways of experiencing life and relationships. In P2, the counselor begins an assessment of the client's motivation to do the work necessary for the construction of a better future.

Tools for Determining with the Client a Preferred or Better Future

These are two strategies that have been used successfully to assist clients with the development of a better path or preferred future:

The miracle question, or dream walking. Forms of the miracle question are as follows:

- If you could snap your fingers and change your world into the ideal you would love to live in, what would that world look like?

- If you had a genie in a bottle who would grant you one wish, what would you ask for?

- Do you daydream of life in a different world? If you do, what is the content of those dreams?

To ask clients to answer the miracle question is to push them immediately into defining what the preferred future or better path looks like for them. The content of their answers, their nonverbal communication, and your further guiding questions will help to clarify...

- the direction the client wants to go

- how realistic or how fantasized and impossible it is to achieve their dream

- whether the client uses such dreaming to escape the suffering of the present

- what they have done recently or in the past to achieve such a dream

- how much hope (and hopelessness) the client has about creating a better future

- what the client must do to start pursuing their dream

Flipping the language upside down. Translating problems into goals, at its simplest, involves flipping problem statements upside down and translating them into goal statements.

The client says...	You respond...
"I'm depressed, and I feel hopeless about change."	"Let's consider how we can reduce or overcome your depression and find hope for getting well."

"I'm so afraid to go outside my own home!"	"Let's explore ways to reduce your fear and help you get out of the house."
"My spouse and I fight all the time."	"Let's find ways to reduce your conflict and introduce better ways to communicate."
"My son was kicked out of school for bullying."	"Let's get him back into school and stop his bullying behavior."
"I can't think straight—my mind is like a fog."	"Let's find out how we can reduce the 'mind fog' and get back to thinking more clearly."

Phase 3 (P3): The Action Plan Phase of the Analysis Grid

The action phase of counseling begins when we have finished P2, agreed on some goals that must be met to achieve the envisioned better future, and collaborated on the specification of steps that must be taken to achieve the goals. In P3, the counseling process hones in on what specific goals the client wants to commit to achieving. Once the goals have been committed to, collaboration focuses on what strategies will most likely bring the client to the successful attainment of the goal. Discussions in P2 reveal what the client has done in the past to address their challenges, what didn't work, and what worked partially. They may need to return to those past actions and reengage them with your help and support in developing a treatment plan or a plan of action. In chapter 9, "Action and Adaptation," we will look more closely at the action phase of our analysis grid. In P2 and P3, our job is to help clients create a preferred future, generate specific goals, and segment the goals to create a plan of action with manageable steps—challenging enough to motivate directed action but simple enough so the client does not feel overwhelmed. Many clients know exactly where they want to go but have failed in their attempts to get there. The best counsel we can give to the clients is to help develop an attainable plan and focus on the building of the resources for its accomplishment.

WISDOM'S REVIEW

Counselors frequently encounter and embrace fundamental misunderstandings about the wisdom of God. True wisdom isn't inside information about why events happened or revelations from a crystal ball about what will happen. Authentic, biblical wisdom is the humble acknowledgment that only God knows and that he cares deeply. J. I. Packer (1973, p. 97) concludes a chapter on God's wisdom with these insights:

> The effect of his gift of wisdom is to make us more humble, more joyful, more godly, more quick-sighted as to his will, more resolute in the doing of it and less troubled (not less sensitive, but less bewildered) than we were at the dark and painful things of which our life in this fallen world is full. The New Testament tells us that the fruit of wisdom is Christlikeness— peace, and humility, and love (Jas 3:17)—and the root of it is faith in Christ (1 Cor 3:18; 1 Tim 3:15) as the manifested wisdom of God (1 Cor 1:24,30).

> Thus, the kind of wisdom that God waits to give to those who ask him is a wisdom that will bind us to himself, a wisdom that will find expression in a spirit of faith and a life of faithfulness.

The goal and responsibility of Christian counselors is to pursue this kind of wisdom with all our hearts. It leads us where God wants us to go: to love him with all our hearts, souls, and strength, and to love others, including our clients, as ourselves.

Responsible living before God is much more than following the dictates of a propositional formula or code of ethics. Ultimately, it is an invitation to a relationship. True, heartfelt obedience is the only reasonable response to the extravagant love of a living God. David wrote, "Blessed are those who keep his statutes and seek him with all their heart" (Ps. 119:2). The truly wise are not just oriented to keeping God's law; they delight in him, and their delight spills over into the lives of those they touch. Jesus is full of love, truth, and beauty. Through his grace, we enjoy the generosity of God, his compassion and care for the smallest details of our lives, his humility, and his deep love, demonstrated by his willing sacrifice on the cross.

People who are growing in God's wisdom have a deep understanding of human evil—not only in others but also in their own hearts. For this reason, they value close friendships and godly counsel. With the support and encouragement of trusted allies, wise counselors can say with the psalmist, "He will make your righteous reward shine like the dawn, your vindication like the noonday sun" (Ps. 37:6).

As we grow in our faith, we bring our deepening wisdom to the assessment process with our clients. We have a balance of concerns for the interior and exterior—issues of the heart and close relationships, the person's thought life and behavior. As we impart wisdom to our clients, we can expect the same kind of responses Jesus experienced. Some clients will gladly accept God's grace and truth, and their lives will be transformed. Some walk away in confusion. And some resist and even attack. Jesus knew what was in every heart (Jn. 2:25). We don't, but in our analysis and assessment, we gain information and make connections so we can be channels of God's wisdom, grace, truth, and power, collaborating with our clients for the building of a better future.

References

American Association of Christian Counselors (2014). *AACC code of ethics*. Retrieved from http://www.aacc.net/about-us/code-of-ethics/

Anastasi, A., & Urbina, S. (1997). *Psychological testing* (7th ed.). New York, NY: Macmillan.

Clinton, T., & Ohlschlager, G. (Eds.). (2002). *Competent Christian counseling: Foundations and practices of compassionate soul care*. Colorado Springs, CO: Waterbrook Press.

Egan, G. (2013). *The skilled helper: A problem-management and opportunity-development approach to helping* (10th ed.). Belmont, CA: Brooks/Cole.

Fonagy, P., & Roth, A. (2005). *What works for whom?: A critical review of psychotherapy research* (2nd ed.). New York, NT: Guilford.

Horvath, A. O., & Symond, B. D. (1991). Relation between working alliance and outcome in psychotherapy: A meta-analysis. *Journal of Consulting Psychology, 38*(2), 139–149.

Keller, T. (2008). *The prodigal God*. New York, NY: Dutton.

Lazarus, A. A. (1981). *The practice of multimodal therapy* (pp. 89–101). New York, NY: Springer.

Packer, J. I. (1973). *Knowing God*. Downers Grove, IL: InterVarsity Press.

Rogers, C. (1951). *Client-centered therapy*. Boston, MA: Houghton Mifflin.

Rogers, C. (1957). The necessary and sufficient conditions of therapeutic personality change. *Journal of Consulting Psychology, 21*, 95–103.

Shaeffer, N. C. (1991). Conversation with a purpose—or conversation? Interaction in the standardized interview. In P. P. Biemer, R. M. Groves,

L. E. Lyberg, N. A. Mathiowetz, & S. Sudman (Eds.), *Measurement errors in surveys* (pp. 367–391). New York, NY: John Wiley.

Strong, S. R. (1968). Counseling: An interpersonal influence process. *Journal of Counseling and Psychology, 3,* 215–224.

9

Action and Adaptation

Counselor Adaptation for Building the Therapeutic
Alliance and Developing Best-Fit Action Plans

As we reflect on the analysis grid—our responsibilities for collaboration with clients to construct new and better paths for clients and
the challenges connected with moving clients to action and accountability (illustration 3, p. 240)—we need to remember that this entire process must be in the hands of a highly adaptive and sensitive guide by the
side of the client.

Counseling must always be client centered. In chapter 7 we intro-
duced the idea that the counselor's role with clients is much like the quarterback's role in college and professional football. When the quarterback
comes to the line of scrimmage near the end of the game with his team
down by four points, he knows he has to get a touchdown for his team.
He has called a running play in the huddle, but when he comes to the

line, he realizes the linebackers have come up and the defense is stacked to stop the run. What he initially thought would work is no longer the best fit for what he is seeing and hearing across the line. He calls out a different play, an audible that he believes will be a winning adaptation. A long pass to the end zone is executed perfectly, and his team wins the game.

Actually, football provides an excellent metaphor for a counselor's adaptation. Before every play, the coaches signal a play from the sidelines, but the quarterback has the discretion to change the play at the line of scrimmage—utilizing insight gained from experience—if he sees that the play won't work against a particular defensive scheme. This adaptation—the audible by the quarterback—changes the play and offers the best hope for a successful outcome. In the same way, we may have a finely crafted treatment plan for our clients, but in appointments we often have to call an audible—we read the situation and make adjustments. As we learn and grow as counselors, we develop the ability to notice new challenges and opportunities, assess them accurately, and adapt accordingly.

Combining Insight With Action and Adaptation

Gerard Egan's (2009) counseling model and similar models (Corey & Corey, 2007; Hill, 2009; Kottler & Shepard, 2011) combine insight and action. These models have significantly influenced Christian counseling. The Rogerian concept of necessary conditions, which include empathy, positive regard, and congruence, must be attached to client action plans for progress to take place. The Rogerian elements are necessary conditions for effective counseling, but they are insufficient without action (Carkhuff, 1969, 1984, 1987). However, we need to be sensitive to the client's disposition, stability, and motivation when we call for action.

Our sensitivity enables us to adapt. Is she ready to act? Is he motivated to change? How clearly is she thinking and reasoning? Is his self-talk hopeful or hopeless?

Be sensitive to the client's need. Some forget the differences between preaching and counseling. Preaching assumes our role is dispensing truth and the client's job is to assimilate and apply it to change outlook and behavior. Change, however, is far more complicated—especially for those who have been deeply hurt, isolated, or enmeshed in difficult relationships, or who are enduring ongoing relational strains or suffering from depression or anxiety. The client's change in behavior may occur only after significant healing has occurred and insight is internalized. We need to assess the client's needs from both a personal and systems perspective. The client's system is often complex and intense. Unraveling the deceptions and attractions takes time and energy. Counseling is more than insightful communication—it is communication with a purpose: to create a positive environment that connects hearts, imparts insight, and facilitates genuine change.

Be intentional and prescriptive. A thorough and accurate assessment is essential in creating an effective treatment plan. Have we identified the client's firing order (such as thinking-feeling-acting or thinking-acting-feeling)? Are we adapting to the way the client habitually thinks and acts? Do we understand the family dynamics (temporal system) that are pushing or pulling the client in different directions? Does the client need medication (body) for depression or anxiety? If someone is suffering from post-traumatic stress, for example, she may not be able to think rationally, make choices, and take action without proper medication. If the person is an addict, are groups available (temporal system) to provide a support network and necessary accountability? Do we have a full-blown addiction with any demonic involvement (supernatural system)?

What kind of trust issues are present, and is the person able to function as an autonomous individual?

While establishing the goals with intentionality, we need to ask two fundamental questions. What kind of change is desired, and what is the direction of the change? The challenge for Christian counselors is keeping two congruent goals in mind. God's goal for every person is to know, love, and honor him in every choice and relationship, but our clients may not have this goal in mind at all—even the clients who are believers. Most of them come to us because they want relief from the pain they are currently suffering. That's their preeminent (and perhaps their only) goal.

A wise counselor understands this gap and knows how to bridge it. Gently, carefully, and boldly, we show our clients how relief from suffering is important although ultimately unattainable in this present age. We must help them see beyond the pain to the meaning it contains for them and to the resources they may utilize to find meaning and purpose amid the challenges they are facing and will face in the future.

Match the language and action plan for change with the client. Just as every person has a love language, every person also has a change language. Some people are motivated by new, lofty goals, but big goals crush others. They need to see the change broken down into bite-sized pieces. Others take steps to change because they want meaningful relationships. They want to stop and correct the destructive patterns they've endured. Some make remarkable progress when they gain new knowledge and insight. For them, knowledge is the springboard of progress. All of these benefit when we spell out the process of change step-by-step in detail. Often, action precedes insight. No matter how much we've explained the benefits of a course of action, clients don't "get it" until they have taken action. For every client and counselor, progress is a process. We need to be patient and persistent, hopeful and helpful, as we point our clients to wisdom-based thinking, choices, and actions.

Phase 3: Translating Client Goals Into Action

Phase 3 in our analysis grid is where we seek to develop best-fit strategies for change with our clients—and where counseling moves beyond being merely a talking cure. In this phase, we encourage clients to collaborate with us to develop reality-based action plans that fit well with the modalities they prefer to utilize in moving into their preferred future.

Gerard Egan (2009) lists six action items counselors need to address as we seek to move our client toward valued action. We have added a seventh principle to honor a strength-based approach to problem-solving.

1. Solve crises first. If the client is experiencing a crisis, seek to engage them in action plans that are strategically designed to define the crisis. The counselor may need to develop a plan of action that makes the client feel safe and make certain the client is in an emotional, psychological, and if necessary, physically safe place.

2. Attend to the client's pain. What is causing the client the most pain? Develop an action plan that is directly aimed at reducing or overcoming this pain.

3. What are the client's priorities? What if there is no immediate crisis? The counselor can begin by identifying the issues that the client deems important. What challenges would the client most like to see resolved? What action has the client taken in the past to address those types of challenges, and what has worked well?

4. Identify manageable pieces. Take action to divide intense and global problems into more manageable ones that aren't as threatening. "Yard by yard, life is hard; inch by inch, life's a cinch." Reduce the problem when possible into manageable pieces and collaboratively develop action plans to manage the pieces.

5. Honor generalizability. Begin with an action plan to address a problem the client is comfortable dealing with and that, if handled well, will lead to general improvement in the client's condition that can be the basis of renewed hopefulness and provide a foundation for bridging other, more complex issues.

6. Assess the cost and benefit. Begin with a problem in which the benefits of a solution most clearly outweigh the costs of energy and time invested to get to the gain.

7. Build on progress that has already started. If you can identify a problem for which clients have already gained some headway, begin there. They have demonstrated some strength, have some hope, and have been successful to some extent. This is a good foundation for progress.

Four Interrelated Action Steps

The successful management of an action-oriented phase 3 is an absolute necessity for distinguishing counseling from simple conversation about the client's life challenges and desires for the future. In this action phase, collaboratively derived goals are pursued and progress is achieved. Discussing preferences and defining goals is effective only if the client takes clear and courageous steps designed to bring into reality new and preferred ways of thinking, feeling, acting, relating to God and others, and managing their bodies. Counseling, then, may begin with comforting, but it's more than comfort. Counseling demands commitment from clients and effort directed at achieving goals. Four steps can be helpful in assisting clients with taking effective action.

1. Brainstorm strategies. Most clients begin therapy hopelessly confused. They often have tunnel vision and believe the way things have been is the way they'll always be. At best, they hope they can discover a single way forward. Brainstorming helps them realize there are usually many ways they can achieve their goals. In this phase, we help clients imagine numerous ways to accomplish their goals. Talking about the possibilities often spurs creative problem solving and fresh motivation.

2. Choose best-fit strategies. From a list of many possible strategies, the next step is to identify one that best fits the client and the situation. Following this strategy may be a daunting challenge, but it is clear, it taps into available resources, and it offers the most hope for success.

3. Link action steps into a focused plan. The counselor assists the client to link the best-fit strategy to a comprehensive, focused plan that stimulates motivation. After brainstorming and choosing the best strategy, the counselor helps the client formulate a multistep program for change. Motivation for change is increased when the client embraces the plan.

4. Encourage and insist on client action. After the plan has been developed, clients need to put their plans into action. As they do this, they are solving the problem—or at least one piece of the problem—they presented when they met you in the first appointment.

When clients are taking action, counseling sessions become valuable opportunities to evaluate the success of the steps and adapt the plan to the changing realities of the situation. The constant cycle—act, adapt, act, adapt, act, adapt—enables clients to operate effectively in phase 3.

True success. From the business literature, Tom Morris (1994) defines the elements that make for true success in business development. We believe they promote therapeutic progress as well.

- Determine what you want—"powerfully imagine" a goal or set of goals.

- Focus on preparation and planning.

- Believe in your ability to accomplish the goals.

- Make a commitment of emotional energy.

- Be consistent, stubborn, and persistent in pursuit of the goal.

- Have the kind of integrity that inspires trust and gets people pulling for you.

- Enjoy the process.

Action and Adaptation in Life and in the Scriptures

Achieving genuine life change requires continued action with constant adaptation. In other words, you and the client are constantly making adjustments as the client moves out in active change. Adaptation is not just something that happens once, and then we are off and running again. The counselor has to be sensitive to the Holy Spirit—to the acquisition and use of biblical wisdom—in order to make the many adaptations required for staying centered on the needs of the person who is moving through the process of change. Action leading to valued change is rarely an outcome when a counselor is committed to a static or nonadaptive process.

Lessons from NASCAR

NASCAR racer Jimmy Johnson once told me (Tim) that during a race, he constantly talks to Chad (his crew chief) on the radio, telling him what he is feeling and giving him constant feedback on his view of what was happening in the race. They constantly communicate about all race conditions. Jimmy then makes the adjustments needed based on what he hears Chad saying back to him. He constantly has to modify things to stay in the race and have a chance to win.

Most people rush through their daily lives at 100 miles an hour with nobody seeing the big picture and nobody to talk to—nobody. All they see is what's right in front of them. Everyone needs somebody who's outside, such as a counselor or God, who can be trusted to provide feedback on the big picture. The counselor and the client need to be in communication with their race manager and be ready to make real-time decisions about modifications in their race plan based on trustworthy information they are receiving. They need guidance to make decisions that will enable them to finish their race well.

When we are troubled and uncertain, we can tell God what we are feeling, confess that we need help, and ask for his direction. God invites us all to ask, seek, and knock (Mt. 7:7-8). When you get attuned vertically, God constantly feeds back to you wisdom about how to direct yourself while you manage the curves and straightaways in your journey.

Another Voice in the Headset—Spiritual Warfare

Some NASCAR events seem to play out like a war on a track. Before we leave our analogy of life as a race, we need to point out that someone else wants to whisper in our ear in the confusion and heat of the race. Paul tells us in Eph. 6:10-12 that we are not wrestling against flesh and blood but against the powers of this dark world and the spiritual forces of evil. We need to be aware that Satan is the enemy of any change that pleases God. He has mastered a number of schemes for taking over the headset and advising change that in the end is always destructive. He is a liar and a destroyer, and he loves to thwart any impulse in the life of a person directed at glorifying God and serving others.

Consider a man who was once a huge winner but then fell very quickly into the loser's column. Notice how adaptive God is in calling him to an action plan directed at his restoration. If the prophet Elijah walked into our office today, we would be in the presence of a deeply depressed man (1 Kgs. 19). Even though he had recently led a great crusade and had experienced one of the most dramatic miracles in the Bible, he was now experiencing total exhaustion, even wishing for his death.

What combination of factors contributed to bringing Elijah to where he is at this moment in his life, and what does he need if he is to be restored? Where should we begin our counsel to him? Let's begin by noticing where God began in his dealings with the depressed and suicidal prophet. God's first concern was with Elijah's physical needs. His physical exhaustion was contributing significantly to his perceptions of himself, God, and his future. When we assess the drastic change in his outlook from Mount Carmel to the cave, we can infer an overwhelming biochemical change. All that fear and running devastated his body and his biochemistry. He needed rest and food, so God sent him to bed and sent an angel to feed him.

Elijah's problem also had social components. He had an enemy who threatened to kill him. Few of us are prepared to face those who oppose us in our ministries and in our daily lives. We deal much better with applause than we do with criticism. Elijah ran in fear from his would-be killer. Eventually he had to face himself. When he does, his words to God are instructive: "I am no better than my ancestors." In other words, "I'm a sinner, just like everybody else, but I've spent my life and ministry thinking I was superior to everybody else." How interesting! He now confesses that even though he has been greatly used by God, he is a prideful person from the top of his head to the soles of his feet. He has not depended on grace every step of his miracle-working journey.

Something else was also going on in Elijah's mind. He had felt indispensable and invincible when he killed the prophets of Baal, but now he felt isolated. With great courage he had stood against hundreds of men and prevailed, but now he faced life alone. God adapts again to his error-based thinking and speaks truth into his life: "I reserve seven thousand in Israel—all whose knees have not bowed down to Baal." God provides a pattern of patiently adapting to Elijah's concerns and addressing the various challenges Elijah must face if he is to be restored to usefulness in God's work. He addresses the prophet's relational, physical, cognitive, and spiritual needs. Elijah's depression had affected every domain of his life.

As we have seen in this book, people are wounded in relationships, and they are healed in relationships. People may learn valuable lessons on their own, but they need other people to step into their lives to love, forgive, encourage, and heal. The Scriptures continually reflect this foundational truth of human nature, and the scientific research concurs. The Basic Behavioral Science Task Force of the National Advisory Mental Council (1996) showed that the quality of a person's social support system was a major contributor in overcoming mental illness. Social support was the main curative factor in 75% of the cases of clinical depression, and it made a substantial difference in the outcome of cases of schizophrenia and alcoholism. The study also recognized that social isolation is a major factor in the maintenance of mental illness. We were created in the image of God, and part of that image is the desire for relationships. In fact, our physical and mental health depend on the quality and quantity of relationships.

The Master Adapter

The master of adaptation was Jesus Christ. He had an accurate assessment of human beings—"he knew what was in each person" (Jn. 2:25)—and he adapted his approach according to the situation and the individual. Jesus performed many miracles out in the open for everyone to see, but sometimes he changed his normal procedure. Mark tells us some men brought to him a man who was deaf and mute. Jesus could have healed him on the spot, but he took the man aside.

> Then Jesus left the vicinity of Tyre and went through Sidon, down to the Sea of Galilee and into the region of the Decapolis. There some people brought to him a man who was deaf and could hardly talk, and they begged Jesus to place his hand on him.
>
> After he took him aside, away from the crowd, Jesus put his fingers into the man's ears. Then he spit and touched the man's tongue. He looked up to heaven and with a deep sigh said to him, "*Ephphatha!*" (which means, "Be opened!"). At this, the man's ears were opened, his tongue was loosened and he began to speak plainly (Mk. 7:31-35).

People had probably made fun of this man his whole life. Jesus didn't have to ask his friends if this was true; he knew people were sometimes cruel to those who face great challenges. To protect the man's dignity, Jesus took him aside. He didn't stand back and loudly pronounce healing for all to see and hear. Instead, he took the man by the arm and led him away so they could be alone, put his fingers in his ears, and touched his tongue with his spit. When Jesus prayed for the man's ears and mouth to be opened, he sighed deeply. When do people sigh deeply? When they are troubled. It was another mark of Jesus's genuine compassion for hurting people.

As we follow Jesus, we'll learn to adapt to different clients and their circumstances. We'll realize two people may need very different approaches. God will use us to step into their lives to care deeply for them, touch them at their point of need, and share God's healing love, truth, and strength. His promise is not that our clients (or we) will avoid crises, but that he will give us the power to face them.

Motivation and Obedience in the Production of Change

It may seem odd that obedience to God can lead to self-pity and bitterness, but that's what we find in Jesus's story of the prodigal and his self-righteous brother. Clearly, obedience isn't the only factor that determines the value of an action. The heart—including motivations, attitudes, and expectations—is crucial. Right actions are noble and good only if they are done for right reasons.

This parable describes three kinds of clients who may come to our offices, and it implies a fourth. The person may be like the repentant younger brother, who came to his senses and returned home to his father. Our task in counseling this client is to represent our heavenly Father's joyful embrace and point the repentant person to love, trust, and honor Christ more each day. The client, though, may be more like the younger brother *before* he woke up in the pigsty and decided to go home. These people have probably been dragged to our offices by a spouse or a parent, and they have no intention of changing—until they wake up and God gets their attention.

Many clients are Christians who, like the elder brother, are angry with God. They accuse him of not coming through to protect and provide. They have obeyed—religiously reading their Bibles, praying, going to church, and helping others—but they think they don't have much to show for it. God seems to be working in other people's lives but not theirs, and they resent it. Jesus's parable, though, implies that even self-absorbed, resentful, religious people have a choice. The Father invites even them—even elder brothers and sisters who are full of self-pity and anger—to respond to his gracious invitation to come to the feast and enjoy his love.

Elder brothers and sisters can be obedient to moral standards and claim they are imitating Christ, but their outward righteousness produces more resentment, entitlement, and anger at God. Only grace produces a transformed heart. Only grace overflows in glad obedience, delight in God, and a desire to please him above all else. Moralism and legalism are outside-in approaches to the Christian life. Grace is the source of love and power for transformational, inside-out change. Author and pastor Tim Keller observes that when we respond to God's kindness, love, majesty, and wisdom, he does wonderful things in our hearts. We may have been strong *or* kind before, but now we gradually become strong *and* kind—like Christ.

> These same radically different traits that are normally never combined in any one person *will be reproduced in you because you are in the presence of Jesus Christ.* You're not just becoming a nicer person or a more disciplined person or a more moral person. The life and character of Jesus—the King who ambles in to Jerusalem on a donkey, then storms into the temple with the audacity to say "This is my house"—are being reproduced in you. You're becoming a more complete person, the person you were designed to be. The person you were ransomed to be (Keller, 2011).

Being conformed to the image of Christ isn't a self-improvement program, and we don't get there merely by gritting our teeth and obeying rules. We are changed as his love floods our hearts, his greatness amazes us, and his kindness transforms our self-pity and resentment into gratitude and joy.

As Christian counselors, our goals are multifaceted. Behind our assessments and treatment planning is the only hope of humanity—the love and forgiveness of Christ. When Jesus talked about the kingdom, he used many different terms and metaphors. In the same way, we draw from the bottomless well of God's truth, creativity, majesty, and compassion, and we tailor our approach to each person. Our immediate goal is often pain relief, but our ultimate goal is for our clients to experience the transforming love of God so they want to follow him with all their hearts. In him, broken hearts can be healed, false thinking corrected, and self-destructive patterns of behavior replaced. But these things happen over time with our clients, just as they have with us.

Faith, Hope, and Love in Client Change

Professor and author Dallas Willard (2002) described the interior work God accomplishes to transform us from the inside out. Our role as Christian counselors is to collaborate with God and our clients in this effort. We are intentional in planning action, but we maintain a commitment to adaptation whenever the Holy Spirit, our internal wisdom, or client feedback signals the need to stop and move in a different direction.

Our adaptiveness is always at the service of the client and designed to support feelings of confidence in the course of action that has been chosen. Quite often, our clients "borrow" our confidence that things can be different. They've tried before, but nothing worked. Now they are looking for hope in our eyes and certainty in our voices. They may not utter these words, but they often feel something like this: "I tried this before on my own, but I didn't make it. Maybe this time with your help—and especially with God's help—maybe this time I can make it."

Channels of faith, hope, and love. If we are to become channels of God's presence, kindness, forgiveness, wisdom, and power, those qualities have to overflow from us. This doesn't happen by magic, and we can't program it to occur by mechanically following a step-by-step plan for spiritual growth. The disciplines are valuable tools to put us in touch with God's heart and his will. We can hear his "still small voice"

(1 Kgs. 19:12 NKJV) only if we are quiet and invite him to speak to our hearts. In the counseling office, we listen to our clients and to God so we have his heart and direction. As we love, know, and follow him, his life flows from us into the lives of those around us—clients, family, coworkers, and friends.

In phase 3, people take action to confront abusers, make restitution for sins, set boundaries, and move forward with their lives. The process of change can be identified and outlined, but most counselors admit it's a struggle to shepherd clients as they take steps forward. In this process, we join our clients' journey, clarify reachable goals that are consistent with their values, and move them forward a step at a time. Throughout this effort, we need to remain focused and determined. Every hope is accompanied by seeds of doubt and threats of discouragement. People need to smell the distant land of strength and joy so they'll keep reaching for it. We try to anticipate difficulties in this process, but we may not become aware of the specific things that block our clients until they are actually moving forward and hitting those obstacles. If they can't identify the barriers, they certainly can't overcome them. They'll stay stuck.

In this phase, clients self-assess and report. They may say, "This is what I said to myself, and this is what I heard from others. I feel that old fear of failure coming back." With this information, we can challenge their thinking and encourage them to take the next step—or maybe the same step again and again.

Seeing past their limits. Counselors model faith, hope, and love (1 Cor. 13) as they create a platform for change that empowers clients to say, "Oh, now I see. You know, I think I can do this!" Hope is essential in counseling (and in every other part of life). We don't just grit our teeth and muster up enough confidence to face life's deepest struggles. Authentic hope comes from a right relationship with God and a sense that he knows and he cares, even if we don't know what's going on.

Paul acknowledged that sometimes our hearts groan in pain and longing for more. He described the sources of hope in his letter to the Romans. He said it is found primarily in the forgiveness and adoption we have through Christ. The Spirit whispers to our hearts that we are God's dear children (Rom. 8:15-17). When we are secure in his love, we don't have to know all the answers and see everything clearly. By faith we trust that God knows and God cares, and that is enough for us. But that's not all. Paul tells us that the Spirit constantly prays for us—not just for our relief but also for us to experience the wonder of God's love, purpose, and power.

> Not only so, but we ourselves, who have the firstfruits of the Spirit, groan inwardly as we wait eagerly for our adoption to sonship, the redemption of our bodies. For in this hope we were saved. But hope that is seen is no hope at all. Who hopes for what they already have? But if we hope for what we do not yet have, we wait for it patiently.

> In the same way, the Spirit helps us in our weakness. We do not know what we ought to pray for, but the Spirit himself intercedes for us through wordless groans. And he who searches our hearts knows the mind of the Spirit, because the Spirit intercedes for God's people in accordance with the will of God (Rom. 8:23-27).

Appropriate self-disclosure. At appropriate times and in appropriate ways, counselors can share their personal story with clients. Clients are relieved to realize someone else has felt as hopeless, unloved, and faithless as they feel. They are encouraged to know counselors have their own struggles. Recounting for them our personal experience with the loss and recovery of faith, hope, and love can give them confidence to take the next step. Counselors believe Paul's teaching in 2 Cor. 1—that God is deeply involved in ministering his grace to those who are hurting. In his planfulness, Paul tells us God strategically brings persons into the experience of particular sufferings, ministers to them in their suffering, and then comforts them so they may seek out and minister to others who are suffering from the identical suffering from which they have experienced God's deliverance. God desires that no suffering be wasted. Often the pain and the grace for endurance that counselors have experienced become the platform for powerfully joining with clients. I call this the comfort chain.

Training Versus Trying for the Production of Lasting Change

As a young counselor I was always greatly encouraged when my clients and I worked out a plan of action leading to valued change and they agreed to try to implement those strategies. But the longer I worked with clients, the more I became convinced that trying just doesn't get it done. Trying for change does not contain a commitment to the rigor required to manage the processes leading to successful and long-term change. Training for change is closer to the biblical and reality-based commitment required for the establishment of real and lasting change.

The apostle Paul was deeply invested in the maturing of his young disciple in the faith, Timothy. Timothy had a problem with fear, and Paul counseled him that God has not given us a spirit of fear but of power and of love and of a sound mind (2 Tim. 1:7 NKJV). The challenge before Timothy and Paul was simply to take Timothy from where he was with his fear to where God wanted him to be with the experience of love and power and sound mindedness. Paul counseled an intensive engagement with the Word of God with its proper division so it could speak with truth to the areas of need in Timothy's life (2 Tim. 2:15). Paul had earlier counseled Timothy to exercise himself toward godliness, for bodily exercise profits a little, but godliness is profitable for all things (1 Tim. 4:7-8), including the dispelling of the fear that plagued Timothy every day of his life. Paul is prescribing a training regimen for Timothy that he has fully committed to in his own life. Writing to the Corinthians, Paul says, "Do you not know that those who run in a race all run, but one receives the prize? Run in such a way that you may obtain it.... Therefore I run thus....I discipline my body and bring it into subjection" (1 Cor. 9:24-27 NKJV).

Can you imagine a person entering a marathon without months of rigorous training and conditioning? This is the quality of commitment required from persons who would know the joy that comes from the actual achievement of valued change. Change is hard work. It requires a commitment to doing the same things over and over again until new habits replace old habits and we are partners with processes that change our thoughts, our wills, our minds, and our relationships.

Dehabituation and Rehabituation to Achieve Lasting Change

Can a leopard change its spots? What an interesting question! The answer seems to be an obvious no. And if he did, would he be a leopard anymore? After working with people for a while, you will probably be gripped by a soberness regarding the issue of change in people. In time, you will undoubtedly be saddened by how little real change you see in people and how little in our world is truly positive. At some point you may even find yourself a bit depressed over the issue of change in yourself and in others. However, people do change. Not everybody and maybe not even lots of people, but some people really do embrace change and become better for themselves, their families, their society, and their God.

When people really change, they share some things in common. One of these is that they have replaced old habits of thinking, behaving, and relating with new ones. The apostle Paul is advocating this very process for achieving meaningful change in his counseling and shepherding ministry to the Ephesian church. Let's look at a couple of examples of his counsel on change found in Eph. 4. Paul's broad counsel included reminding the Ephesians of what they had been taught: "Put off...the old man which grows corrupt...and be renewed in the spirit of your mind, and...put on the new man" (vv. 22-24 NKJV). Then, so there can be no question regarding exactly how he envisions this process working, Paul gets down to specifics.

Suppose your client is a crook. He has problems taking what he has not earned and worked for. In fact, he gets an adrenaline rush out of being smart enough to function in this manner while all the stupid people he is stealing from are getting up early and going to work. So when is a thief not a thief? When he is not stealing anymore? Wrong. How about when he gets a job and stops taking what doesn't belong to him? Wrong. When he has done all that, he has fixed some stuff in his brain, made his body get out of bed, started paying taxes, and so on. But that isn't what Paul has in mind.

The dehabituation/rehabituation change Paul envisions impacts the total person. A thief is no longer a thief when he labors with his own hands and takes a portion of what he has earned by the sweat of his own brow and gives it to a person who is in need. This person who once received joy and an adrenaline rush by stealing now gets his joy and his adrenaline rush by giving to those in need. The deeply engrained habits of the old man have been replaced by the now deeply engrained habits of the new man, "which after God is created in righteousness and true holiness" (Eph. 4:24 KJV). A lot of training and self-denial have gone into the forming of the new habit, but once that new habit is formed, it dominates the person's thoughts, spirit, feelings, will, and relationships.

Paul explores this dehabituation/rehabituation model of change with several examples. Let's examine one more of my favorites. This one has to do with a person's speech. The Bible makes so much of the person's use of words. We are told the power of life and death is in the tongue (Pr. 18:21). Paul counsels that the goal for the disciple of Christ should be the dehabituation of the use of words that corrupt, cut, or wound another person (Eph. 4:29-30). Every counselor has experienced the power of words to destroy marriages, families, and friendships. So now a series of questions. Am I using my tongue appropriately if I simply refrain from the use of any words that hurt my marriage partner or others? The answer is no. Is the kind of change we wish to see in our clients and our personal lives characterized simply by the absence of the negative? The answer again is no. As we have seen with the thief, what we desire to achieve through our counsel is not merely the absence of the negative but additionally the habituation of the positive.

In the matter of communication we counsel training, disciplining the tongue for restraint of words that cut or wound, a disciplined investigation of the other person's life for the determination of needed words, and then a commitment to gracing the person with words that edify or build up the hearer. The psalmist prayed, "Set a watch, O LORD, before my mouth; keep the door of my lips" (141:3 KJV). Paul sees the person who was the master of sarcasm and cutting speech transformed into a communicator of a grace message that encourages and edifies the recipients. How marvelous and how redemptive when people witness that kind of change in others and experience it in themselves.

Where does the power for this kind of change come from? Primarily it comes from the Holy Spirit. This is why Paul says in the very next verse,

"Do not grieve the Holy Spirit of God, with whom you were sealed" (Eph. 4:30). He has already reminded them, "When you believed, you were marked in him with a seal, the promised Holy Spirit" (Eph 1:13).

Consider for a moment what the word *sealed* signifies. When you buy a bottle of Tylenol, it is sealed. The therapeutic power of the Tylenol has been sealed in, and you can trust that nothing impure has been added to diminish its power for healing your pain. Paul is saying to all who will receive the message that the Holy Spirit has come into your life to empower dehabituation and rehabituation for the purpose of living a life that glorifies God, developing productive grace-based relationships, and living in the imitation of the Christ, who happens to be the most fully human person who has ever walked the earth.

You can trust the Holy Spirit to furnish you with that power. He is the anchor point of our belief in change as Christian counselors. Nothing is too difficult for him, and when we and others engage his person and power in a disciplined model of training, the outcome is truly transformational.

Client Pain in the Production of Lasting Change

Battered but not broken. The Scriptures aren't full of cotton candy. They communicate the honest truth of God's purposes and plans for his people. In this life, we can expect difficulties, but God has a purpose for them all. We don't have to waste our pain, as Paul explained.

> But we have this treasure in jars of clay to show that this all-surpassing power is from God and not from us. We are hard pressed on every side, but not crushed; perplexed, but not in despair; persecuted, but not abandoned; struck down, but not destroyed. We always carry around in our body the death of

Jesus, so that the life of Jesus may also be revealed in our body
(2 Cor. 4:7-10).

People naturally try to avoid pain, and deeply wounded people try even harder to deny, minimize, or rationalize their pain. But God often uses difficulties to show us our need for him, to draw us closer, and to teach us life's most important lessons. As we learn to trust God in them, the life of Christ is slowly, gradually, and haltingly revealed in us.

God is at work even when it doesn't go away. A few years ago, psychologist Larry Crabb talked about his dad, who was dying. Larry said that his father was a sailor and that old sailors can smell land before they see it. They can see something beyond the limits of this life. God is at work whether we realize it or not. If we don't trust him to be at work behind the scenes, we'll worry and complain, and we'll manipulate people to get what we want from them so we'll feel more secure. But if we trust that God is always at work, we can relax. We can embrace God's love even when we don't see evidence of it and "let grace abound yet more and more" (Montgomery, 1880). With renewed hope, God gives us the power to break through walls of doubt and discover the joys on the other side. Paul reminded the Romans, "I consider that our present sufferings are not worth comparing with the glory that will be revealed in us. For the creation waits in eager expectation for the sons of God to be revealed" (Rom. 8:18-19). And in the next life, the new heaven and new earth, "everything sad [is] going to come untrue," mercy and justice will rule, and we'll experience the fullness of joy in the presence of God.

Short-circuiting God's work. Sometimes, our best intentions are misdirected and harmful. Larry Crabb (2001) cautioned counselors against focusing too early on symptom reduction. Pain can be an effective stimulus for change. The prodigal didn't come to his senses until he had wasted every dime and experienced the humiliation of feeding pigs and longing to go to their trough for lunch. When our compassion surpasses our wisdom, we might try to alleviate a client's pain before God has done his holy surgery to change a heart. We need to ask, "Is intervention getting in the way of what God is actually trying to do in this client's life?" People usually need to "come to the end of themselves" before they're willing to take steps to change.

Enablers often "fix" addicts' problems and prevent them from hitting bottom. In the same way, some counselors enable their clients by giving relief too quickly and therefore short-circuit God's deeper, more lasting work to transform the person's heart, character, and life. This is a delicate decision. We need wisdom to know when to step in to comfort and when to let a client wrestle with the consequences of past choices. Crabb suggests we ponder the value of letting them stay in the ditch of their own making and stew in their troubles for a while. Then they may be more willing to listen and take steps to change.

Adaptiveness requires counselors to balance God's goals with the client's aims. Accurate perception requires clinical skills and a heart in tune with the Holy Spirit. We adapt our approach to both purposes and hope to find the right blend so the client is most benefited by their present experience. Scripture and life teach us that the crucible of suffering has provided some of our most valuable life experiences.

Resistance to Change

The process of change sounds easy, but nearly all counselors admit it is very hard to pull off. You are joining your client's journey, delivering doable goals that are consistent with their values, and attempting to move with them through a successful process of change. A lot of encouragement and hope building is associated with this phase of the counseling process. As the counselor, you need to envision what's ahead for the client and believe for them in a brighter and more fruitful future. Ultimately, however, they must own the power for change. They hold the key to the successful achievement of the desired change. As counselors, we need to be comfortable with that reality. We must never attempt to coerce them into change that they are not ready for or willing to own. If they do not want the change they once planned for, the counselor needs to be comfortable with giving them that right. I sometimes have told clients, "I really believed in our plan of action, but now I believe you are choosing not to pursue it. I know you have your reasons, and I choose to respect those. The responsibility for these choices and the power to make them rest with you. Either we need to decide on another collaboratively established plan of action, or we need to stop here until such time as you think I can be of further assistance to you." A client's readiness for embracing change through a collaboratively agreed-on plan of action is critical to the success of the counseling relationship.

Adapting to client resistance is always an extremely complicated challenge. We are frequently not given sufficient information regarding the blockages the client is experiencing that have precipitated the resistance or the decision to discontinue counseling. Sometimes our clients need better information, and we can attempt to provide that. Sometimes they just need to be affirmed and loved while they negotiate a particularly difficult time in the cycle of change, and we can provide that. Sometimes they need to be pushed and confronted with the need for repenting of error-based thinking or blaming that has got them stuck in a nonproductive pattern of behaving and relating to themselves and others, and we must provide that.

Paul confronted such a situation while relating to the Corinthians. He found himself in the very sensitive and uncomfortable situation of having to confront them with the need for repentance and to counsel them that only in repentance could the blockages in their relationship with him and others be removed (2 Cor. 7).

WISDOM'S REVIEW

To negotiate the challenges inherent in phase 3 and move clients to action leading to valued change, we need wisdom, skill, and patience. Adaptation and action require counselors to be insightful, thorough, and nuanced in their approach to each client. As we become increasingly skilled and wise, we can forget about ourselves and devote our attention to listening more carefully to our clients and God in the counseling sessions. We become excellent listeners. We hear the client's story, and we find ourselves hearing the real story beneath the words. As we move from assessment to goal-setting to action, we are able to be more confident that we are planning for change that can truly make a difference in the quality of life the client is experiencing personally and in relationships.

Paradoxically, we become stronger and more effective counselors as we increasingly recognize our weakness and invite God to be truly present with us in every moment of the session. As we grow, then, we become more dependent on God, not less. Even when our clinical skills are at their peak, we realize we can't force change to occur. Apart from Christ, we can't change a client's heart or instill courage and wisdom. We provide the environment for the Holy Spirit to work, and we invite him into the triad of connections. When appropriate, we also encourage the client to be sensitive to the voice of God in the session. As we attempt to manage the change process with clients, it is totally appropriate at times to ask the client, "What is God saying to you right now?"

When clients come to us, they need to perceive a certain amount of power in our lives and practices. This is what Strong (1968) recognized as social influence. However, Fiedler (1950) recognized that congruence and expertness are actually the direct result of the therapist's expressed weakness. When counselors expressed their humility and vulnerability in appropriate ways, clients often concluded, "I can trust this person. I'm going to listen so he can help me."

From change to maintenance. In phase 3, we adapt to help clients respond to challenges and opportunities. This is not a simple, straight-line approach. Their challenges and opportunities vary from week to week as they take action, and we adapt accordingly. At each point, we are prescriptive in helping the client take steps forward. Like the parents of adolescents, we need to promote healthy independence so our clients become self-sufficient and strong. If they remain immature and dependent too long, we haven't fulfilled our God-given role. Near the termination of counseling, our task is to prepare them for a lifetime of growing in grace, wisdom, and glad obedience to Christ.

A foundation of hope. It is a dictum of counseling that people without hope don't make progress, but those who find hope muster the courage to scale the tallest obstacles. Hope isn't found in simplistic formulas and answers. We can't offer peace and blessing that God hasn't promised. Our hope—and the hope we offer our clients—is based on the cross and the resurrection of Jesus Christ. The cross shows the depth of God's amazing love, and the resurrection is the promise that eventually, everything will be made right. Christ's resurrection is the firstfruits, and someday we'll stand with him in the glorious new heaven and new earth. Today, we stand in the middle ground, looking back at the cross and ahead at the promise of unmeasured mercy, justice, and fulfillment. Life is messy today, but someday it will be glorious and beautiful. The Spirit of God is the down payment for all that is to come. In him, we have at least a taste of our wonderful future.

In his famous sermon "The Weight of Glory," C. S. Lewis made this comment:

> At present we are on the outside of the world, the wrong side of the door. We discern the freshness and purity of morning, but they do not make us fresh and pure. We cannot mingle with the splendors we see. But all the leaves of the New Testament are rustling with the rumor that it will not always be so. Some day, God willing, we shall get in.

References

Basic Behavioral Science Task Force of the National Advisory Mental Health Council. (1996). Basic behavioral science research for mental health: Sociocultural and environmental processes. *American Psychologist, 51*(7), 722–731.

Carkhuff, R. R. (1969/1984). *Helping and human relations* (Vol. 1). *Selection and training* (p. 21). Amherst, MA: Human Resource Development Press.

Carkhuff, R. R. (1987). *The art of helping* (6th ed., p. 44). Amherst, MA: Human Resource Development Press.

Corey, M. S., & Corey, G. (2007). *Becoming a helper* (5th ed.). Belmont, CA: Brooks/Cole.

Crabb, L. (2001). *Shattered dreams* (pp. 52–53). Colorado Springs, CO: WaterBrook Press.

Egan, G. (2009). *The skilled helper: A problem-management and opportunity-development approach to helping.* (9th ed.) (pp. 358–361). Belmont, CA: Books/Cole.

Fiedler, F. (1950). The concept of an ideal therapeutic relationship. *Journal of Consulting Psychology, 14,* 239–245.

Hill, E. H. (2009). *Helping skills: Facilitating exploration, insight, and action.* (3rd ed.). Washington, DC: American Psychological Association.

Keller, T. (2011). *King's Cross* (pp. 161–162). New York, NY: Dutton.

Kottler, J. A., & Shepard, D. S. (2011). *Introduction to counseling: Voices from the field.* Belmont, CA: Brooks/Cole.

Lewis, C. S. (1941, June 8). The weight of glory [sermon]. Published in *Theology, 43*(257), pp. 263–274. Available online at http://tjx.sagepub.com/content/43/257/263.full.pdf+html

Montgomery, J. (1880). Prayer for power to give our hearts to God. *The poetical works of James Montgomery: With a memoir* (Vol. 2, p. 119). Cambridge, MA: Riverside Press.

Morris, T. (1994). *True success: A new philosophy of excellence.* New York, NY: Berkley Books.

Strong, S. R. (1968). Counseling: An interpersonal influence process. *Journal of Counseling Psychology, 3,* 215–224.

Willard, D. (2002). *Renovation of the heart: Putting on the character of Christ.* Colorado Springs, CO: NavPress.

10

Community and Accountability

The majestic God who communicates his character and passions to us in the Bible exists in the context of rich community. We call that mysterious community of intimacy the Trinity.

> The doctrine of the Trinity forms the heart of the Christian conception of God. Rather than being of secondary importance, this doctrine is central to our faith. The implications of this conception are immense. Above all it suggests that God is himself relational. The Father, Son, and Spirit are the social Trinity. Therefore, community is not merely an aspect of human life, for it lies within the divine essence (Grenz, 1994, p. 76).

In his high priestly prayer recorded in John 17, Jesus petitions the Father on behalf of those who would believe in him. He asks that they might be one even as he and the Father are one. This intercessory prayer on our behalf demonstrates Jesus's celebration of his relationships in the Godhead and points out the importance of intimate relationships among his disciples for the achievement of psychological, physical, and spiritual well-being.

Relationships hold great power for wounding and healing persons for one primary reason: Humans are created in the image of God. Just as God exists in community, so those whom he has created in his image find the need for intimacy embedded in their DNA. The Creator announces, "It is not good for the man to be alone. I will make a helper suitable for him." Man alone is incomplete, just as God without community would be a violation of his divine and Trinitarian nature. Solomon will later add, "Two are better than one...a cord of three strands is not quickly broken" (Eccl. 4:9,12).

Without a doubt, when we speak of the triunity of the biblical God, we are in the realm of mystery. Although many teachings of the Bible are clear as crystal, other biblical truths always contain an element of mystery. The triune nature of the Godhead is one of those things. Another is the teaching that a man and a woman who come together in the covenant of marriage become one flesh. Yet another is that persons who confess faith in the work of Jesus Christ on their behalf are baptized by the Holy Spirit into one body, that Christ is the head of it, and we are members of one another regardless of gender, ethnicity, age, and a host of other variables that distinguish and sometimes isolate us from one another.

In every culture throughout history, human beings have defined themselves by their relationships. From ancient Sparta to the jungles of New Guinea to the cities and towns of North America, people derive meaning and worth from the quality and nature of their connections to others. We long for love, laughter, and validation, and we suffer when these needs aren't met. Actress Celeste Holm reportedly stated, "We live by encouragement, and we die without it—slowly, sadly, angrily." Psychologists and sociologists have observed that embedded relationships give our lives value (described as "meaning systems" by Slattery & Park, 2011). The family system is the network of core social relations. This web of connections forms the foundations of human identity, security, creativity, beliefs, and satisfaction for every person on this planet.

True community—experienced in families, neighborhoods, schools, and churches—makes life rich and reinforces resilience. In all forms of communication, the context is more important than the content. To put it another way, communication is more about ethos than mere logos. The nature of people's relationships causes them to thrive or suffer. When connections are loving, consistent, and strong, every participant feels more secure, and from a secure base, is willing to take risks.

Most of the clients who come to see us, however, have been damaged and disappointed in their most important relationships. They feel insecure, anxious, and defensive because trust has been eroded or shattered. They experience the trajectory of pathology in family and social systems that were abusive, enmeshed, or isolated. These families tend to reproduce themselves.

In counseling, therapists provide the nucleus for a new community, a new model, a new vision of what relationships can be, and a new hope for the future. For clients, isolation or extreme dependence prevent gains in therapy. Quite often, the client's first relational hill to climb in counseling is learning to trust the therapist. As trust in this relationship produces security, courage, and hope, the client then is able to move into deeper, healthier relationships with others in the family, church, and community. With support from all these sources and accountability from one or two, treatment gains can be anchored and growth can be realized.

One of the primary goals in treating our clients is to help them build a social system of support and accountability. The grand purposes we long to see accomplished in the lives of our clients require that much of the relational work be accomplished outside of the weekly sessions they have with their counselor. Some counselors desperately need to build these systems too. The Christian faith has always been, and continues to be, highly relational. The apostle Paul uses the metaphor of human anatomy ("the body of Christ," 1 Cor. 12) to describe our interconnectedness. One part simply can't function effectively unless all parts are healthy, communicating well, and coordinating their efforts—all under the authority and direction of the head, Jesus Christ. Relationships are vital to every person in every culture, but studies reveal a quantifiable strength in the network of Christian connections.

Relationships, Religion, and Life Satisfaction

Contemporary research shows that religious people are more satisfied with their lives than nonbelievers (Koenig, McCullough, & Larson, 2001). A recent study by Lim and Putnam (2010) finds that it is not the relationship with God that makes the devout person happy; higher satisfaction comes from close ties to friends in the church. These findings applied to both Catholics and Protestants. (The number of Jews, Mormons, Muslims, and people of other religions interviewed was too small to draw definitive conclusions, although these groups showed the same trends.)

Most of the studies exploring the link between religion and life satisfaction have faced a chicken-and-egg dilemma. The research did not answer the directionality question: Does religion make people happy, or do happy people become religious? Lim and Putman developed a longitudinal study to explore this directionality. Using panel data analysis, they explored an additional question: If religion leads to life satisfaction, which aspect of religion makes people happy? Is it private religious practice (prayer and Scripture reading)? Is it subjective spiritual experience (feeling the presence and love of God)? Is it theological beliefs (for example, evangelical theological constructs, such as the deity of Christ, inerrancy of Scripture, and so on)? Or is it the social network and fellowship with other people of faith that most significantly influences life satisfaction?

Lim and Putnam used a representative sample of 3,108 adults of different faith traditions. In 2006, participants were asked a set of questions concerning their religious activities, beliefs, and social networks. In 2007, the same participants were contacted again and asked the same set of questions (the researchers received 1,195 responses). Generally, the survey confirmed other studies: Religious people are more satisfied than nonreligious people. Those who identified themselves as religious showed higher life satisfaction than those who declared themselves as nonreligious.

The study showed that frequency of attendance at religious services accounted for most of the difference in life satisfaction between people with religious affiliation and those without. While controlling other factors, 28.2% of participants who attended a religious service weekly professed to be "extremely satisfied," compared with 19.6% of those who never attended services. Lim and Putnam said this statistic is roughly equivalent to the difference between "a family income of $10,000 and of $100,000."

Lim and Putnam found the most important socializing factor in church participation is not broad involvement (sitting in church services as well as social contact outside of church), but the significance of more intense, meaningful, close relationships—the participants' close friends in their congregation. "People who frequently attend religious services are more satisfied with their lives not because they have more friends overall (when compared with individuals who do not attend services), but because they have more close friends in their congregation" (p. 920). The causality (having friends in the congregation leads to higher life satisfaction) was supported in the second study. The number of friends in a participant's congregation in 2006 contributed to the level of life satisfaction in 2007.

Lim and Putnam show that life satisfaction is much more about the social aspect of religion—specifically the number of close friendships in congregations who engage in religious activities that enhance their Christian identity—rather than the theological or spiritual aspects of religion. In other words, quality relationships with fellow believers produced positive life satisfaction more than nonreligious involvement, but also, more than attachment to and closeness to God.

> Our analyses suggest that social networks forged in congregations and strong religious identities are the key variables that mediate the positive connection between religion and life satisfaction....For life satisfaction, praying together seems to be better than either bowling together or praying alone (Lim & Putnam, 2010, p. 927).

This research confirms the therapeutic value of attachment theory, and it also raises some intriguing questions for Christian counselors and everyone else in Christian ministry. Does the influence of the therapeutic alliance—the unique supportive relationship between counselor and client—mirror close, religious-based friendships that are found in church? And we might ask more philosophical questions: Why did God declare it was not good for man to be alone in the Garden when he lived in a perfect relationship with God and was untainted by sin? If we have God, why do we need people?

We are forced to conclude that God created us with the inherent need for human relationships. Alfred Adler was right to emphasize "social interest" as a key variable in mental health. People require meaningful relations with other people to experience the best in life. For this reason, alienation, separation, and strained and broken relationships devastate people. The pain, emptiness, anger, and fear generated by torn relationships can't be mended with only cognitive restructuring. Learning to think correctly is important, but people also desperately need the existential, heartfelt connections of love, affirmation, and validation (Clinton & Sibcy, 2009).

Of course, as Christian counselors we offer our clients supportive and accountable relationships with us and with God. People need both, but they may have to be convinced by the ones they can see before they find the faith to trust the One they can't see. A positive horizontal relationship, then, may be the first step in the establishment of a vertical relationship with the God who cannot be seen.

Effective relationships are multifaceted, containing elements of encouragement and accountability. Some counselors gravitate toward encouragement, and others toward accountability. Both, however, are essential for the building of a productive therapeutic environment. Clients need to sense our unconditional love, but they also need to be held accountable for building new habits of thinking, acting, and reacting. Some of us think of accountability as a wagging finger, a stern look, and demands for compliance, but holding people accountable is an act of service. It honors their choices and loves them enough to help them succeed. To be effective, we tailor our approach to meet the needs of the moment. Tenderhearted people need only gentle reminders, but habitual liars and deceivers require love's firm hand.

One Another

In dozens of passages using the term "one another," the Bible gives direction to meaningful relationships. Some of these directly connect our experience with Christ to our motivation and capacity in human relationships. For instance, John wrote that we are to "love one another" because Jesus loved us first (1 Jn. 4:10-11). Paul instructed us to "forgive one another...as the Lord forgave you" (Col. 3:13), and "accept one another, then, just as Christ accepted you" (Rom. 15:7). These and similar passages prescribe our relationships with clients, and they give clear directions for clients as they try to reframe and restore strained relationships in their lives. These passages remind us that people have vital connections in a vast web of relationships. Growing in our abilities to relate in healthy ways isn't negotiable. With support, honesty, and encouragement, anything is possible; without these things, few positive outcomes are likely.

Our ability to relate in meaningful ways is a product of God first working his grace into us. Most of the "one another" passages are found in the second half of New Testament letters. In the first half, the writers describe the wonders of God's grace, which we internalize by faith. In the second half, they describe the logical ethical, moral, and relational implications in our attitudes and actions. First God works his grace into us, and then we are required to live it out with the goal of providing our world with an accurate representation of the God of the Bible (Eph. 5:1). Counselors and clients who can live out these "one another" imperatives are demonstrating to themselves and others that they have broken the power of negative addictions and idols in their lives and found the freedom to act for others in a manner that is possible only through the empowering presence of the Holy Spirit operating from their core being.

These are some of the most common "one another" passages in the New Testament:

- Confess your sins to each other (Jas. 5:16).

- Forgive one other (Eph. 4:32; Col. 3:13).

- Encourage one another and build each other up (1 Thess. 5:11; Heb. 3:13).

- Carry each other's burdens (Gal. 6:2).

- Pray for each other (Jas. 5:16).

- Offer hospitality to one another (1 Pet. 4:9).

- Accept one another (Rom. 14:1; 15:7).

- Be devoted to one another in love. Honor one another (Rom. 12:10).

- Serve one another (Gal. 5:13).

- Admonish one another (Col. 3:16).

- Stop passing judgment on one another (Rom. 14:13).

- Do not put any stumbling block in each other's way (Rom. 14:13).

- Value others above yourselves (Phil. 2:3).

Learning to Live It

God wants his people to practice the "one another" principles in every relationship and at all times. They are the oil in the machinery of life and the glue that holds everything together. The challenge, of course, is to practice them when it's most difficult—to love people who are unlovely, to forgive people who have hurt us and don't care, to serve gladly even when people aren't appreciative, to be kind when we'd rather run away or ridicule people, and to honor people when we long to be honored.

When relationships are based on these spiritual principles, they provide a secure base that affirms identity and capability. Those who are anxious about being accepted by others gradually realize they can relax and trust someone—perhaps for the first time in their lives. Avoidant people recognize the self-protective walls they have built, and they slowly become more perceptive about their own hurts and the value of others. Disorganized people have felt incompetent, isolated, and ashamed. In a secure, affirming environment, hopelessness and shame are gradually replaced with warmth and a new sense of confidence.

Let's look more closely at how believers can apply these principles.

Confess your sins to each other (Jas. 5:16). In most families, clubs, businesses, civic groups, and even churches, the last thing people want is to be vulnerable enough to confess their sins to other people. Without the firm foundation of proven love, forgiveness, and acceptance, self-disclosure seems foolish and even dangerous. James encourages us, "Therefore confess your sins to each other and pray for each other so that you may be healed" (Jas. 5:16). Healing can occur in the context of affirming, forgiving relationships, but only if people are convinced that it's safe to be honest.

What are the sins people need to confess? They are much more than violating some restriction from an arcane moral code. The code may identify the wrong, but the heart of sin goes deeper. Every sin is our desire to be our own god, to be in control, to run our lives the way we want to. We put something other than God in the center of our affections. Some of these, such as drugs or sexual addictive behaviors, are obviously destructive. But other "lesser gods" are good things we've turned into ultimate things, including money, prestige, power, and approval.

Nothing is inherently wrong with them. If we receive them as gifts from God, we can use them as stewards of God's generosity. But if those things have captured our hearts, they have become our gods. We live to get them, we invest time and money in them, and acquiring them becomes the highest goal of our lives. And they destroy us just as surely as cocaine or meth destroys an addict.

Confession has external and internal aspects. Sins have a clear behavioral component, but the heart is even more important. When we confess our sins, we need to look for the underlying thirst, the drive that led to the sinful behavior. Only when this motivation is exposed, labeled, and confessed can there be a genuine renovation of the heart. In the dehabituation and rehabituation process, external change in behavior is always connected to internal change in disposition. Identifying and confessing the internal drive is necessary for genuine repentance to take place.

Forgive one other (Eph. 4:32; Col. 3:13). The hope of our confession rests on the assurance of God's forgiveness. Our experience of God's rich, wonderful forgiveness provides the motivation we need to move beyond bitterness and blame when others have hurt us. As we draw from the deep well of God's grace in our lives, we can extend grace and forgiveness to those who have hurt us.

Many of our clients are confused about forgiveness. They assume that to forgive is to act as if the offense didn't happen or to forget it happened. Some live in a cloud of bitterness; others implode in depression. People need clear teaching about the power and process of forgiveness. Pastor and author Lewis Smedes offers this explanation and encouragement:

> When we forgive evil we do not excuse it, we do not tolerate
> it, we do not smother it. We look the evil full in the face, call
> it what it is, let its horror shock and stun and enrage us, and
> only then do we forgive it (Smedes, 1984, pp. 79–80).

Forgiving does not erase the bitter past. A healed memory is not a deleted memory. Instead, forgiving what we cannot forget creates a new way to remember. We change the memory of our past into a hope for our future (Smedes, 1996, p. 171).

Encourage one another and build each other up (1 Thess. 5:11; Heb. 3:13). Therapy groups are designed to create a social microcosm (Yalom & Leszcz, 2005) so counselors could encourage members to replace existing, self-destructive behaviors with new, healthy ones. The goal is to teach, model, and process in the group and then to release people to apply their new skills in every other relationship. In counseling offices, therapy groups, Bible studies, and support groups, the goal is not only to impart information but also to provide a hothouse environment for growth. In many cases, the combination of individual therapy and group support is especially powerful in creating the conditions for progress. Principles and skills are learned in therapy, affirmed and modeled in a group, tried in outside relationships, and evaluated and supported back in the office or group environment. In this way, incremental steps are encouraged, taken, and reinforced.

In *Theory and Practice of Group Counseling*, Gerald Corey (2011, p. 15) observes that the leader sets the pace in learning and growth.

Leaders bring to every group their personal qualities, values, and life experiences and their assumptions and biases. To promote growth in the members' lives, leaders need to live growth-oriented lives themselves. To inspire others to break away from deadening ways of being, leaders need to seek new experiences themselves. In short, group leaders become an influential force in a group when they are able to model effective behavior rather than merely describe it.

Carry each other's burdens (Gal. 6:2). Some Christians have the spiritual gift of showing mercy to those in need. This God-given talent involves the powerful blend of compassion and caring action. All believers, though, are called to resemble Christ in caring for hurting people around them. One of the most memorable stories in the Gospels describes four men who wanted to take their paralyzed friend to Jesus. When they couldn't get through the crowd into the house, they didn't give up. They tore a hole in the roof and lowered him at the feet of Jesus, who forgave him and healed him (Mt. 9:2-8; Mk. 2:1-12; Lk. 5:17-26).

Many people are like the paralyzed man—they can't make it on their own. They need someone to help them. When we care for hurting, needy, sick, thirsty people, we "fulfill the law of Christ" (Gal. 6:2). Jesus told his disciples that the greatest commandment was to love God with all their hearts, and the second was like it—to love their neighbors as they love themselves. As we follow Christ, we fulfill his law by devoting as much energy, creativity, and resources to meet the needs of others as we invest in meeting our own needs. That's a high standard of love and care—the one Jesus modeled for us.

Pray for one another (Jas. 5:16). Prayer is a significant part of spiritual, emotional, relational, and physical healing in the Christian community. James asked and instructed, "Is anyone among you in trouble? Let them pray. Is anyone happy? Let them sing songs of praise. Is anyone among you sick? Let them call the elders of the church to pray over them and anoint them with oil in the name of the Lord" (Jas. 5:13-14). We pray for protection from the evil one (1 Thess. 3:1-5), and we ask God to give us more knowledge of his will, his wisdom, and his love (Eph. 1:17). We pray for God to open the eyes of our hearts so we can hope in him and experience his power (verses 18-19).

Paul tells us to pray for all people, and especially our leaders (1 Tim. 2:1-2). Paul often asked others to pray for him and for his ministry. As Christ's body, we put on the armor of God to fight for truth, mercy, and justice in our spiritual battle (Eph. 6:10-20). After Paul listed the full armor he concluded, "And pray in the Spirit on all occasions with all kinds of prayers and requests. With this in mind, be alert and always keep on praying for all the Lord's people" (verse 18).

In counseling, we respect the wishes of our clients by asking them if they feel comfortable with us praying with and for them. If they do, we have the opportunity to go before God's throne with our clients' needs, trusting God to reveal his great love, to give us wisdom to know his will, and to impart the courage to do it.

Many clients don't know how to pray, or they feel defeated and discouraged because God hasn't answered their prayers. We can point them to Paul's prayers in Eph. 1 and 3, Phil. 1, and Col. 1. They (and we) can use these beautiful, inspiring prayers to guide them as they connect with God.

Offer hospitality to one other (1 Pet. 4:9). In the first centuries, kindness was often linked to the traditional Jewish virtue of hospitality, but it is much more. Social graces are important for the engine of culture to run smoothly, but genuine kindness appears at crucial times when people feel most vulnerable. Jesus displayed kindness when he touched a leper, held children in his arms, stopped to relate to a woman who had been healed, and raised a widow's son from his coffin. He demonstrated kindness to his disciples by patiently explaining himself over and over again, and he was kind to the Pharisees by continually engaging them and offering them his grace. And on the cross, he was incredibly kind by asking the Father to forgive his tormentors.

Our clients may present as wounded and withdrawn or perhaps as angry and self-protective. Every client needs our kindness. Mercy is an expression of value, love, and attention, and it communicates empathy and intention. Kindness connects with the hidden fears and highest hopes of a client's heart.

Kindness isn't weak and blind, and it's not manipulative. Our clients are sometimes too quick to let those who have harmed them off the hook and settle for something far less than a loving, supportive, kind relationship. If an addict, abuser, or prodigal stops lying, stealing, cursing, and hitting, clients feel relieved. That's the cessation of abuse, but it's not the presence of kindness. Authentic displays of kindness put salve on wounds, serve, give, and sacrifice for others. If those traits aren't present, the person isn't truly kind.

Genuine kindness isn't earned. Most relationships are conditional. They are based on a mutually beneficial transaction. But kindness is different. It is love poured out with no ulterior motives. God's kindness is produced in us and through us by the Spirit of God. It is part of the fruit of the Spirit, so it grows as we stay vitally connected to Christ, our source.

Accept one other (Rom. 14:1; 15:7). People instinctively wonder if they are acceptable. A host of people's pathological behaviors are their attempts to hide from the fear of being unacceptable, the compulsion to prove they are worthy of acceptance, and bitterness and shame because they don't feel accepted. When we accept one another as Christ has accepted us, we don't close our eyes to sin, destructive behavior, and immaturity. God lavishes his grace on us, but he loves us so much that he doesn't let us remain selfish and childish. In the same way, when we accept people the way Christ accepts us, we step into the messiness of their lives, love them deeply, speak truth with grace, and point them to choices and a lifestyle that pleases God.

Honor one another (Rom. 12:10). Some people see accountability as rigorous and oppressive: "I'm telling you what to do, and you'd better do it!" In Christian counseling, however, accountability isn't ownership or control; it's a way to honor our client's desires, values, and future.

Accountability, then, is never demanding. It helps a client overcome fears, face goals, and take courageous steps forward.

When we look at the life of Christ, we see that he honored people by taking them as they were and speaking grace and truth into their lives. He didn't demand that they jump through any hoops before he related to them. He listened, validated their needs, and let them make their own choices. Some responded in joyful faith, others walked away confused, and some despised him. Still, he honored their right to choose.

Serve one another (Gal. 5:13). As the Lord of glory, Jesus deserved to be worshipped and served, but he humbled himself to be the servant of all. He told his disciples that he didn't come to be served but to serve (Mt. 20:28). When the disciples bickered about who was going to take the top positions in Jesus's cabinet in the new kingdom, Jesus corrected them. He contrasted the way they should think and act with the normal behavior of people who demand to be served.

> The kings of the Gentiles lord it over them; and those who exercise authority over them call themselves Benefactors. But you are not to be like that. Instead, the greatest among you should be like the youngest, and the one who rules like the one who serves. For who is greater, the one who is at the table or the one who serves? Is it not the one who is at the table? But I am among you as one who serves (Lk. 22:25-27).

We discover the nature of our hearts when we serve but our efforts aren't appreciated. In other words, how do we act when we're treated like servants? Jesus continued to give and serve even when his closest friends ran away, his enemies tortured him, and the fickle crowd turned from singing, "Hosanna!" to yelling, "Crucify him!" We won't be able to serve selflessly and consistently if we feel spiritually empty. This kind of humility comes only from strength—a vibrant, powerful love relationship with

God that meets our deepest needs so we don't have to jockey for power and acclaim.

Whom do we serve? Before his arrest, Jesus told a story about a king whose followers were caring for the hungry, thirsty, naked, homeless, and imprisoned. The king praised them for loving and serving him. When they responded with surprise at his appreciation, the king explained, "Truly I tell you, whatever you did for one of the least of these brothers and sisters of mine, you did for me" (Mt. 25:40).

Serving our clients is sometimes a thankless task. We need to remember that we are actually serving Christ. That realization humbles us, inspires us, and gives us renewed energy to bear our clients' burdens.

Admonish one another (Col. 3:16). To admonish others is to caution, to gently correct, and to challenge faulty thinking and misguided behavior. In our culture, tolerance is considered the highest virtue, especially among the young. No one is supposed to make any value judgments about another person's choices. This limitation, though, isn't found in the life of Christ. He poured out his life as a sacrifice, but he also gave clear directives and warnings. Admonitions were expressions of his love. The tone of correction is very important. Correction given with a harsh or demanding sound creates fear, shame, and resentment, but when it is given with kindness and hope, the hearer is invited to respond. There are, of course, no guarantees of a good response to our cautions and corrections, but we can control how we deliver them.

Do not judge each other (Rom. 14:13; Jas. 4:11). Many people misunderstand Jesus's warning, "Do not judge, or you too will be judged" (Mt. 7:1). They assume it prevents any analysis or assessment of another person's behavior or attitude. (And of course, many people use this verse to stop people from assessing their selfish, destructive behavior: "Don't judge me! It's not right to judge anybody. Jesus said so.")

This conclusion, however, can't be what Jesus meant. The Scriptures are full of evaluations of people. Paul pointed out the Corinthians' many sins in detail and with clear warnings to change. God wants us to have our eyes open in relationships, to assess, to be discerning, and to evaluate accurately—but without condemnation. When we delight in blasting people for their faults and gossiping about them, we have crossed the line into condemnation.

In every culture, city, family, business, and friendship, we encounter differences of opinion and taste. Disagreements aren't wrong, and they don't have to be destructive. If we value other people, disagreeing can be a wonderful, creative process of learning and growing. However, insecurity often is a fuse that causes disagreements to explode into attacks and resentment. In the body of Christ, division often occurs because people insist on their own way, they don't listen, and they don't love, value, and respect other people's views. Paul often wrote about the value of unity—not uniformity, but unity of heart based on our shared experience of God's grace. He warned the Roman Christians to avoid petty bickering, and he reminded them that each person is ultimately accountable to Christ, not to us. He wrote, "Who are you to judge someone else's servant? To their own master, servants stand or fall. And they will stand, for the Lord is able to make them stand" (Rom. 14:4).

In difficult family relationships, many people try to avoid painful realities (and control other family members) by insisting that any honest evaluation of behavior is judging and therefore off-limits. This enables abusers, addicts, and others to continue in their pathological, destructive behavior. In counseling people from these families, take time to explain the difference between compassionate assessment (which can lead to honest communication, healthy boundaries, change, and growth) and harsh condemnation (which enflames fear, shame, anger, withdrawal, and attack).

Do not put any stumbling block in each other's way (Rom. 14:13). Paul instructed, "Stop passing judgment on one another. Instead, make up your mind not to put any stumbling block or obstacle in the way of a brother or sister." In counseling, we can put obstacles in our clients' way by having expectations that are too high or too low. If they are too high, we come across as demanding. If they are too low, we don't offer enough hope for real change. We can also become an obstacle to our clients if we take too much responsibility for their growth. Clear boundaries and responsibilities lower our levels of stress and protect our clients from us becoming too controlling.

In the same way, our clients often put obstacles in their relationships. They can be too controlling or too disconnected. They can add to the stress of a family situation by trying to fix every problem. This prevents others from being honest about their flaws and taking responsibility for their choices. In counseling, we need to be alert for the many and varied stumbling blocks in our clients' lives—and we need to avoid adding any!

Value others above yourselves (Phil. 2:3). Some people feel comfortable only when they occupy a one-up position in relationships. They insist on being in charge, commanding attention and respect. Ironically, people on the other end of the spectrum—those who appear weak, crippled with self-pity and shame—also want attention, not for their power or success, but for how much they've suffered. It is human nature to want to be the center of attention. In Paul's letter to the Philippians, he explains that the gospel of grace fills the hole in our hearts with Christ's love, encouragement, and joy so we can look beyond our own needs. Instead of "selfish ambition and vain conceit" (which are characteristics of both one-up and one-down clients), we value others above ourselves and look out for their interests as well as our own.

As counselors, we value our clients by caring for their needs as we listen intently and have empathy for their pain. We pray for them, we study our notes to prepare for sessions, and we devote ourselves to their care. One of our goals in therapy is to help them experience the wondrous love of Christ so hurts are healed, hearts are filled, and our clients can be free to care for others without strings attached.

The Role of the Church

Counselors and their clients often have mixed views of the local church. Some feel loved and supported by their churches, but some have been deeply wounded by Christians who were supposed to love and support them. The "one another" passages describe the way God designed Christian relationships to operate in the church, but when we read Paul's letters, we can deduce that many of these churches experienced significant relational struggles. In counseling, we often need to address our clients' experiences in church because they powerfully shape the clients' view of God and important relationships.

We also may need to address our clients' expectations of the church. Every body of believers is made up of fallen people living in a fallen world. We are all, as Paul said about himself, in process, and we all have a long way to go in our spiritual growth. Wounded people are often the most demanding because they have unrealistic expectations about the way others should treat them. The church simply can't measure up to those demands. There will be a time when all wrongs will be made right and all hurts healed, but that won't be until the new heaven and new earth. Until then, even the best churches are mixed bags.

Of course, a few churches are genuinely oppressive. Leaders in these churches use positions of authority to dominate, intimidate, and fleece their people. These situations are rare, but they occur. If your client comes to you from this environment, treat it like an abusive family. Help the client see things clearly, respond with grace and strength, and confront wrongs. The process may result in healing and repentance, but the leaders may not change. In fact, like many addicts, their oppression may get worse when they are confronted. In this case, our role may be to help the client leave gracefully and find a safer, more supportive spiritual home.

The purpose of the church is to provide an atmosphere that encourages honesty, love, and devotion to God. The writer of Hebrews zeros in on the necessity for the church and the true role of the church:

> Let us hold unswervingly to the hope we profess, for he who promised is faithful. And let us consider how we may spur one another on toward love and good deeds, not giving up meeting together, as some are in the habit of doing, but encouraging one another—and all the more as you see the Day approaching (Heb. 10:23-25).

Churches fulfill their God-given role when they balance encouragement with accountability and point people to the matchless grace, wisdom, and majesty of Christ. He is the source of joy, peace, forgiveness, and strength.

Affluent communities, including much of our country, need a particular warning. The comparative wealth and freedom of American culture can be subtly confused with the promised blessings of heaven. When we look around our nation and our communities, we enjoy economic prosperity, health, and technology that were inconceivable only a generation ago. These are wonderful gifts from God, and we are stewards of his blessings. But when people demand more and more, they've lost any sense of perspective and gratitude. They live for themselves instead of living to honor Christ and serve their neighbors. Pastor G. Campbell

Morgan explained, "Your purpose in life is not to find your freedom, but your Master" (cited in Carmichael, 1997, p. 255).

This cultural analysis can have a significant bearing on counseling because a selfish preoccupation with affluence creates a pervasive, poisonous sense of entitlement. Comparison ruins our perspective because it leaves us always dissatisfied. Our clients (and perhaps we) are rarely grateful for God's grace, care, and love, and they don't respond well to difficulties because they believe problems should never happen. In this environment, the idols of the heart—power, positions, possessions, and popularity—promise to fulfill us, but they leave us empty and angry. We may need to address client expectations of a happy American life as we address other presenting problems in therapy.

Accountability for Counselors

An article by Miller and Hubble (2011) in *Psychotherapy Networker* compared cultures of excellence across many fields in America. In the past, the United States scored at or near the top in almost every category, but in 2011 Americans were 17th in science, 25th in math, 28th in overall life satisfaction, and 37th on access to and quality of health care. Alarmingly, the overall trend was downward, suggesting that these rankings will be worse in the future. Miller and Hubble reported a similarly daunting decline in the public perception of psychotherapy.

In contrast to these scores, therapists' self-perceptions are more positive. A 20-year international study of 11,000 therapists was reported in *How Psychotherapists Develop* (Orlinsky & Rønnestad, 2005). These are some of the more intriguing findings.

- Contrary to all the turf-protecting wars of the various disciplinary groups, psychotherapy is viewed by most practitioners as "a unified field." This finding is in stark contrast to psychiatrists defending their field against psychologists, psychologists defending themselves against social workers, and social workers feeling superior to licensed professional counselors and licensed marriage and family therapists.

- Therapists stay in the profession and find vocational satisfaction not for money or fame, but because they value connections with clients that lead to genuine change and improvement.

- Those who remained in the field were motivated by a desire to excel in their craft.

- These two factors are major buffers against counselor disillusionment and burnout in all the counseling disciplines.

The authors coined a new term, *healing involvement*, to describe what therapists pursue in their work, and they noted both a long-term outcome—*cumulative career development*—and a short-term outcome—a sense of *currently experienced growth*—as reasons for pursuing healing involvement. Therapists expressed a deep desire to consistently improve their skills to increase the inherent satisfaction of healing involvement.

How do we maintain growth that leads to healing involvement and vocational satisfaction? We can measure outcomes in sessions—questioning clients about what works and what doesn't work in therapy and then making immediate adjustments according to the clients' feedback. This isn't rocket science. It is an intuitively obvious and effective means of accountability for therapists to be sure they are on track with their clients. However, many therapists don't follow this simple but profoundly effective course because they are afraid of negative feedback, which fuels their own fear of failure, shame, and loss.

Objective accountability. Immediate, reflexive accountability prevents false assumptions of the client's assessment of counseling. Duncan (2010, p. 34) reviewed literature that indicates therapists' self-reported views of success are often inaccurate and biased. One study reported therapists' self-grading from A-plus to F. Fully 66% of the respondents gave themselves an A, and no one gave himself an average grade. The bell curve didn't exist in these self-reports. In another study rating client deterioration in 550 cases, therapists predicted deterioration in just one case, but 40 cases—equaling the actuarial rate of 8% decline—showed actual deterioration.

Tracking outcomes for therapeutic mastery. Counselors tend to avoid objective measures of accountability, but these are vital for excellence in our work. For those who measured change, client outcomes improved more than fourfold over those who didn't measure change, and nine out of ten therapists who used objective measures significantly improved their skills (Duncan, 2010, p. 89). Tracking outcomes helps therapists go beyond intuition and subjective impressions of clients' experience in therapy (Duncan, 2010). Obtaining feedback helps therapists align with clients and serve them more effectively—which, of course, leads to better outcomes (Anker, Duncan, & Sparks, 2009).

Creating a culture of excellence. Paradoxically, counselors who try to portray an image of perfection are often threatened by cultures of excellence, and they discount the value of objective measures. We grow in our skills, however, when we have the security to admit we could have done something better, we've failed, or we needed expert consultation. We develop a culture of excellence when we recognize our limitations and deficiencies, seek help, and incorporate new insights and skills into our practices. As we invite honest assessments—from our clients and peers— we create a positive, supportive community of learners.

These cultures require a high degree of trust, assurance that honest reporting of failures are not held against them, and leaders who are willing to be transparent about their mistakes and failures. In this environment, every person is committed to measuring outcomes on a case-by-case basis, learning from mistakes, and celebrating successes. Sadly, this kind of professional alliance is rare. Strong, affirming, consistent leadership is needed to overcome resistance of professional staff who expect condemnation if case outcomes are measured and reported.

A supportive culture of excellence can't be imposed by an outside agency. An Oregon state statute, HB 2059, mandates that all health care professionals, including psychotherapists, report to the state any conduct seen in colleagues that is "unbecoming a licensee." Some professionals in Oregon have reported that the new law has significantly curtailed professional communication, and some health care professionals fear losing their licenses (Miller & Hubble, 2011). Cultural change must come, instead, from leaders modeling honesty, compassion, and therapeutic excellence—a blend of attractive, powerful traits that makes anything less unattractive.

Globally, leaders in our field have created a virtual community to improve their impact in counseling and psychotherapy—the International Center for Clinical Excellence (centerforclinicalexcellence.com). This website has more than 100 forums for articles, discussions, and videos of masters doing therapy.

> Without taking a chance, venturing beyond the tried and true, nothing happens. It's only through difficulty that you learn. It's precisely for this reason that the members and associates continue working very hard at making the ICCE a safe place for clinicians to share openly and be pushed and stretched (cited in Miller & Hubble, 2011, p. 6).

WISDOM'S REVIEW

One of our goals is creating a therapeutic relationship that provides safety, encouragement, and hope for our clients. As extensions of this connection, we point them to groups and church environments where they will feel supported and where they can pour the grace they've experienced into the lives of others.

A person alone may initially experience the redemptive love of Christ, but significant growth never occurs in isolation. Every person in the community of faith contributes to the building up of the body in love...

> until we all reach unity in the faith and in the knowledge of the Son of God and become mature, attaining to the whole measure of the fullness of Christ.
>
> Then we will no longer be infants, tossed back and forth by the waves, and blown here and there by every wind of teaching and by the cunning and craftiness of people in their deceitful scheming. Instead, speaking the truth in love, we will grow to become in every respect the mature body of him who is the head, that is, Christ. From him the whole body, joined and held together by every supporting ligament, grows and builds itself up in love, as each part does its work (Eph. 4:13-16).

These relationships are countercultural. Human nature pushes people to attack or withdraw, to intimidate or cower. It takes security and courage to move toward one another with open minds, compassionate hearts, and the intention to serve. This pursuit doesn't come naturally. It is the product of a heart being transformed by the grace of Christ. The beautiful truth is that gracious, courageous actions in relationships often produce gracious, courageous responses from the recipients, and the cycle can continue. The Scriptures and history tell us that the default mode of the human heart is to dominate or hide, but with God's help, we can take steps to build communities of authentic affection, honesty, and mutual accountability.

References

Anker, M., Duncan, B., & Sparks, J. (2009). Using client feedback to improve couples therapy outcomes: A randomized clinical trial in a naturalistic setting. *Journal of Consulting and Clinical Psychology, 77*(4), 693–704.

Carmichael, W. (1997). *Seven habits of a healthy home: Preparing the ground in which your children can grow.* Carol Stream, IL: Tyndale House.

Clinton, T. & Sibcy, G. (2009). *Attachments: Why you love, feel, and act the way you do* (pp. 3–33). Brentwood, TN: Integrity Media.

Corey, G. (2011). *Theory and practice of group counseling.* Independence, KY: Brooks/Cole.

Duncan, B. (2010). *On becoming a better therapist.* Washington, DC: American Psychological Association.

Grenz, S. J. (1994). *Theology for the community of God.* Nashville, TN: Broadman and Holman.

Koenig, H. G., McCullough, M. E., & Larson, D. B. (2001). *Handbook of religion and health* (p. 117). New York, NY: Oxford University Press.

Lim, C., & Putnam, R. (2010). Religion, social networks, and life satisfaction. *American Sociological Review, 75,* 920.

Miller, S., & Hubble, M. (2011, May). The road to mastery: What's wrong with this picture? *Psychotherapy Networker.* Retrieved from http://www.psychotherapynetworker.org/magazine/recentissues/1298-the-road-to-mastery

Orlinsky, D., & Rønnestad, M. (2005). *How psychotherapists develop: A study of therapeutic work and professional growth.* Washington, DC: American Psychological Association.

Slattery, J., & Park, C. (2011). Meaning making and spiritually oriented interventions. In J. Aiten, M. McMinn, & E. L. Worthington, Jr. (Eds.), *Spiritually oriented interventions for counseling and psychotherapy* (pp. 15–40). Washington, DC: American Psychological Association.

Smedes, L. (1984). *Forgive and forget.* New York, NY: Harper & Row.

Smedes, L. (1996). *The art of forgiving.* New York, NY: Ballantine Books.

Yalom, I. D., & Leszcz, M. (2005). *The theory and practice of group psychotherapy* (5th ed.). Cambridge, MA. Basic Books.

11

Spiritual Interventions

*Interventions Directed at the Provision of the Holy Spirit
and the Nourishment of the Human Spirit*

Many of our clients come to us with the expectation that we integrate our faith and biblical concepts into our therapeutic approach. They want to understand their predicaments from God's point of view, and they hope we can point them to his wisdom, love, and power.

We need to be careful, though, that we don't blindside anyone when we bring up the subject of God, his grace and purposes, and the biblical principles of healing and growth. On our consent forms and during the first session, we need to make our position and intentions clear— we are thoroughly professional *and* distinctively Christian. On the consent form, we may want to list the many spiritual interventions we may use, such as prayer, use of the Scriptures, and meditation. Some clients, of course, are familiar with some or all of these practices, but many are not. And even those who have been in church for years may not understand how these spiritual disciplines can profoundly help them resolve their problems.

Like gifted surgeons, Christian counselors need to develop skills, find resources, and gain experience so we can expertly use spiritual interventions to cut into our clients' hearts to expose sins and wounds and help bring the healing of God's love, grace, wisdom, and power. In this chapter, we will examine some of the most common and effective spiritual interventions.

Using the Scriptures With Wisdom, Grace, and Power

The Bible is an amazing document. It was penned over the course of 1,500 years by many different authors, and it was completed almost two millennia ago. Yet it is remarkably perceptive about the complexity and drives of human nature—ancient and contemporary. Guided by the Holy Spirit, the authors clearly identify the misguided thirsts of the human heart and how our pursuit of lesser gods leads to relational, spiritual, personal, and cultural devastation.

And the Bible doesn't stop with an accurate diagnosis of the problem. From the opening chapters of Genesis to the closing chapters of Revelation, the writers describe the wonder of God's grace, the transforming power of his redeeming love, and the efficacy of that power and love for promoting healing in human souls and relationships. Our task as counselors is to correctly handle the word of truth (2 Tim. 2:15).

David Powlison (2010) asserts that Christian counselors need to establish a clear biblical hermeneutic, including Christology, anthropology, and soteriology. Every person is created in the image of God, is accountable to God, is a "deviant from God" because of sin, but is "renewable by God." These concepts guide Christian counseling, and they are not negotiable.

> [God as] Maker, Judge, and Savior orients us as we seek to make sense of the psychological functioning of creatures....The implications hold true down to the microscopic individual details of human psychology. Of course, this credo supplies none of the myriad psychological facts and details— far from it....But the credo orients, teaching us to see facts in their true context (pp. 246–247).

Few issues are more important in Christian counseling than the need for the counselor to be properly oriented as she approaches her work. The ability to see the elements of the client's story in their proper context requires that the Christian counselor possess the ability to set the narrative within a framework of biblical truth. In order for Christian counselors to accomplish that objective, we must direct our attention to several intermediate accomplishments.

Christian counselors must become experts on the gospel and its implications. We can't assume our clients—even those who have been in church for many years—grasp the beauty and transforming power of the gospel of grace. Like the prodigal and his brother, people try to find meaning and personal worth in two very different ways—through self-indulgence or through a sterling moral record. In self-indulgence, people try to fill their lives with anything and everything that will make them happy for the moment. Eventually, many prodigals and moralists come to their senses and realize they've wasted their lives.

The gospel of grace isn't a balance or a blend of these two wrong views of life and God. It's a completely different way, as author and pastor Tim Keller (2008) makes clear.

Jesus does not divide the world into the moral "good guys" and the immoral "bad guys." He shows that everyone is dedicated to a project of self-salvation, to using God and others in order to get power and control for themselves. We are just going about it different ways....

The gospel is distinct from the other two approaches: In its view, everyone is wrong, everyone is loved, and everyone is called to recognize this and change....Jesus says, "The humble are in and the proud are out" (see Lk. 18:14). The people who confess they aren't particularly good or open-minded are moving toward God, because the prerequisite for receiving the grace of God is to know you need it (pp. 44–45).

The Bible paints a bleak picture of those who insist on self-indulgence and those who try to impress with their moral excellence. Both are helpless, hopeless, and doomed. But the message of the gospel is that the God of the Bible didn't leave us in our dire predicament. He took the initiative to step out of heaven and into earth, become a servant, and die the death we deserved. Jesus Christ, the glorious Lord of creation, became our substitute by suffering abandonment and death on the cross. This is the greatest message and marvel of the ages! God's grace is, indeed, amazing. To experience this grace, we have to realize two things: We are more wicked than we ever imagined, and God loves us more than we ever dared hope.

The gospel of grace humbles us because we realize we're helpless, hopeless sinners, unable to earn God's acceptance. The message, though, doesn't leave us in despair. We are raised to the heavens as we realize we are completely forgiven, deeply loved, and wonderfully adopted by the God of Scripture, who is the Creator, lover, and pursuer of a humanity created in his image.

Grace is where a relationship with God begins, and it is the sustaining force that empowers us to live for the one who paid the ultimate price for us. We never outgrow our need to experience God's love, forgiveness, and strength. God's staggering love is the source of delight and discipline as we obey God and live to please him.

Most of our clients come to us as both sinners and victims. They need the cleansing power of Christ's sacrifice for their sins, and they need the comfort and assurance that God won't waste their pain. God's grace brings comfort—not an escape from pain, but the strong confidence that God has far deeper and higher purposes for our suffering than we ever imagined (2 Cor. 1).

In counseling, we need to perfect the skills required for sharing the message of the good news of God's redemptive, boundless love in appropriate, powerful ways.

As we reflect on spiritual interventions, we are impressed that all of them hold significance for moving clients forward in certain modalities more forcefully than others. Consider the importance of knowing and experiencing the certainty that I am loved regardless of past or present behavior. This truth brings a new way of thinking about myself! My mind informed by the gospel is more at peace; my emotions are more positive. My actions are now under the umbrella of a relationship with an all-knowing and all-powerful God. I am safe! I have a future that is secure!

The gospel is not just about the now. I remember hearing John Eldredge speaking about the hope that we who have believed the gospel have regarding our future. He shared his thoughts about Heb. 6, where the writer states, "We have this hope as an anchor for the soul" (verse 19). Then he referred to Acts 3:20-21, where we read, "...that He may send Jesus Christ, who was preached to you before, whom heaven must receive until the times of restoration of all things" (NKJV).

The grand hope for those who follow Christ is for that time when

Christ will return and restore all things. Broken bodies and minds will be restored. Nothing good, beautiful, and just will be lost. This is the power of the gospel. This good news of the ultimate restoration of all things is an anchor for our souls in the darkest times.

The gospel is wonderful news that, when believed, serves as an anchor in the redeemed soul. The gospel brings the believer to a safe place where all the hell of the past, the present, and the future cannot sever the line securing us to the knowledge that we are loved with an everlasting love. Anchored in that love and the certainty of a participation in a future filled with the promise of the restoration of all things, souls find a rest they have never known before. This is the benefit of bringing clients under the umbrella of experiencing the gospel. Tranquillity in the core of the human soul provides fertile soil for the commencement of processes that may lead to the transformation of the total person.

Christian counselors must possess a rich knowledge of the Bible and its relevance for solving the challenges of life. Christian counselors need a firm grasp of the truth communicated in the Scriptures. The sweep of the scriptural narrative includes four acts: creation, Fall, redemption, and restoration. Most of the Bible focuses on God's work to redeem wayward people—the children of Israel and the nations in the Old Testament, and the Jews and Gentiles in the New Testament.

The Bible includes rich instruction on many aspects of God and spiritual life, including the nature of God, the role of the Holy Spirit, how people grow in faith, the expectations of spiritual life, man's free choices and God's sovereignty over all, the nature of the church, our new identity as God's children, how to overcome indwelling sin, and many other topics.

One of the most important elements that the Christian counselor brings to the counseling process is our concept of how transformation takes place. Some teach that God does it all—we passively trust while

God does his work in and through us. Conversely, others focus on our obedience as the key. In Philippians, Paul provides a simple, profound insight. After beautifully describing Christ's incarnation, sacrifice, and return to glory in heaven, Paul gives this instruction:

> Therefore, my dear friends, as you have always obeyed—not only in my presence, but now much more in my absence— continue to work out your salvation with fear and trembling, for it is God who works in you to will and to act in order to fulfill his good purpose (Phil. 2:12-13).

New Testament scholar N. T. Wright uses a metaphor to help us understand that we don't experience spiritual transformation by rigidly following rules or hoping change will magically happen. He compares the process of spiritual change to learning a new language. Unless we've carefully learned the language of a foreign country, we can't expect to feel comfortable when we travel there. To relate to people in the foreign land, we have to do the hard but rewarding work of learning the vocabulary, conjugating the verbs, and practicing our pronunciation. At first, the new language is strange and difficult, but it can become second nature if we practice it long enough. Then we feel comfortable in the new land. The process is never easy or quick.

N. T. Wright and Paul both advise that persons interested in soul growth must work at it. Learning the "language of life" in the new land of the transformation requires effort. The effort is directly tied to our view of Scripture and the Holy Spirit. Scripture and the gospel are birthed through the work of the Holy Spirit. Scripture is the work of the Spirit of God in the hearts and minds of the authors who have given us our Bible. The regeneration of the human spirit accomplished by the indwelling presence of the Holy Spirit in the core of the human soul is the work of that same Holy Spirit. This is the same Holy Spirit who is the third person of the Trinity and who, according to Paul in Rom. 1, brought Jesus back from the dead. He is then the Creator of the resurrection life of Jesus, the Holy Scriptures, and the regenerated human spirit.

The Holy Spirit in the core of the human soul is the key ingredient in the restoration of the image of God in the core self, the learning of the "language of the kingdom," and the ultimate transformation of the total person. However, the Holy Spirit is not the only ingredient required for an inside-out transformation. Provisioned with the Word of God, the Holy Spirit works to carry out the transformation of the soul, which is the ultimate purpose of his indwelling presence and the true objective of the gospel.

Paul emphasizes this relationship between the Spirit provisioned and the Word richly indwelling the mind of the believer in Eph. 5 and Col. 3. Briefly note the fruit of a rich relationship with the Scriptures expounded in Col. 3. The word of Christ (Scriptures) richly indwelling results in thankfulness, singing, order in the home, and the peace of Christ ruling in our hearts (Col. 3:15-25). All of this leads to the putting on of "the new self, which is being renewed in knowledge in the image of its Creator" (Col. 3:10).

When we move to Eph. 5, Paul teaches us that the will of God is that we be continually filled with the Holy Spirit of God. The consequence of this filling is that we are energized to live a life of singing, thankfulness, mutual submission, order in the home, and the ability to be God imitators living a life that is wise because the days are evil (Eph. 5:1–6:17).

To us the conclusion is inescapable that the Spirit's continuous ability to work with power from the core of the human personality is dependent on a commitment to the continuous and planful focus of the brain on the intake of the Word of God and an unswerving loyalty to obedience to the Word of God processed through the brain.

Christian counselors celebrate and give attention to the gospel as the forerunner to the Spirit's indwelling, the Spirit as the sole possessor of the power to bring us from death to life, and the Scriptures as the "food" provisioning the Spirit of God to do the work of inside-out transformation that he alone can perform. What we have covered in these past few paragraphs is at the heart of a Christian counselor's approach, focused on a collaborative effort engaging a caregiver in the effort to equip a care seeker for the possession of the soul under the authority of the Word of God, empowered by the Spirit of God, committed to working with a community anchored in the gospel, and directed by the goal of achieving the imitation of the Christ.

In the same way, we have to do the work of learning "the language of life" so we can experience and internalize the love, kindness, knowledge, and power of God. Spiritual transformation isn't easy, but it's the most important thing we'll ever do (Wright, 2010, pp. 39–42).

Christian counselors must cultivate the ability to communicate God's promises and purposes with sensitivity. Many (if not most) Christian clients—and even some who aren't believers—instinctively ask, "Why? Why did God let this happen to me? What about all the promises in the Bible? Why are they not working in me?" The Scriptures tell us that God is the sovereign ruler over all things and yet look at all the evil we see in the world.

For centuries, theologians have tried to answer the question of evil and human suffering and reconcile it with belief in God's sovereignty. Human suffering is probably the number one reason why people turn away from belief in God. To some, the problem is answered simply by ascribing all evil and human suffering to human free will. The brilliant British apologist G. K. Chesterton suggested we give up on blending and balancing God's sovereignty and our free will. Both are clearly taught in the Scriptures. "Christianity got over the difficulty of combining furious opposites, by keeping them both, and keeping them furious" (Chesterton, 1908/1959, p. 95).

God's promise and purposes rarely operate as smoothly as even we counselors would like, but the hope of the restoration of all things includes the biblical faith that our sins, the sins of others, and cataclysmic events we encounter can't thwart God's ultimate aims. These things may cause delays and detours, but God eventually brings good out of evil.

Perhaps no story in the Bible displays as many twists and turns as the saga of Joseph, Jacob's 11th son. His brothers hated him. They sold him to a passing caravan, and Joseph became a slave in Egypt. His master's wife tried to seduce him, but the young man refused. For his integrity, he was thrown into a dungeon. For many years, he languished, until stunning events gave him a platform as the prime minister of Egypt. His deft administration saved the nation, and it also saved his family, who came to Egypt for grain. His brothers had committed evil, but God had used even their sin as part of his divine plan to rescue countless lives.

What do we make of stories like these found in Scripture? Do they mean sin doesn't matter? No, of course not. A theology of sin and suffering requires serious reflection. Simplistic answers do more harm than good. We probably will never receive adequate answers when we ask, "Why?" We have to focus on the majesty of God and his infinite wisdom. We remember that not all prayers are answered the way we'd like.

Jesus's own prayer for rescue from the horrors of the cross was turned down in the Garden of Gethsemane. God hasn't promised to keep us from pain or even to give us quick relief. But he has promised his presence amid our suffering, regardless of the cause, and he promises to use it to soften our hearts and give us compassion for others who are hurting. Someday, it will all make sense. On that day, we'll see our lives from God's point of view.

One day we shall see that nothing—literally nothing—that could have increased our eternal happiness has been denied us and that nothing—literally nothing—that could have reduced that happiness has been left with us. What higher assurance do we want than that? (Packer, 2009, p. 303).

Christian Counselors Must Appreciate the Role of Prayer in Therapy and Personal Transformation

Amazing as it may sound, God delights in connecting with us through prayer. Abraham, Moses, David, Paul, and many other mighty prophets and ordinary people have come to God with prayers filled with a blend of wonder and intimacy. In his seminal work on prayer, Richard Foster (1992) comments on the delight and distress associated with prayer.

> We today yearn for prayer and hide from prayer. We are attracted to it and repelled by it. We believe prayer is something we should do, even something we want to do, but it seems like a chasm stands between us and actually praying. We experience the agony of prayerlessness....

> The truth of the matter is, we all come to prayer with a tangled mass of motives—altruistic *and* selfish, merciful *and* hateful, loving *and* bitter. Frankly, on this side of eternity we will *never* unravel the good from the bad, the pure from the impure. But what I have come to see is that God is big enough to receive us with all our mixture. We do not have to be bright, or pure, or filled with faith, or anything. That is what grace means, and not only are we saved by grace, we live by it as well. And we pray by it (pp. 7–8).

Prayer for Ourselves and Our Clients

As we consider the spiritual intervention of praying for clients and with them, we first need to focus on praying for ourselves. If we grasp our need for God to give us wisdom, we'll express our dependence by praying. We ask God to cleanse our hearts, to help us see our clients the way he sees them, and to let the love of Christ overflow from us into the lives of those we counsel.

Before we begin the day, we can use our schedule of appointments as our prayer guide. And as we pray, we stop to listen to the Spirit. He may remind us of a need, a passage of Scripture, or a word of encouragement we can offer. We bring each client before the throne of God and ask him for wisdom, strength, and courage. During appointments, we may offer silent prayers for insight or clarity. After a while, we find a rhythm in prayer that fits our personalities, our schedules, and our role as God's servants to our clients.

Teaching Our Clients to Pray

Some clients use prayer as a magic incantation to force God to bless them. They are often disappointed and confused. Many others have given up on prayer because the pressures and hurts of life overwhelm their trust in God's nearness and his desire to bless them.

The book of Psalms is the Bible's prayer book and hymnal, but it's not all about praise. Fully half of the psalms are outpourings of honest, painful emotions. We can help our clients learn to pray their fears, tears, discouragement, and anger as well as their thanksgiving and praise.

People often make one of two mistakes in dealing with damaged emotions. They either stuff them or vent them. Many clients want to be seen as good Christians, and they're convinced that good Christians aren't ever angry, afraid, or sad. They repress these emotions and put on a smile, but the feelings fester and poison the heart. Others go to the opposite extreme—they've never met a feeling they didn't let out. They loudly and proudly tell everybody how they feel, but they offer very little to the resolution of problems. For both kinds of clients, recognizing and praying about painful emotions can be a positive step in the therapeutic process.

Praying their fears. In Psalm 56, David was in trouble, and he feared for his life.

> Be merciful to me, my God,
>> for my enemies are in hot pursuit;
>> all day long they press their attack.
> My adversaries pursue me all day long;
>> in their pride many are attacking me (verses 1-2).

David didn't hide his fears. He prayed them, and God strengthened him:

> When I am afraid, I put my trust in you.
>> In God, whose word I praise—
> in God I trust and am not afraid.
>> What can mere mortals do to me? (verses 3-4).

Praying their tears. The psalmist felt abandoned by God.

> As the deer pants for streams of water,
>> so my soul pants for you, my God.
> My soul thirsts for God, for the living God.
>> When can I go and meet with God?
> My tears have been my food
> day and night,
> while people say to me all day long,
>> "Where is your God?" (Ps. 42:1-3).

We sometimes use the first verse as a praise song, but it's the opposite. Deer pant only when they are dying of thirst! Often in the psalms, the writer's heart longs for God, but the Lord seems terribly distant. Even in despair, however, the psalmist continues pursuing God.

> My soul is downcast within me;
>> therefore I will remember you
> from the land of the Jordan,
>> the heights of Hermon—from Mount Mizar.
> Deep calls to deep
>> in the roar of your waterfalls;
> all your waves and breakers
>> have swept over me.
> By day the LORD directs his love,
>> at night his song is with me—
>> a prayer to the God of my life (verses 6-8).

Praying their discouragement. At one point, David felt abandoned by God.

> How long, LORD? Will you forget me forever?
>> How long will you hide your face from me?
> How long must I wrestle with my thoughts
>> and day after day have sorrow in my heart?
>> How long will my enemy triumph over me?
> Look on me and answer, LORD my God.
>> Give light to my eyes, or I will sleep in death (Ps. 13:1-3).

Sooner or later (the psalms seldom give a sense of how long it took), David resolved to trust God even in his pain.

> But I trust in your unfailing love;
>> my heart rejoices in your salvation.

I will sing the LORD's praise,
>   for he has been good to me (verses 5-6).

Praying their anger. Several of the psalms are shockingly full of anger. The writers' expressions of outrage can make us feel uncomfortable, but we need to remember that this is God's songbook. Somehow, raw honesty draws us closer to God and puts us in touch with his righteous anger at injustice. At a point in his life, David's enemies attacked him without mercy. He took his anger to God:

> Break the teeth in their mouths, O God;
>   LORD, tear out the fangs of those lions!
> Let them vanish like water that flows away;
>   when they draw the bow, let their arrows fall short.
> May they be like a slug that melts away as it moves along,
>   like a stillborn child that never sees the sun.
> Before your pots can feel the heat of the thorns—
>   whether they be green or dry—the wicked will be swept
>   away.
> The righteous will be glad when they are avenged,
>   when they dip their feet in the blood of the wicked.
> Then people will say,
>   "Surely the righteous still are rewarded;
>   surely there is a God who judges the earth" (Ps. 58:6-11).

And of course, the psalms are also full of wonder, praise, and thanksgiving—sometimes at the end of the prayers expressing painful emotions.

Don't Jump Too Quickly to Comfort

One of our goals in counseling is to help clients be honest about their emotions without letting painful feelings dominate them. The psalms provide encouragement to be open and honest about every emotion, and they consistently point people to God's sovereignty, love, and wisdom. Our task is to be guides in this process and to invite God to work in his way in his timing. We want to offer genuine hope, not quick, simple solutions. Quite often, people learn the richest, deepest lessons as they wrestle with their doubts and disappointments. We need spiritual discernment and clinical skills to know when to comfort and when to let clients dig a little deeper into their pain. We do well to remember that emotions are often the first clue we have regarding the deeper motivations and thoughts of our clients. The Christian counselor works with clients' emotions to discover the truth and lies that are filling their minds and fueling their behaviors.

Provide Models of Prayer

Jesus's disciples asked him to give them a prayer like rabbis gave their followers. The pattern of prayer he gave them is called the Lord's Prayer. N. T. Wright explains that the prayer immediately points us to the reality that "there's a larger God out there."

> If we linger here, we may find our priorities quietly turned inside out....
>
> The Lord's Prayer is designed to help us make this change: a change of priority, not a change of content. This prayer doesn't pretend that pain and hunger aren't real. Some religions say that; Jesus didn't. This prayer doesn't use the greatness and majesty of God to belittle human plight. Some religions do that; Jesus didn't. This prayer starts by addressing God intimately and lovingly, as "Father"—*and* by bowing before his greatness and majesty. If you can hold those two together, you're already on the way to understanding what Christianity is all about (Wright, 1996, pp. 6–7).

We also find other patterns of prayer in the Bible. All of the psalms are useful as guides and motivation to connect with God. In the New Testament, Paul prays exultantly in Romans (11:33-36), and he prays for believers to grow in their faith (Eph. 1:15-23; Phil. 1:9-11; Col. 1:9-14). Each of these points us to Christ, shows the supreme value of knowing him, and reinforces our motivation for making choices that honor God.

These prayers, then, can be instructive to correct clients' misguided views of God. They may see him as a harsh judge, a senile grandfather, or a detached god on another planet. When our clients adopt these prayers as their own, they invite God to bring light into their darkness so they gradually see him as he really is.

In the middle of his letter to the Ephesians, Paul breaks into prayer again. This time, he asks God to flood his readers' hearts with his overwhelming love. We might want to use this to guide our prayers, and we can invite our clients to pray this way, too.

> For this reason I kneel before the Father, from whom every family in heaven and on earth derives its name. I pray that out of his glorious riches he may strengthen you with power through his Spirit in your inner being, so that Christ may dwell in your hearts through faith. And I pray that you, being rooted and established in love, may have power, together with all the Lord's holy people, to grasp how wide and long and high and deep is the love of Christ, and to know this love that surpasses knowledge—that you may be filled to the measure of all the fullness of God.
>
> Now to him who is able to do immeasurably more than all we ask or imagine, according to his power that is at work within us, to him be glory in the church and in Christ Jesus throughout all generations, for ever and ever! Amen (Eph. 3:14-21).

We can point out these prayers to our clients and ask them to focus on one and pray over it as a homework assignment, or we can use it as a teaching tool to reveal a bit of God's heart and his purposes for them.

Praying With Clients

One of the most powerful things we can do as Christian counselors is to actually pray with and for our clients. If prayer has been clearly explained as a possible intervention on the consent form, our desire to pray with them shouldn't come as a surprise. Still, it's wise to ask for permission. The prayer doesn't have to be long and involved. We simply take our clients to Christ and ask him to do what only he can do in their lives. Some counselors pray at the beginning of an appointment to indicate their reliance on God for wisdom and insight; others pray at the conclusion. Still others choose to pray at different times during sessions when a particular hurt or need is expressed. The goal is to use prayer in a way that is therapeutic and instructive. Counselors must be sensitive to clients' responses to the times when they initiate prayer.

If and when it is appropriate, you might want to ask clients if they want to pray aloud before or after you. This may seem awkward for many clients, but for a few it may open a door of healing and honesty.

Laying On Hands

The laying on of hands often occurs in Scripture. It is always a symbol of affection and an expression of desire for God's special anointing and empowering of the person who is being prayed for. Human touch is powerful, but it can be misused or misunderstood. If you want to "lay hands on" a client as you pray, be sure to ask for permission and explain your rationale for doing so. It is often better to lay hands on a person only when three or more people are involved, such as in a support group, and the objective and rationale for doing so is clearly understood.

Laying on of hands, in our experience, has often been accompanied by anointing with oil and a prayer for healing deliverance (Jas. 5:14-16). The rationale and benefits of this anointing should also be clearly explained to, understood by, and requested by the client. We have usually performed or participated in this anointing in the presence of a group of intercessors.

Journaling and Storytelling

When people put a pen to paper (or fingers to a keyboard), amazing things can happen. The process of formulating thoughts and writing them often clarifies confused thinking, brings hidden thoughts to the surface, and stirs long-buried emotions. Writing can enhance a client's ability to be objective about past hurts and present difficulties.

A timeline may be a good beginning point. Ask clients to spend some time listing major life events, including births, deaths, marriages, divorces, separations, moves, successes and awards, failures and disappointments, and anything else they feel is important in their story. When they share the timeline with you, they often realize they forgot a number of important events—even seminal events that shaped their lives in extraordinary ways. This, you can assure them, is completely normal.

Another effective strategy for journaling is to ask clients to schedule an extended, uninterrupted time alone and ask God to bring to mind events from the past that were particularly hurtful. Often, people report thinking of several in the first few minutes, and then after a gap of time, they think of a few more. After a longer lapse of time, they remember something that hasn't come to mind in years. The ones that clients remember last are often ones buried in their subconscious because they were too painful to remember. These become the fodder for the therapeutic progress. Also, this process often stimulates the client to be open to further exploration in the future. Some clients remember important events "out of the blue" weeks or months after this exercise.

Taking possession of the soul often involves the discovery of items long buried in the mind that are contributing to the client's present negative emotions and relational challenges. Journaling can help peel back the layers of information stored in the brain and open the way for the reshaping of the mind. Through journaling we are usually able to connect with the metacognitive dimension of our thoughts. This may then lead to deeper levels of understanding regarding the beliefs that are driving our behaviors and impacting our relationships with ourselves, others, and God.

By helping clients to tell their life stories, we invite them to reinterpret their lives from God's perspective. This is often difficult but wonderfully helpful. When we read the Gospels, we see that the disciples didn't understand Jesus's mission throughout his life. The disciples on the road to Emmaus were heartbroken by Jesus's death and needed help figuring out who he was and why he came. They needed to know he was alive and continuing his work in their world. In the same way, our clients need help (from God and from us) to discern what God has been making of their lives.

Paul explained to the Corinthians that God uses suffering to give us compassion for others who suffer (2 Cor. 1:3-7) and to deepen our faith (2 Cor. 4:7-18). Our task is to help our clients look at their lives from the same point of view that Joseph (Gen. 50:20), Paul, and the heroes of faith (Heb. 11) used. All of them sometimes felt confused or overwhelmed, but they persisted in trusting God. We won't have the full picture on this side of eternity, but we can be sure that God is always up to something good, right, and valuable. Connecting deeply with this truth, we are able to begin the journey toward higher levels of emotional, psychological, and spiritual health.

When we give an assignment to create a timeline, write in a journal, or reinterpret a life story, we need to realize that even if this activity is familiar to us, it is nevertheless new, awkward, and threatening to some of our clients. They may fear they will fail and lose our approval, or they may be afraid of what they'll uncover. Be patient, explain things carefully (and often), and encourage them with each of their forward steps.

Music and Imagery

The arts connect with our souls. Music, drawing, painting, and dance are sometimes doors to our deepest emotions. In therapy, music and visual arts can play vital roles as spiritual interventions.

Music. Music has an innate power to capture our hearts. In *The Power of Music*, Elena Mannes reports that music stimulates more parts of the brain than any other human function. It's possible, then, that soothing, inspiring music can actually help change the hardwiring of psychopathology. Mannes's research also suggests music has the potential to affect people with neurological problems, such as strokes, Parkinson's, and even Alzheimer's (Mannes, 2011, p. 1). Music can raise and lower our blood pressure. It can create a calm in the brain, allowing for the enlargement of the soul's capacity to respond to thoughts, feelings of somatic addictions, and relationships in new and healthier ways.

Culture, age, personality, and experience determine which songs of faith inspire our clients and which ones bore them. As we become familiar with different genres of Christian music, we can make informed suggestions. Some clients will be moved by the old hymns, but others prefer a more modern beat and lyrics. Those who prefer "Be Still My Soul" may not appreciate a song that describes God's love as a hurricane.

Ask your clients if they listen to music, if they have a preference in Christian hymns and songs, and how they like to listen. Some have

MP3 players and listen to music when they exercise, commute, or work around the house. Others listen to background music all day, and others make music a part of their worship and prayer each day.

Imagery. Visual arts are often used to help children express their emotions, but adults can benefit from painting and drawing too. For children, drawing is often used in cases of abuse and trauma because the child has difficulty verbalizing painful feelings. For children as well as adults, visual arts invite several senses (tactile, visual, and kinesthetic) and stimulate neurological processes in more and different ways than conversation does.

Counselors can ask clients to depict actual events in their lives. The drawing can show how clients have experienced events and related to other people who were involved. This activity can bring new insight to clients and the counselor, which then facilitate more progress in therapy.

To use visual arts effectively, counselors need to be trained by competent, experienced professionals. Drawing and painting can be effective tools for intervention if they are used wisely.

Meditation

In many Eastern religions, meditation is used to empty the mind. In Christianity, meditation is used to fill the mind with accurate thoughts of God and our relationship with him. In many cases, Christian counselors can ask clients to find a quiet place and reflect on a certain passage of Scripture or biblical concept and its application to their lives. Meditation is an invitation to think, pray, and use the imagination to enrich our relationship with ourselves and with our God. God has an amazing imagination. Consider how many different colors and types of flowers he created. Humans have that same power of imagination. It can be used for good or evil. When used for good, it is an effective agent in the quest for soul possession. The Bible contains many admonitions to consider, reflect, and think deeply about God and his ways. Christian counseling is more than teaching people to think correctly, but it certainly includes this vital practice.

Edmund Clowney (1979, pp. 12–13) identifies three dimensions of Christian meditation that give substance and direction to the practice. First, it is always focused on the truth of the Scriptures and assumes that God is relational and wants to communicate with his people. Second, the pursuit of God is a response to the love, forgiveness, and acceptance of God. Believers are invited to come to their heavenly Father with a blend of boldness and humility. Third, the process of connecting with the heart of God often includes confession and repentance, but it inevitably results in thanksgiving and praise.

A client doesn't have to become a desert father to practice meditation. A passage, a few pointed questions, and some unhurried time are all it takes to contemplate God's character, his presence, his grace poured out in our lives, and his "good, pleasing and perfect will" (Rom. 12:2). Meditation can be as structured or as relaxed as the counselor and client want it to be. Some people come from liturgical church backgrounds, so rituals and written prayers are familiar and meaningful to them. Others need a more fluid, contemporary, and personalized approach.

As people reflect on a passage and pray, they aren't alone. The Holy Spirit enlightens the eyes of their hearts to grasp the glory of God's truth (Eph. 1:18). He encourages, affirms, and corrects the person who is seeking God. Meditation, then, is as much confession as praise, as much looking back as looking forward.

Fasting

Solomon provides advice on the control of the body appetites: "When you sit to dine with a ruler, note well what is before you, and put a knife to your throat if you are given to gluttony. Do not crave his delicacies, for that food is deceptive" (Pr. 23:1-3). Solomon calls for drastic action when we discern that we are in bondage to any substance, including food. Put a knife to your throat! Fasting is a way that the mind functions against the cravings of the body and brain to say no. The choice is to deny what has enslaved the soul to fulfill a higher purpose. The purpose is the pursuit of the imitation of God. Fasting is most powerful when it is accompanied by Bible study, prayer, silence, meditation, and solitude. (Always seek medical advice first.)

WISDOM'S REVIEW

The Christial counselor uses spiritual interventions to go deeper into God's heart. This movement into the heart of God moves the focus from self to God and others.

Every client who comes to see us has the potential for becoming, in Henri Nouwen's famous phrase, a wounded healer. As God's love flows into us, it eventually overflows from us into the lives of others. This transformation may not happen soon, and it may not occur while clients are in counseling. Sooner or later, however, real healing and health are inevitably expressed in efforts to comfort others. The overflow of God's grace is a sign of spiritual health. At some point, emotional, spiritual, and relational growth is arrested if people don't turn the corner and become givers as well as takers.

> In a fundamental human paradox, the more a person reaches
> out beyond herself, the more she is enriched and deepened,

and the more she grows in likeness to God. On the other hand, the more a person "incurves," to use Luther's word, the less human she becomes. Our need to give is as great as anyone's need to receive (Yancey, 2000, p. 239).

Most of us know the story behind Horatio Spafford's hymn "It Is Well With My Soul." After the Great Chicago Fire, he sent his wife and three daughters to Europe for an extended vacation. He planned to join them after he finished some business arrangements. When their ship sank, the three girls perished. His wife sent him a two-word telegram: "Saved alone." He sailed at once to join her. On the voyage, the captain informed him when the ship arrived at the spot where his daughters drowned. There, he wrote his song.

The story doesn't end there. The Spaffords didn't wallow in self-pity and heartache. During World War I, they and some friends cared for Christians, Muslims, and Jews on the Eastern front. They established soup kitchens, hospitals, and orphanages. Through their deep grief and loss, the Spaffords experienced God's compassion, and they became channels of love and hope for people in need (Ariel & Kark, 1996).

The transformation from helpless, angry victims to wounded healers isn't a rare occurrence. It's the story of most Christian counselors, and most of us will testify to the value added we discovered in our lives when we practice some of the spiritual disciplines outlined in this chapter.

The treasure. In the gospel of grace, we offer people the greatest treasure in the universe. The love, forgiveness, and power of Christ heal broken hearts, put steel in the backbones of those who feel weak, and provide limitless resources as clients follow Christ's lead. The love of God melts insecurity and replaces it with joy and hope. When people get a taste of God's magnificent grace, they feel strong enough to face their emotional wounds, tangled relationships, deepest disappointments, and shattered dreams. The growing experience of God's majesty and grace gradually gives them something to live for.

Jesus is the treasure hidden in a field and the pearl worth any price. Knowing him is the supreme value in all of life. Ultimately, our spiritual interventions invite people to experience the gracious *presence* of God, and we model the *pursuit* of God. These interventions are spiritual disciplines in action. As we practice them with our clients, we need to tread lightly. We are walking on holy ground.

Today, we offer the assurance of God's presence and power without promising total relief from pain or complete clarity about the future. But we also offer the strong and secure hope that someday, all will be made right. Our spiritual interventions are always on the platforms of the gospel, God's good news on the restoration of all things in the kingdom to come and his redemption of a people for himself in the now.

References

Ariel, Y., & Kark, R. (1996). Messianism, holiness, charisma, and community: The American–Swedish colony in Jerusalem, 1881–1933. *Church History, 65*(4), 641–657.

Chesterton, G. K. (1908/1959). *Orthodoxy.* New York, NY: Image.

Clowney, E. P. (1979). *Christian meditation.* Vancouver, BC: Regent College Publishing.

Foster, R. (1992). *Prayer: Finding the heart's true home.* New York, NY: HarperCollins.

Keller, T. (2008). *The prodigal God.* New York, NY: Dutton.

Mannes, E. (2011). *The power of music.* New York, NY: Walker.

Packer, J. I. (2009). *Knowing God devotional journal.* Downers Grove, IL: InterVarsity Press.

Powlison, D. (2010). A biblical counseling view. In E. L. Johnson (Ed.), *Psychology & Christianity: Five views* (2nd ed., pp. 245–287). Downers Grove, IL: InterVarsity Press.

Wright, N. T. (1996). *The Lord and his prayer.* Grand Rapids, MI: Eerdmans.

Wright, N. T. (2010). *After you believe.* New York, NY: HarperCollins.

Yancey, P. (2000). *Reaching for the invisible God.* Grand Rapids, MI: Zondervan.

12

New Horizons—the Way Forward

Today's Christian counselors have a God-given calling. The biblical concept of calling is as old as the ancient prophets and as fresh as today's sense of purpose. In *The Call*, Os Guinness (1998, p. 4) defines the spiritual calling of every believer as "the truth that God calls us to himself so decisively that everything we are, everything we do, and everything we have is invested with a special devotion and dynamism lived out as a response to his summons and service."

As counselors, we have received an invitation and a summons to join God in a unique, case-based form of discipleship. We serve God, our clients, our communities, and the church to fulfill the Great Commandment and the Great Commission. We fulfill the Great Commandment as we love God with heart, mind, soul, and strength—and love our neighbor as we love ourselves. We do our part to fulfill the Great Commission as we spread the gospel and make disciples in our offices and across the globe. In every culture and every age, our calling is pursued one person at a time.

We are joined with Paul and Jesus in their vision for all who are followers of Christ. Paul shared his vision for the creation of a community of God imitators with the Ephesians when he exhorted his followers, "Be imitators of God as dear children. And walk in love, as Christ also has loved us and given Himself for us, an offering and a sacrifice to God for a sweet-smelling aroma" (Eph. 5:1-2 NKJV). Jesus, while preparing his disciples for the many challenges they would face as his followers, spoke with them about the process by which this imitative community is to be created across all time and cultures. His exhortation on the process to be followed in the pursuit of the life that glorifies God is this: "By your patience possess your souls" (Lk. 21:19 NKJV).

Our purpose in this book has been to equip Christian counselors with a better understanding of the elements to be considered in order to fulfill this exhortation. We have specified the components that define and shape the soul. We created the concentric circles to illustrate these components (illustration 2, p. 205). We also set those elements in an analysis grid (illustration 3, p. 240) to provide a strategic and structured approach for organizing the client story in a way that will promote efficiency and effectiveness in the gathering and organizing of significant elements of the client's story contributing to his present experiences. This information gathering is set in illustration 3 against the backdrop of six more A's. We believe the entire counseling process for Christian counselors rests on this foundation—creating the right atmosphere and using authority appropriately. Next in importance for us is the counselor adaptation and alignment throughout the counseling process (P1, P2, P3, P4). We also believe that counseling must lead to meaningful change. Therefore the essential elements of the counseling process include the creation of best-fit action plans and accountability for the practice of change that is believed to be meaningful for and owned by the client. Thoughtful attention to all of these elements has contributed to our understanding of Christian counseling as a collaborative engagement involving care seeker and caregiver laboring together under the authority of the Word of God, in dependence on the empowering work and presence of the Holy Spirit, within the larger context of the church for encouragement and accountability, with the goal of assisting men and women to possess their souls, for achieving the imitation of God and heightened levels of spiritual, psychological, physical, and relational health. In brief, we believe that an ever deepening mastery of the processes and strategies connected with achieving this outcome will help move clients from their present story, to a preferred one, to a plan of action, and into a community of encouragement and accountability. This, we believe, is at the heart of fulfilling our calling as Christian counselors.

We carry out our calling to Christian counseling with a group of colleagues who have enabled us to make remarkable strides in the past three decades, but we can't afford to rest on our accomplishments. The movement needs to stay on the cutting edge. "The time has come to facilitate the deliberate and systemic development of competent Christian counseling.... [It is] necessary to help [Christian counseling] grow from a dynamic but disorganized movement into a more disciplined and self-directed profession." This effort has seen success, but it has experienced opposition. In the last decade, we've seen positive changes as well as threats "in the Church, in the health and mental health care marketplace, in the legal and regulatory environment, among the counseling and mental health professions, and in [our profession] itself." In our culture and in our profession we need to take advantage of the "driving forces that will significantly transform [Christian counseling] in the 21st century" (Clinton & Ohlschlager, 2002; see also Ohlschlager & Mosgofian, 1992/2012).

For our profession to thrive, we need to focus resources on professional development—planned, rational, and actively directed efforts, as opposed to passive, unplanned, or random growth—to keep Christian counseling grounded in the Scriptures and in effective spiritual practices. We value the advances of the scientific community, but we have no intention of abdicating our God-given role to adversarial, antichurch institutions. The future is always uncertain, and the way forward is challenging. As Christian counselors, we need to sharpen our skills, deepen our faith, and work together to shape the development of our profession.

A clear, compelling vision of the future is essential. When Disney World opened in Florida a few months after the death of Walt Disney, one of the media visitors reportedly remarked to a park designer, "It's sad that Mr. Disney didn't live to see this."

"Oh, but he did see it," replied the designer. "That's why the park is here."

Each of us needs a vision for the future—for the movement of Christian counseling and for our calling within it.

Trends in the Movement

The future of Christian counseling is bright. Gifted leaders, professors, and practitioners are doing excellent work to integrate faith with clinical insights. We can identify several significant trends currently occurring or on the horizon.

Advocacy for clients and the marginalized. With our commitment to compassion, Christian counseling should be in the forefront of client advocacy. We need a "patient Bill of Rights" outlining services to our clients, the poor and disenfranchised, those persecuted and suffering around the world because of their faith, and victims who are too abused and marginalized to speak out for themselves. In this effort, leaders in the

Christian counseling movement are working with such organizations as World Vision, the Salvation Army, the International Critical Incident Stress Foundation, World Help, and Compassion International.

Code of ethics. The American Association of Christian Counselors Code of Ethics (American Association of Christian Counselors, 2014) is becoming the standard of care for Christian counseling agencies in the United States and worldwide. It has been translated into eight languages and adopted by Christian counselors in more than a dozen other countries.

National credentialing. The International Board of Christian Counselors (IBCC) delivers four baseline credentials to Christian counselors worldwide, as well as credentials for crisis intervention and Christian coaching. The IBCC and the Christian Counseling Code of Ethics are designed to complement one another, becoming the primary sources of credentials and ethical standards representing the American Association of Christian Counselors specifically and Christian counseling generally.

Faith-based initiatives. Christian counselors are collaborating intentionally across the full range of service modes, including outpatient treatment, residential and day-care programs, hospitalization, and intensive aftercare treatment. Partnerships are proving to be effective. For example, Meier Clinics and John Brown University have received major grants for faith-based initiatives in marriage counseling and care. Many different organizations, agencies, and colleges will continue to partner with faith-based programs in the future.

Intensive care for counselors and pastors. Pastors and Christian counselors need to be aware of the threat of burnout. Too many are suffering from the devastating effects of unrelieved stress. To combat this growing problem, a network of centers provides intensive, high-quality care to the shepherds of the church. Exhausted pastors and burned-out counselors experience relief and renewal in these intensive retreat experiences.

Distance and online education. Increasingly, colleges and universities are using distance and online educational programs that allow students to develop and maintain their careers and nurture their home and work environments. For example, Light University, an extention of the American Association of Christian Counselors, has trained hundreds of thousands of students around the world in a variety of certificate-based counseling and coaching programs. Accredited colleges and universities are joining this effort through degree-based education. Advanced technologies continue to expand the scope and variety of accredited courses and enrichment programs.

Continuing education and certificate programs. Continuing education and postgraduate certificate programs equip Christian counselors in specific modalities and skills. These programs are designed for licensed practitioners and pastoral counselors. In addition, certificate programs in applied ministry train lay helpers around the world. "On demand" training will offer counselors everywhere the opportunity to always be current and to specialize in areas of need and interest.

Doctoral programs. A growing number of PhD programs in counseling, pastoral counseling, marriage and family therapy, and counselor education and supervision now offer the finest professional training in Christian counseling, Bible and theology, research and policy, spiritual formation, pastoral care, and the sciences of biology, psychology, sociology, and spirituality.

Heightened multicultural sensitivity. Christian counseling is making significant advances in bridging cultural differences in our communities. Part of our role is to break down cultural, racial, and economic barriers, find common ground, and build communities of love and respect.

As leaders in diversity, the movement is advancing advocacy against all forms of prejudice—including religious prejudice—in the mental health professions.

Advanced research. Pioneers in research are advancing on the empirical frontiers of Christian counseling. Establishing a proven database for the validity of Christian counseling is a priority in the development and defense of our movement. Faith-based variables correlate significantly with better health and well-being, and research on treatment and outcomes is coming into its own. Competent clinicians and professors are actively researching applications that will reveal the BEST therapies in and for Christian counseling (**B**iblically informed, **E**mpirically **S**upported **T**herapies).

Lay helping ministries. As our culture has become more aware of pressing needs in the lives of families and individuals, many pastors and church leaders are facilitating the rapid growth of lay helping ministries. Agencies, denominations, and counseling organizations are dedicated to train and supervise people in the church to care for friends and neighbors in an expansion of our unique calling in discipleship. These church-based efforts often partner with local counselors for training, referrals, and consultation.

Spiritual formation. In recent years, *spiritual formation* has become a common term for discipleship. Today's principles and practices are less programmed than some of the older forms, so many postmodern people feel more comfortable with the term and the process. Actually, Christian counselors often prefer the nuanced approach of spiritual formation. Their sensitivity to people's needs, process orientation, listening skills, and insights into rich biblical applications give these counselors a platform to be leaders of spiritual formation in their churches.

Biblical and theological depth. Christian counseling is becoming more biblically grounded and theologically astute. Professional courses, articles, books, and workshops educate counselors in theological models and spiritual applications. Many pastors are benefiting from this synergy. Christian counselors often offer pastors a richer grasp of the effects of sin, distorted desires, and misguided motivations, as well as the process of transformation. With these insights, Christian leaders can apply the Scriptures more effectively in their teaching and ministry. When Christian counselors and church leaders work together toward common goals of honoring Christ, healing emotional wounds, reconciling broken relationships, and helping people grow in their faith, everybody benefits.

Internet technologies. Recent years have seen the rapid growth of online counseling and web-based resources for education, coaching, consulting, mentoring, and spiritual formation. Christian counselors and training programs that once functioned locally are now reaching across the nation and around the world. Seminars on the web are inspiring and equipping thousands of clinicians, pastors, and lay helpers globally. These technologies will continue to expand in the future, immediately and conveniently providing a widening array of outstanding resources.

Cutting-edge modes of care. Counselors increasingly utilize innovative practices beyond traditional office-based psychotherapy. Some are doing therapy in homes, in businesses, and in church settings. In addition, therapists are actively involved in a wide range of services, including mediation and peacemaking, coaching, consulting, teaching, training and supervising lay helpers, and intensive weekend marriage workshops.

Interprofessional collaboration. Efforts to enhance collaboration among disciplines of care are producing many benefits. In many cases, cooperation has improved client access to counseling services, provided empirical validation of treatments and outcomes, and curbed abuses and limitations of care by managed care and the insurance industry. In some cases, however, tensions over conflicting values have increased among professions, especially regarding antireligious prejudice and the explicit integration of spiritual and Christ-centered practices in counseling. In our advocacy of Christ-centered therapy, we have a lot of remedial and pioneering work to do to reasonably present the hope that lies deep within us.

The Manhattan Declaration. In 2009, this "call of Christian conscience" was signed by more than 150 evangelical, Catholic, and Orthodox leaders. The declaration supports the sanctity of life, traditional marriage, and religious liberty. Most Christian counselors find common cause with these leaders and the values they uphold and protect. The Declaration provides a solid foundation widely varied groups can share as they work together in the future.

Glocalization. A global extension of local ministry to a worldwide audience is known as *glocalization*—in other words, "think globally, act locally." Leaders in our movement are in the vanguard of vision and technology to articulate concerns and marshal resources to care for people who need help (victims of sex trafficking, refugees, political prisoners, AIDS/HIV patients, and persecuted and tortured Christians) and to address global environmental concerns. Modern communication technology has brought the needs of the world to our desktops and phones. Today, Christians want to help, and they have more resources than ever before. Virtually every believer can be involved in prayer, targeted giving, short-term missions, disaster relief, and long-term vocational missions. We can care for people next door or on the other side of the world.

Specialization. In every field of science, the proliferation of new information requires increased specialization. In Christian counseling, advances challenge therapists to become specialized in education, training, theory, and practice. Some in our profession prefer the status quo, but we need to be at the forefront of this opportunity as visionary leaders instead of reluctant followers.

Theoretical integration. In recent decades, outstanding work has been done to anchor our work biblically and theologically as well as integrate the worlds of counseling and psychology. The coming years should see more research and a sharper focus on many elements of common ground. For many generations, psychology has been a shrewd observer of the human condition, but secular theories didn't address and incorporate ultimate biblical truths. On the other hand, Christian counseling has sometimes been too reactionary and simplistic in its approach. Respect for the value of each discipline facilitates integration so that accurate assessment can be blended with genuine forgiveness, the power of spiritual transformation, and a strong foundation of hope.

Integration with medicine and law. By its nature, Christian counseling has always valued theology. In recent years, law and medicine have begun incorporating psychosocial data into their training and practices. Attorneys increasingly value Christian perspectives in mediation, jury selection, and sentencing guidelines. And medicine sees inherent value in health psychology, psycho-cardiology, cancer and geriatric counseling, treatment compliance, and the spiritual and emotional components in exercise and nutrition.

Brain imaging and neuroscience. Psychiatrist Daniel Amen asks, how can we be serious professionals unless we look at the organ [the brain] we are purporting to treat? (Amen, 2001). Brain imaging and the neuroscience revolution are transforming modern psychiatry and the mental health professions. These may be the most exciting and important advances in our field in the next generation.

Positive psychology. For more than a century, the clinical mental health sciences have focused on the pathology of human behavior. Recently, however, a different philosophy has emerged. Positive psychology invites therapists to focus on the best about human nature and social behavior. A strength-based therapy influenced by positive psychology is consistent with the faith, hope, and love we find in the Scriptures, and it provides a powerful motivation for change.

Spiritual hunger. Western culture is the richest, most advanced society the world has ever known, but the accumulation of wealth, power, comfort, and prestige eventually leave people feeling empty and confused. They long for more. Many in the postmodern culture—young and old— are turning away from traditional forms of religion. They want a genuine connection with God. Christian counseling stands at the intersection between their existential longing and authentic Christian experience. We play a crucial role in bringing the Bible alive to today's generations and offering the majesty and grace of God to people who have turned away from traditional church structures.

Be Ready, Stay Sharp

This is an exciting time to be a Christian counselor. We have more resources than ever before to equip us to be effective, but there are many distractions. To take advantage of the opportunities God gives each of us, we need to sharpen our clinical skills, deepen our walks with God, and be actively involved in mutually encouraging relationships.

Sharpening our skills. Staying sharp is a challenge. We face pressures to keep up with a client load, stresses at home, financial difficulties, and many other problems. Like our clients, we can get overwhelmed. We may not reach the point of burnout, but we may become restless and chronically dissatisfied. When this happens, we lose our cutting edge. Our goal changes. Rather than trying to stay informed and astute in our clinical skills, we simply try to get through each day.

In academic training, we are exposed to many different theories and models of counseling. By the time we emerge with a degree, some of us have a clear model we plan to use, but some continue to experiment for many years. As we gain experience, get feedback from supervisors, and see many different clients, we adopt or adapt a model that works best for us. Still, we need to stay abreast of new discoveries in the field. Continuing education units keep us informed, but we need to remain lifelong learners who soak up insights from leaders we respect. As our practices grow, many of us realize we are gifted in helping clients with a particular profile. To become better equipped, we may receive additional training and certification in such fields as marriage and family therapy, adolescents, geriatrics, addictions, or sexual abuse. Books, conferences, articles, and online resources continually stimulate us and allow us to stay engaged.

Deepening our faith. When Jesus described the range of responses to his message, he used the agrarian metaphor of four types of soil. One kind is hard as a concrete road, and the seed of the gospel doesn't penetrate at all. The second is the coarse, rocky soil found throughout Palestine. The seed sprouts, but the poor soil allows few roots, so the plant soon withers in the heat of the sun. The third soil has the potential to be productive, but weeds choke out the valuable wheat. The fourth kind is "good soil" that produces a harvest.

Many Christians—including counselors—fall into the third category. About them, Jesus explained, "Still others, like seed sown among thorns, hear the word; but the worries of this life, the deceitfulness of wealth and the desires for other things come in and choke the word, making it unfruitful" (Mk. 4:18-19). We can't stop weeds of discontent, worry, and an inordinate thirst for prestige, power, and possessions from spouting in our hearts—those are natural and spontaneous results of fallen people living in a fallen world. But we don't have to let them grow and choke out the fruit of the Spirit.

Growing Christians are good at digging out the weeds. They aren't shocked to find those weeds growing in their minds and souls. They realize their hearts are still desperately wicked, even though they are chosen, adopted, forgiven, and sealed in Christ. As Martin Luther observed, we are *simul iustus et peccator*—simultaneously saints and sinners. Observant, growing believers remain alert. They notice the yellow flags of discouragement and doubt, and they are alarmed when they see the red flags of self-defeating behaviors in themselves. They see these weeds, and they do whatever it takes to yank them out.

The default mode of the human heart is to drift away from God. To be the counselors God wants us to be, we need to pull weeds, put on armor, fill our tanks, stay connected to the head...and use any other biblical metaphor that describes a rich, vibrant love for Christ. The spiritual disciplines are essential means to the end of knowing, loving, and obeying God out of an overflowing heart. If we neglect prayer, Bible study, worship, confession, fellowship, service, fasting, and the others, we may not notice for a while. Sooner or later, however, we begin to feel spiritually flabby, lethargic, and slow.

Each of us can establish a rhythm of spiritual disciplines that keeps us close to God's heart and Word. The things that keep us freshly connected to God may be very different from the practices that help others, but we can't afford to be complacent. If we neglect them, our hearts gradually grow cooler. The practices themselves aren't the end. We practice them so we experience more of the delight of God.

The Christian life certainly is demanding. Jesus said that if we want to follow him, we need to follow his example by taking up our cross and dying to our selfish desires. But the Pharisees oppressed people by presenting obedience as a grind—more duty than beauty (today's moralists do the same). Knowing Christ is the most thrilling, exhilarating, inspiring, and challenging experience we'll ever know! The more intimately we know him, the more we realize his greatness and grace are beyond comprehension. Christ is the bread that satisfies, the living water that quenches our thirst. He is the good shepherd, the light of life, and our most loyal friend. Philosophy, theology, and religion are valuable only when they point us to him. Our hearts are empty and restless until they are filled with his love. As pastor John Piper has often stated, "God is most glorified in us when we are most satisfied in him" (Piper, 2011, p. 10).

When we find Christ delightful, he gives us courage to face the inevitable opposition, distractions, disappointments, and darkness we encounter. Like Christ in the garden, we sometimes want to bail out, but we choose to stay because we want the Father's will instead of our own. But to be honest, sometimes we turn and run from God and his purposes. Even then, we have the assurance that Jesus will welcome us back and forgive us, just as he forgave Peter after his friend denied him three times. No one and no sin are beyond the grace of God. That's comforting for us as well as our clients.

Mutual encouragement. A burning log set aside on the hearth soon cools, and the fire dies out. In the same way, we need people around us who will fan the flame of God's love in our lives—not occasionally, but regularly. Paul had this kind of relationship with Timothy, as we see in his second letter to his protégé:

> You then, my son, be strong in the grace that is in Christ Jesus. And the things you have heard me say in the presence of many witnesses entrust to reliable people who will also be qualified to teach others (2 Tim. 2:1-2).

We need someone like Paul in our lives to be our mentor. We don't need many people like this—maybe only one at a time. Mentors are perceptive about our motives and wise to see our direction, and they love us enough to tell us the truth. We need a group of peers around us—other Timothys—who are trusted friends and partners in life. And we also need a few people who see us as their mentors. We pour into their lives, just as our mentors pour into ours. Soon, those whom we disciple want God to use them in the lives of still more people, and the cascade of love and devotion continues. When we have these three layers of encouraging, accountable relationships, we seldom feel alone.

WISDOM'S REVIEW

Christian counselors have an incredibly important calling. God wants us to step into people's lives at their point of desperate need. We are the hands, feet, and voice of Jesus to these people as we represent his love and strength. This is the highest honor anyone can imagine, and it carries the weight of responsibility to represent him well. We treat each client the way we'd treat Jesus Christ if he were sitting in the chair across from us—with respect, love, humility, and honor.

The people who come through our doors are much like the disciples in the Gospels. They may mean well, but they may also be slow to catch on. We might have begun our careers with unrealistic expectations for clients' quick growth, but now we know better. We realize we are just like them, so we feel compassion for them.

In our love for our clients, we speak the truth—sometimes hard truths that should be shared only with a tear in our eye. But we communicate the truth of the gospel of grace with genuine hope that God will use our message to touch a heart and change a life.

Our ultimate aim is the one God has given for centuries—to know him, to love him, and to let him transform us and our clients from the inside out. David had many pressures, but he wrote that the only thing of primary importance is beholding the beauty of God (Ps. 27:4). Through Jeremiah, God said that people may boast about many things, but the only thing that matters is knowing him (Jer. 9:23-24). Jesus said that experiencing his love is like overflowing with a flood of living water (Jn. 7:37-39). And Paul wrote the Philippians about the "surpassing worth of knowing Christ Jesus my Lord" (Phil. 3:7-10). The one who has revealed himself to us as our Savior is the Creator and King of the universe. His greatness and grace are beyond comprehension. He is the healer, provider, and protector, the Lion of Judah and the Lamb of God.

What is God's desire for us? In Paul's powerful description of grace at work in us, he exposed a bit of God's heart: "In order that in the coming ages he might show the incomparable riches of his grace, expressed in his kindness to us in Christ Jesus" (Eph. 2:7). For all of eternity, beginning now, we will marvel at God's amazing grace. He's not stingy. He lavishes his love on us, and he delights in revealing the riches of his grace in kindness to us. Who wouldn't want to know someone so powerful yet so loving? Who wouldn't open his heart to a King who demonstrated the depth of his love by dying for us? As Christian counselors, this is the one we represent and introduce to our confused, wounded, angry clients. He is their hope.

Christian counseling is noble work, but it's difficult. We didn't go into this field to make millions or to see our name in lights. We're following the Lord's path to sacrifice, give, love, and serve. As Paul traveled to Jerusalem after one of his journeys, he met with the elders from the church in Ephesus and explained to them his motivation.

I only know that in every city the Holy Spirit warns me that prison and hardships are facing me. However, I consider my life worth nothing to me; my only aim is to finish the race and complete the task the Lord Jesus has given me—the task of testifying to the good news of God's grace (Acts 20:23-24).

As we care for people and extend God's grace and truth to them, our goal is the same—to faithfully complete the task God has entrusted to us, namely, to proclaim the transforming love and power of God found in the gospel of Jesus Christ. We are partnering with God to help others possess their souls and grow in Christ. In that role, we find more meaning than we ever imagined.

References

Amen, D. (2001, February).Why don't psychiatrists look at the brain? The case for greater use of SPECT imaging in neuropsychiatry. *Neuropsychiatry Reviews 2*(1), 19–21.

American Association of Christian Counselors. (2014). *AACC Christian counseling code of ethics.* Forest, VA: American Association of Christian Counselors.

Clinton, T., & Ohlschlager, G. (2002). *Competent Christian counseling: Foundations and practice of compassionate soul care.* Colorado Springs, CO: WaterBrook Press.

Guinness, O. (1998). *The call.* Nashville, TN: Word.

Ohlschlager, G., & Mosgofian, P. (1992/2012). *Law for the Christian counselor* (p. 156). Eugene, OR: Wipf & Stock.

Piper, J. (2011). *Desiring God.* Colorado Springs, CO: Multnomah.

The Popular Encyclopedia of
Christian Counseling
Tim Clinton and Ron Hawkins,
general editors

A Definitive Resource on the
Rapidly Growing Field of Christian Counseling

Academically sound and yet easy to read, this concise, practical, and comprehensive reference includes more than 250 articles organized topically under 26 headings, exploring...

- foundations of Christian counseling and the process of change

- various kinds of disorders

- modes and applications of Christian counseling

- counselor skills, theories, and therapies

- ethical issues, education, and research

Whether you're a counselor, pastor, lay helper, or counseling student, you'll find the reliable and up-to-date information you need to be effective as you help people heal and grow.

145 contributors, including...

Gary Chapman, PhD • Henry Cloud, PhD •
Archibald Hart, PhD • June Hunt, MA • Ian Jones, PhD
• Diane Langberg, PhD • Michael Lyles, MD •
Frank Minirth, MD • Linda Mintle, PhD • Joni Eareckson Tada
• Siang-Yang Tan, PhD • John Townsend, PhD • John Trent, PhD
• Everett Worthington, PhD • Mark Yarhouse, PsyD